THE BIG WALKS OF THE SOUTH

Including: The South Downs Way, The Cotswold Way, Offa's Dyke Path, The South West Coast Path, The Pembrokeshire Coast Path

DAVID BATHURST

THE BIG WALKS OF THE SOUTH

Material revised and updated from THE BIG WALKS OF GREAT BRITAIN, published by Summersdale Publishers Ltd in 2007 (first published as THE BEATEN TRACK by Summersdale Publishers Ltd in 2001)

Summersdale Publishers Ltd
46 West Street
Chichester
West Sussex
PO19 1RP
UK

www.summersdale.com

Printed and bound in Great Britain

ISBN: 978-1-84953-024-8

Back cover photo courtesy of www.nationaltrail.co.uk/offasdyke

THE BIG WALKS OF THE SOUTH

DAVID BATHURST

About the author

David Bathurst has been a keen walker all his adult life, and as well as his completion of numerous long-distance routes has also walked the entire coastlines of Sussex and Kent. By profession David is a solicitor and senior legal adviser to the magistrates sitting in Chichester and Worthing, and he has written several other books on a wide range of subjects. His chief claim to fame is the recitation of the four Gospels from memory in July 1998 and then the recitation of the complete surviving works of Gilbert and Sullivan from memory in August 2004.

By the same author

The Big Walks of Great Britain, Summersdale 2007
The Big Walks of the North, Summersdale 2010
Walking The South Coast Of England, Summersdale 2008

Contents

About this Book

Despite the increasingly sophisticated range of leisure pursuits and interests available to us, walking still enjoys huge popularity as a form of recreation. People like to walk for different reasons. Some do it simply for the health benefits, and aren't fussy where their walk takes them. Some like to have a definite objective, such as a place of historic interest or a hilltop. Some will want to use their walking to trace our rich industrial, social or cultural heritage. Some like to walk long distances as personal challenges and/or to raise money for deserving causes. And some walk for all these reasons. As the popularity of walking has increased, so has the number of 'name' long-distance walking routes across Great Britain, providing challenging, invigorating and often exciting walking to and through numerous places of immense scenic beauty and historic interest. In short, all the reasons people like to walk come together in the walking of a long-distance route. The purpose of this book is to provide an overview of what can be described as the Big Walks, namely the top long-distance walking routes, in the south of Great Britain. Included either in this book, or in the companion volume covering the north of Great Britain, are all 15 of the National Trails of England and Wales, the four Scottish National Long Distance Walking Routes, and the Coast To Coast Walk which although without official National Trail status is one of the best-loved routes in the Great Britain. They are all tremendous walks, each with their distinctive character. Take the South West Coast Path with its spectacular cliff scenery; the Cotswold Way with its breathtaking panoramic views and cosy honey-coloured towns and villages; the Thames Path through the heart of London; or the Ridgeway Path, transporting walkers back into prehistoric times. Each has its store of treasures, waiting to be explored and to provide an unforgettable tapestry of magical walking memories.

This book aims to provide a succinct and light-hearted description of each route covered, providing information as to the nature and relative difficulty of the terrain, highlighting places of scenic and historic interest and offering advice to those contemplating the challenge. It does not pretend to give every route detail, but to be a reference work providing an accessible and user-friendly guide to the relative merits of each Big Walk so you can decide which one you like the look of the most from the detail given. And if for whatever reason you are unable to undertake any of them, you can enjoy following each route from the comfort of your armchair. A chapter is given over to each route: each chapter begins with the route length, overall assessment of difficulty, and highlights of the walk to be described. The walk is then broken down into sections. There is no magic in the section divides: the aim is for each section to start and finish at a place that is reasonably easily accessible by road or rail, and to equate to what a fit walker should be able to accomplish in a day. Where a section is very long, it will be because of the lack of amenities or transport opportunities available on it. Mileages are given for each section and cumulative mileages given in brackets throughout the narrative. All this will assist in the planning process. Please note that every effort has been taken to ensure the accuracy of the information in the book, so that you know exactly what you're taking on, but inevitably there are changes to routes and land use which could not be anticipated at the time of writing.

Becoming a Big Walker

Bearing in mind the shortest route in this book is 85 miles, and the longest is 628 miles, you'll quickly appreciate the magnitude of the task facing you should you decide to take one of them on. You may be an experienced rambler who simply wants some focus for your walking, in which case you may be able to tackle any of these Big Walks with ease and with little need to peruse the rest of this introduction. But if your idea of a long hike is the 200-yd walk up the road to buy a carton of milk, you clearly have some work to do before tackling even the easiest of the described routes. You need to get properly fit. Don't pigeonhole it with all your other New Year's resolutions (come New Year's Day, it's bound to be pouring with rain or freezing cold anyway). Start now! Begin by aiming for 30 minutes' brisk walking every day – don't skip it one day and tell yourself you'll make up for it the next, as the chances are you won't. Having established the minimum, make time to take yourself off on longer walks, up to say three or four hours at a stretch, aiming ultimately to manage a full day's walk. Where you go is up to you – you may be happy tramping round the vicinity of your home town or village, but you may wish to explore further afield. You might of course hate it (in which case you probably wouldn't be reading this book). On the other hand, you may get hooked. Romantic evenings out are ditched in favour of intensive studies of Ordnance Survey maps. Weekend shopping trips revolve round visits to outdoor shops in search of a particular brand of hi-tech bootlaces. You actually read the care instructions that come with a new pair of gaiters. You startle fellow commuters by trying out new walking boots with your suit when hurrying to catch the 7.39. You start subscribing to a walking magazine and are able to answer a few clues of the walker's crossword. You no longer feel self-conscious in a bobble hat. You bore your dinner guests with statistical and photographic records of your most recent walking endeavours. And the present that excites you most on Christmas morning is a gift-wrapped multi-pack of perfumed sneaker balls.

Whether you've become an obsessive or just an enthusiast, once you've achieved the necessary levels of fitness you may be ready for your first Big Walk. Remember, though, that tackling any of the walks in this book will require several days' hiking, over terrain which may be more demanding or inhospitable than any you've tackled from home. There's no reason why the whole of any Big Walk needs to be done at once – in fact, virtually nobody will have the resources to do, for instance, the South West Coast Path in one go. Indeed you may prefer to do your first one in segments, maybe just a day or two at a time, only increasing the number of consecutive days' walking when you're sure you are ready for it. It's a good idea to start with one of the easier walks such as the Peddars Way & Norfolk Coast Path or The Ridgeway Path, where not only is the terrain less demanding than on other Big Walks but transport links are always reasonably accessible. Remember, though, that even the easier Big Walks have their remote stretches with no access to wheeled transport, and if you don't feel up to negotiating them, you need to think again. Once you've successfully completed the shorter and easier walks, you can start thinking about one of the stiffer challenges in this book. We all have different levels of fitness – a 12-mile walk will be a half-day stroll to some and a never-ending slog to others – so ascertain your level before committing yourself. Then and only then should you get down to the exciting business of planning your travel arrangements and your accommodation, which of course will be a matter of personal taste. The Internet and local tourist information offices will give you all the information you need on that aspect. You also need to think about when to go: you may conclude that there is never a right time to walk, with unpredictable weather and short days in winter but crowds and inflated prices in summer. Unless and until you are an experienced and confident walker, and better able to cope with the unexpected, the summer months with longer days and better weather are undoubtedly to be preferred.

Equipment

Having decided on your Big Walk, and when you're going to do it, the next question is what to wear and what to take, and this will depend very much on the nature of the terrain and length of your walk. There's a huge market for walking equipment of all kinds, the claims made in support of the various available products growing seemingly more overblown and pretentious with the passing years. Before parting with large amounts of money, prioritise and consider what you really need. Footwear is of prime importance. Those trusty walking brogues you purchased from a backstreet gents' outfitters in Swindon in 1957, and which haven't needed as much as a new pair of laces since, may be quite adequate for an easy day's pottering on the Thames Path but will be totally useless for a winter day's assault on the Pembrokeshire Coast Path. The choice of footwear is huge, so rather than befuddle your senses by scanning the 30 pages of walking boots in your monthly walking magazine or a million pages of the things on the Internet, seek advice from a reputable outdoor wear shop. Just beware of being talked by target-driven salesmen into buying any number of expensive but unnecessary accessories, from pocket handwarmers to luxury loganberry-flavoured foot gel, at the same time. Clothing is also important: if it's cold or there's rain about, a decent breathable waterproof jacket is a must, and in cold weather you will also need gloves as well as plenty of layers. In hot weather, you must avoid sunburn so loose fitting long-sleeved shirts and trousers are better than T-shirts and shorts (which in any case are, shall we say, less than flattering on those of a certain age or above), and you shouldn't forget a sunhat. As to what to take with you, water is a must, especially in warm weather: thirst (dehydration) is to be avoided at all costs, so drink lots, especially early in the day. Even if you're hoping to find a pub or cafe en route, have a supply of high-energy food as well – bananas or dried fruit are to be preferred to chocolate. For day-long walks, a small day pack to carry your supplies may be all you need, but for several consecutive days, even if you're B & B'ing or hostelling rather than camping, you'll need a much bigger backpack capable of containing all you need for your trip including changes of clothes, toiletries, maps and essential food, drink and emergency supplies (see below). If once you've packed your rucksack you find you can't lift it off the floor, don't panic. Remove all the stuff you really feel you can do without. If having done that you find you still can't lift it off the floor… then you can panic. That said, bag-carrying services do operate on some of the walks described in this book, enabling you to enjoy your Big Walk unencumbered. Failing that, you can always go along to weight-training at your local gym. And it's as well to remember Sod's law of backpackers – it'll always be the item you need the most that finds its way to the most inaccessible corner of the rucksack.

Highs and Lows

The lows first. Embarking on a big walk does carry certain risks. The route descriptions provide bracketed mileage indicators so you can work out how far it is from one significant location to another, and you can therefore get some idea of how far you may need to walk in one day to be sure of reaching somewhere with an adequate range of amenities. There are some very lengthy amenity-less and remote sections; Hartland Quay to Bude on the South West Coast Path is just one example of a section of route where you could find yourself in real difficulty if you were insufficiently fit to complete the walk in a day. Some of the climbs and descents are very steep, with the attendant risk of accident and injury; mist or heavy rain can transform a benign landscape into a hostile wilderness; the simple act of missing a signpost and drifting off course could leave you stranded, miles from anywhere, at nightfall. You need to minimise these risks. Pace yourself carefully, planning to do slightly less than you think you can manage in a day. Start the day with a decent breakfast including lots of high-energy food. Have with you proper mapping of the route. (The Aurum Press and Cicerone Press guides to individual routes contain all the mapping you'll need.) Equip yourself with a compass but make sure you know how to use it first. If you can't comprehend even the English part of the 60-page multilingual instruction manual, and were unable to concentrate on the outdoor shop assistant's impromptu lesson as you were worried your lunch hour was almost up, maybe it's best not to attempt any of the tougher walks, especially in the winter months. Make sure someone knows where you're going to be walking and where you're aiming for. Have a mobile phone (although a signal can't always be guaranteed) and local taxi firm numbers with you. Keep not only an emergency food supply but first aid materials, a torch and a whistle as well. And prevention being better than cure, consider cancelling your walk if the weather is bad. On a more prosaic note, even if you never put yourself in danger, your resolve may be tested by blisters, aching muscles, or just general fatigue. Don't force yourself to carry on if you really can't bear to – remember, it's not an Army endurance test, and the path will still be there next year – but don't give up too easily either. A sudden great view, a nice meal, even just a beer or a pot of tea, can transform your whole attitude to the walk, and give you the impetus to complete the journey.

Having dwelt for a few moments on the negatives, let's finish on a positive note. To accomplish a Big Walk, even one of the lesser routes in this book, is no mean achievement. If you've got people to sponsor you to complete it, you may make a nice sum for charity (doubtless wishing the person who sponsored you 50 p a mile had signed his name at the top of the form, thus setting the standard for others to follow, rather than the person who sponsored you 50 p to complete the whole walk). You may make some great friendships that will last the rest of your life. You'll get to see some fantastic scenery, some beautiful towns and villages, and, if you're observant, a huge variety of plant life and wildlife. Having completed one Big Walk, you'll be hungry for more, and find you've fresh impetus to rise to new walking challenges. And you'll have learnt a lot of valuable life lessons. The virtues of self-reliance, patience and determination to complete the course. The knowledge that in our technology-dominated society the simplest things are the best – a dewy valley in the morning sunshine, a snow-capped mountain top, a babbling stream refreshed by last night's rains. And acceptance of the inevitability with which the pub your friends recommend as the best they've ever been to, and which you've made a two-mile detour off the path to visit, has been turned into a block of luxury flats.

Happy walking.

The South Downs Way

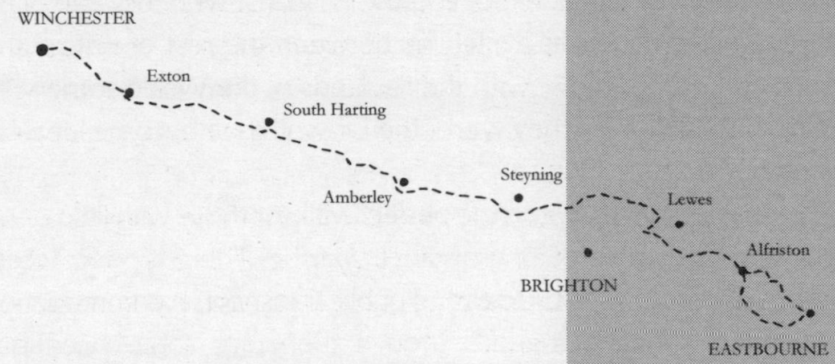

Designation: National trail.
Length: 99 miles (main route) or 96 miles (via alternative bridleway from Alfriston).
Start: Winchester, Hampshire.
Finish: Eastbourne, East Sussex.
Nature: A well-defined route along the chalk ridges of the South Downs with spectacular views to the sea and across the Weald.
Difficulty rating: Moderate.
Average time of completion: 7–9 days.

HIGHLIGHTS OF THIS WALK:

- **Winchester**
- **Harting Hill**
- **Chanctonbury Ring**
- **Steyning**
- **Devil's Dyke**
- **Ditchling Hill**
- **Alfriston**
- **Seven Sisters**
- **Beachy Head**
- **Long Man**

It was some sixty million years ago that great chalk deposits on the seabed bulged up into a great dome, the crest of which eroded over time to leave two chalk masses which form the North and South Downs. When the first settlers arrived on the Downs some six thousand years ago, they and their descendants preferred the drier, safer hills to the swampy Weald below. Thus originated the long, unerring tracks over the South Downs, which were to be used by generations of settlers, including Bronze Age traders who used them for the transport of minerals such as jet and gold, and the Romans, who fully exploited the downland routes as a vital link between the rest of Britain and mainland Europe. Now, with the flat lands of the Weald somewhat more hospitable than they were, the Downs have become ideal for recreational use.

The South Downs Way is the perfect walk for those with little or no previous experience of long-distance walking. There is good access to all parts of the route by road and public transport, accommodation is plentiful throughout and, although there are some strenuous climbs, it is reasonably easy to accomplish, with well-signposted and well-defined paths and tracks. On days of clear visibility the march across the chalk downlands of Hampshire and Sussex, described by Kipling as 'our blunt, bowheaded, whalebacked Downs,' brings massive rewards. From this platform of chalk you can gaze across the English Channel towards France, across the endless patchwork of fields, forests and villages of the Weald, or perhaps down to the great valleys of the South Downs, with their lovely rivers – the Arun, the Adur, the Ouse and the Cuckmere – that have cut through the soft downland chalk. You can enjoy the multitude of bird, insect and animal life on the Way, which may include skylark, linnet, yellowhammer, corn bunting, Adonis blue butterfly, rabbit, common shrew, harvest mouse, brown hare, badger, and of course the famous black-faced Southdown sheep. You can gaze down at the chalk grassland, bedecked with squinancywort, knapweed, wild thyme, vetch, trefoil and speedwell. Whilst looking groundwards you may find a shallow depression of chalk or clay constituting a dew-pond, of which there are many on the South Downs, created to provide drinking water for sheep. You can descend to a multitude of delightful villages with their solid Norman churches, indicative of the commitment of the Normans to Christianity after their invasion, and the cottages of that vital local building material, downland flint. Indeed there is so much to see off route, including a wealth of fine churches and other historic buildings, that copious detours are to be recommended in order to get the best out of what the Way has to offer. A further advantage of a detour to a small town or village is that, having gained a hearty appetite by the satisfying march along the roof of Hampshire and Sussex, you can enjoy a drink or a meal at one of the many pubs and tearooms that are available.

Most of the guidebooks describe the route from east to west. My opinion, however, is that the walk works far better in reverse. The prevailing wind will be on your back, and there is something rather special about ending at the seaside, in the delightful and hospitable town of Eastbourne. It has to be said that the final few miles of the main route, across the Seven Sisters chalk cliffs and past Beachy Head, are as thrilling a climax as can be imagined.

Winchester to Exton (12 miles) via Chilcomb

ENJOY: Winchester, Cheesefoot Head, Lomer, Exton

The walk starts at Winchester, the ancient capital of Saxon England, and worth a day of any walker's time. Anyone entering the city from the east cannot miss the massive statue of King Alfred, who was largely responsible for Winchester's prominence in pre-Norman times. The city's chief glory however, is its cathedral, begun in 1079 and, at 556 ft end to end, one of the longest in Europe. It is renowned for its magnificent chapels and medieval wall paintings. Nearby is a thirteenth-century deanery and a Pilgrims' Hall where pilgrims lodged in the Middle Ages on their way to Canterbury. You will not have been the first walker to set off from this city on a long journey eastwards.

The Way uses metalled roads to head eastward out of the city and, having crossed the M3, sets off into the countryside. Close by is Twyford Down, scene of bitter protests as the M3 was being built. Indeed, traffic noise seems to dominate as the Way follows a field-edge path eastwards, then turns left onto a metalled road that enters Chilcomb, a pretty village with an early Saxon church. After leaving Chilcomb you carry on along a metalled road, turning left to join a track, climbing all the time. Proceeding over Telegraph Hill, from which Winchester can be viewed, the Way crosses the busy A272 and reaches Cheesefoot Head (3.5), the first significant viewpoint of the walk, with fine vistas across Hampshire. It is the site of a great natural amphitheatre and it was here that General Eisenhower addressed the Allied troops in 1944 before the D-Day landings. From Cheesefoot Head the Way descends, heading north-east, then turns right onto a track and strikes south-eastwards across Gander Down. The A272 is crossed again, and good firm tracks are followed southwards and uphill to reach Milbury's, a popular pub whose name is presumably derived from the ancient burial mound known as Mill Barrows, lying immediately to the south. The Way turns left at the crossroads by the pub and follows a hilltop road, rounding Kilmeston Down. Good views are available from here towards Hinton Ampner House, a rebuilt eighteenth-century manor house close to Cheriton, the site of a major battlefield in the English Civil War.

For a couple of miles you lose the views as you join a track to head south-eastwards towards Beacon Hill. The highlight here is Lomer, the site of a lost medieval village, and its picturesque pond immediately adjacent to the path. Then suddenly, by Beacon Hill, the ground seems to fall away; the Way turns right then left along metalled roads and plunges off the plateau and steeply downwards, offering splendid views to Old Winchester Hill and the Meon valley. Exton (12), in this valley, is a village with an attractive church and pretty cottages, while the Meon is a lovely chalk stream, praised by seventeenth-century angling author Izaak Walton for its fishing.

The Meon valley railway

Opened in June 1903 and closed in February 1955, this picturesque line linked Alton with Fareham. The hilly terrain meant that construction was not always straightforward and a number of navvies were killed or injured in the building work. Drunken fights were commonplace and it is reported that one very drunken navvy was stripped of his clothes and thrashed by his mates with stinging nettles.

Exton to A286 for Cocking (22.5 miles) via *HMS Mercury*, Queen Elizabeth Country Park, Uppark and Didling Hill

ENJOY: Old Winchester Hill, Butser Hill, Queen Elizabeth Country Park, Uppark, Harting Hill

This is a long section, but it could conveniently be broken at Queen Elizabeth Country Park or the B2146 above Harting. Having followed a road north-east out of Exton, the Way crosses the busy A32, crosses the Meon and follows a succession of narrow, stony tracks eastwards out of the valley, in the shade of trees and under the old Meon Valley Railway. You then head south-eastwards steadily and directly through more open countryside to reach Old Winchester Hill (14.7), at 648 ft the most elevated ground so far. The summit is noteworthy for its Iron Age fort and associated defensive earthworks which date back to around 200 BC. However, you can enjoy the summit simply for its wonderful views which on a half-decent day extend as far as the Isle of Wight, and also the nature trail and reserve that are situated here.

Sadly, the airy hilltop grassland walking does not last; the Way reaches a road, turning left onto it and then right onto a path that plunges downhill again to pass Whitewool Farm, just beyond which you turn right onto a metalled road, and shortly left onto a track leading to Henwood Down. There is then another right turn onto a track, crossing a minor road at Coombe Cross. By turning left, however, you may soon reach East Meon and its beautiful church, famous for its magnificent Tournai font of black marble, depicting the Creation. It has been described as 'a Bayeux Tapestry in stone'.

Returning to the route, further climbing leads to the good viewpoint of Salt Hill (well over 700 ft) and, beyond Wether Down, the stark buildings comprising the former naval base of *HMS Mercury* (18.9). You reach a metalled road and turn left onto it to pass this. At length you reach a road junction, cross straight over and head eastwards, beginning the final march on Butser Hill. You proceed initially on a track and then turn left to proceed beside a road. The rise of the ground towards Butser is almost imperceptible – the hard work has been done reaching the top of Salt Hill – and you can enjoy the lovely views to East Meon Church. As the summit draws closer it is likely that you will not be alone enjoying the hilltop (20.4) that, at 888 ft, represents one of the major summits of the South Downs Way. Only those walkers who are very pressed for time, or those urged on by inclement weather, will not stop here. The hilltop is a magnet for hang-gliding and kite-flying enthusiasts, its Bronze Age tumuli will interest the archaeologist, and its panoramic views across Hampshire and to the Isle of Wight will impress anybody fortunate enough to be there on a clear day.

The Way swings to the south-east and a glorious downhill plunge on springy grass takes you underneath the A3 London–Portsmouth road. Beyond the underpass you reach the information centre and cafe on the edge of the huge woodlands making up Queen Elizabeth Country Park (21.2). The Park not only has good facilities but also a huge range of very well-marked walks amongst the woodland. The network of paths hereabouts can be a little bewildering to the walker who may search in vain for the familiar acorn symbol or simply the words 'South Downs Way'.

There is then a long climb through the forest, heading north-east on a good track, and on fine weekends there are certain to be other walkers and cyclists for company. At last, at Faggs Farm, things level out, the trees relent and you reach some excellent, well-signposted eastward walking on good paths and metalled tracks above the pretty village of Buriton, with its fine Georgian manor house and rectangular pond. The views from the Way are improving all the time. At Sunwood Farm (25.3), you reach the border with West Sussex. Until the extension to Winchester was opened in 1989, this used to be the western end of the route, and although it is a pleasant enough spot, it seemed a lame start or end to a great walk. At length you cross the B2146, where you can detour to the left to visit the pretty village of South Harting, which offers both accommodation and refreshment. Nearer at hand, and accessible by a detour to the right down the B2146, is Uppark. Built around 1685–1690, it has been described as a copybook example of the Wren-style country house. The author H. G. Wells spent part of his boyhood there. The house was very badly damaged by fire in 1989 but has been miraculously restored, and you may well wish to break off from your exertions to enjoy a tour of the house. However, you'll find that in the course of any long-distance walking, shuffling slowly from room to room can feel as exhausting on the feet as actual path walking, and you may be forgiven for being one of the less appreciative students of the set of paintings in the Long Gallery or the detail on the ornamental vase which Lady Emprynghame-Beaumont brought back from Outer Mongolia in 1739.

Beyond the B2146 you enter thick woodland, climbing up in a south-easterly direction to reach the B2141(the main Chichester–Petersfield road) then, having crossed this road, you go forward to reach Harting Hill, the first real highlight in West Sussex. Though at roughly 750 ft it lacks the loftiness of Butser Hill, there are splendid views to the north of the escarpment, most notably to the village of South Harting, whilst looking back there are views which can extend as far as the Isle of Wight and Portsmouth. Harting Hill, like Butser Hill, is a popular haunt for day-trippers, perhaps because its superb views are obtainable within a few yards of the well-used car park. It is also the start of a magnificent seven miles of South Downs Way walking, on a succession of well-marked paths that are free from road tramping or traffic noise. After following the top of the escarpment on excellent tracks, with more splendid views to the north, the Way turns sharp right and changes direction to go round the western side of Beacon Hill. You then turn abruptly from south/south-east to due north to contour the hill's eastern side. There seems no obvious reason why Beacon Hill, with its Iron Age summit fort, is bypassed by the route, although it has to be said that the traverse of it is very demanding and you may be glad to be spared its rigours. Having met the path coming down off Beacon Hill, you have a short descent followed by a swift climb to the summit of Pen Hill. Ahead you can make out the beautifully-shaped downland slopes, largely wooded, that comprise Treyford Hill and Didling Hill; moreover, on a clear day it is possible to identify Bognor Regis on the Channel coast.

There is a less interesting interlude as the Way descends to pass Buriton Farm, turning left then almost immediately right onto a good track, and there follows a climb through the woods of Philliswood Down. A sharp left turn at a crossroads of paths brings a clearing in the woods revealing five Bronze Age round barrows known as the Devil's Jumps (31.3). The woodland thickens for a while as you pass the grounds of Monkton House, once lived in by the art collector Edward James, and you may hear the shrill cries of the resident peacock. At length, the woodland relents and there is a sequence of magnificent open walking, heading just south of east, with breathtaking views to the Sussex countryside including some tremendous panoramas of Chichester harbour. Indeed, one of the most satisfying moments on your entire journey is to emerge from the trees and find yourself on the open ridge, high above the Weald, with the spire of Chichester Cathedral soaring proudly from the flatlands close to the harbour and, in the immediate foreground, the tree-clad slopes of Treyford Hill, Didling Hill, Linch Ball and

Cocking Down. A footpath leading off to the left soon after you clear the woodland will take you to the so-called Shepherd's Church of Didling. Started by the Saxons, only the font remains from that time. The rest is early thirteenth-century. Its gnarled bench-ends are its most remarkable internal feature, but its field setting gives it a beauty and solitude that is timeless. When the field is not cultivated, another possible detour is to the triangulation point at Linch Ball at just over 800 ft. On a clear day not only can you see across the Solent to the Isle of Wight, but you can also identify Chanctonbury Ring to the east.

Shortly after Linch Ball, the path drops to the A286 just above Cocking, and on the descent you may be accompanied by vanloads of marksmen travelling to or from shooting butts on the Downs. At the A286 (34.5) the bus company have kindly placed a stop right on the route, and there are regular buses to Cocking. It is fairly easy for the purist, who will insist even on off-route diversions being walked, to stick to his principles for the descent to the village for rest and refreshment. His principles will be more severely tested next morning on the realisation that after a steep climb *up* on a pavement-less main road, there is another climb to regain the height lost since Linch Ball, and twelve miles to the next pint of beer.

A286 to Houghton (12 miles) via Crown Tegleaze and Littleton Farm

ENJOY: Bignor Hill, Upwaltham, Toby Stone viewpoint, Amberley Working Museum

The Way continues in an easterly direction with a long climb from the A286 via Manorfarm Down onto Heyshott Down, with only very restricted views to the south. However, a short detour takes you to the triangulation point at the summit of Heyshott Down, from which there are fine views to the north. Thereafter, you enter another thickly forested section. The going is very fast at most times of year, as the trees provide welcome shelter from summer heat and reasonable protection from the rain. You continue over Graffham Down, above the attractive village of Graffham which is hidden from view by the trees, although easy footpath access to the village is possible. As you reach Woolavington Down, the woodland begins to thin out and a slight upward incline takes you to the summit of this section, the 830 ft junction of paths known as Crown Tegleaze. There is an elegant signpost here but the views are still limited because of the thickness of the surrounding forests. However, beyond this point you leave the dense forest behind and suddenly the ground falls away, your route dropping steeply through fields to reach the A285 Chichester–Petworth road at Littleton Farm (39.8). If there is time to spare, it is worth walking a short way down the main road to the right to view the little flint church of Upwaltham. Originally built in the twelfth century, the nave and apse have remained completely unchanged since.

Downland churches

Visits to downland churches such as Didling and Upwaltham are an integral part of walking the South Downs Way, and you should try to include time to explore them in your itinerary. Sadly, access to churches on this or indeed any other national trail can be something of a hit-and-miss affair in these days of vandalism, and the building may be locked with no information as to how to gain legitimate entry. Thankfully, there do remain many churches around which you are able to wander at will, with literature to assist and enlighten you, whether a glossy guidebook or a selection of ageing copies of the monthly church magazine.

After crossing straight over the A285 the route climbs again, following a wide track which passes the edge of woodlands on Burton Down, and emerges just south of two prominent masts signifying the advent of Bignor Hill from which there are superb views on a clear day. These will include the spire of Chichester Cathedral and the coastal settlements of Bognor Regis and Pagham, with the sea forming a rich blue backcloth. Nearer at hand, but worthy of a photograph or two, is Halnaker Windmill, sitting proudly on its hilltop; it dates back to 1750 although it has been heavily restored since. Shortly, the Way meets Stane Street, a Roman road constructed to link Chichester with London. The area is steeped not only in history but pre-history; just south-east of the junction with Stane Street is the site of a neolithic camp, and there are numerous tumuli nearby. The Way passes across a car park, with a very steep road running down to Bignor and its Roman villa which was discovered in 1811. Wooden buildings with thatched roofs have been built over the exposed foundations to give some idea of what the villa may have looked like, and there are also some fine mosaics to see.

Back on the Way, an airy walk on a wide track just north of east takes one to Toby's Stone (42.5), a memorial to a well-known local huntsman. Here is one of the best views so far, encompassing the Arun valley and downland beyond, the Sussex coastal plain, and the sweep of countryside north of the Downs. It is at its most spectacular when the Arun has flooded and many parts of the valley are under water, but on any clear day the views to the coast and the sea are stunning. Reluctantly, you have to drop down to the foot of Westburton Hill, then after a sharp right turn the Way gradually climbs once more onto Bury Hill, skirting the extensive woodlands of Houghton Forest to the immediate south. Excellent views open up once more, the most enticing prospect being the Arun valley straight ahead. There is a slight descent to cross the very busy A29, then the Way plunges down to the flat valley bottom and having reached and crossed the Arun, follows alongside it for a short while before rising to meet the B2139 and turning right. A left turn here takes you to the village of Amberley which contains an imposing castle ruin dating back to 1380, thatched cottages and a Norman church.

The Way follows alongside the B2139 (46.5) briefly before branching left on a country lane, but by continuing straight on you arrive at the railway station and the refreshment facilities at Houghton. Adjacent to the station is the Amberley Working Museum, a magnificently comprehensive array of exhibits, memorabilia, crafts and trades of yesteryear, with a particularly fine display of old buses. The sight of a double-decker bus parked close to the route should not therefore encourage you into thinking that you have an easy ride back to base, for it may simply be the museum's latest exhibit, having been declared unroadworthy over forty years ago and not been driven at all since ferrying a troop of Girl Guides to Butlins in 1965.

Houghton to Adur Crossing (12.8 miles) via Washington

ENJOY: Sullington Hill, Chanctonbury Ring, Steyning Bowl

The initial climb out of the Arun valley consists of a gentle incline up the lane, with the added bonus of a free glimpse at some of the exhibits of the Amberley Working Museum. Then, having turned right at a T-junction of roads, you leave the road by turning left, and make a long steep ascent on farm tracks to the top of Rackham Hill. You should watch out for cyclists coming down the hill towards you at enormous speed. It is a relief to reach the top of the escarpment, now proceeding more decisively eastwards again. The reward for the effort, apart from the satisfaction of reaching the halfway mark on the route, is a splendid view of the Arun valley and the hills that have been left behind, and a return to ridge walking, where views to the Weald and the sea are equally impressive. You can clearly make out the towns of Bognor Regis and Littlehampton, as well as the medieval ruins of Arundel Castle.

The whole of the six-mile stretch from Amberley to Washington is South Downs Way walking at its very best, with no significant undulations and good open walking on wide tracks, virtually free from woodland. In fact woodland is much sparser on the second half of the walk. The Way passes close to Parham Park, and the beautiful Elizabethan mansion of Parham House, and then goes on past Springhead Hill and Chantry Post on Sullington Hill (50.3), where in each case the presence of a nearby car park and access road brings a brief spate of casual walkers. In due course another break in the ridge signals another sharp descent, not to a river valley but the dangerously busy A24 London–Worthing road (52.4) which has to be crossed. (An alternative route, leaving the main route at Barnsfarm Hill, takes you down the north side of the escarpment onto a track, and in due course over a footbridge across the A24 into the picturesque village of Washington.) Having crossed straight over the A24, you briefly join a metalled road then turn right, but by continuing on the road downhill you reach Washington. Though you may immediately think of the American city, this 'Washington' actually means a Saxon settlement of the sons of Wassa. The church is largely uninteresting but the village is undeniably picturesque and there is a welcome pub where admirers of Hilaire Belloc still gather to sing his West Sussex Drinking Song, ending with the words, 'The swipes they take in at Washington Inn is the very best beer I know.'

There follows a short but steep climb to the Iron Age hill fort of Chanctonbury Ring (54), the path following a clearly defined but somewhat winding course to the summit. The Ring actually consists of a clump of beech trees, planted within the oval-shaped hill fort in 1760. It is still possible to make out parts of the low bank and ditch. Although many of the trees were lost in the great storm of October 1987, it remains a useful shelter on a wet day as well as a splendid viewpoint. There is another prominent Iron Age fort, Cissbury Ring, clearly visible nearby, and this is worth a detour if time permits. The Way proceeds in a south-easterly direction, and you will enjoy another splendid high-level promenade which soon passes the grand (but strictly private) buildings of the sixteenth-century stately home, Wiston House.

The walk arcs in a crude semi-circle round Steyning Bowl then changes direction from south-east to north-east to go over

Annington Hill and then descend gradually, by means of a track and along a minor road, to the next big valley, the Adur (pronounced 'Ada'), just below Upper Beeding. You enjoy a short riverside stroll before crossing the river by means of a footbridge (59.3), immediately beyond which is a most useful tap, provided by the Society of Sussex Downsmen; it is one of a number of water points on the South Downs Way. Buses are available to Steyning from the nearby A283. Steyning is a beautiful little place, its finest corner being Church Lane which shows off virtually every form of local building material – timber, flint, brick, tile, thatch, Horsham stone and slate – with some houses dating back to the fifteenth century. Arguably the finest building in the town is the part twelfth-century St Andrew's Church, which contains fine Norman carvings. The original building was founded in the eighth century by St Cuthman; legend says he arrived and settled in Steyning having pushed his invalid mother in a wheelbarrow from Devon.

Adur Crossing to A27 Crossing for Lewes (15.3 miles) via Truleigh Hill, Devil's Dyke and Pyecombe

ENJOY: Fulking Escarpment, Devil's Dyke, Ditchling Beacon

Most walkers will agree that the Adur valley, rather disfigured hereabouts with industrial workings, lacks the appeal of the Arun valley. Fortunately, perhaps, you do not linger here long, but after proceeding quickly to the busy A283 and crossing it, you immediately climb back onto the escarpment. Your reward for this brisk ascent will be the good views back to Chanctonbury Ring as well as Lancing College Chapel. This Gothic-style building dates back to 1848 and in this country is beaten for height by only three other ecclesiastical buildings, namely Westminster Abbey, York Minster and Liverpool Cathedral. As you near the top of the hill, you reach Truleigh Hill with its rather untidy assembly of buildings, amongst which is a most useful youth hostel (60.9).

Once past the buildings, fine eastward ridge walking returns with the crossing of Edburton Hill and the Fulking escarpment. The best views lie northwards to the Weald, a vast area of woodland, farmland, small villages and towns which separate the South Downs from the North Downs. Immediately below you are the villages of Edburton and Fulking. Edburton boasts an excellent fresh fishery, and Fulking is a beautiful village with a very popular pub. These pleasant hills, however, serve merely as appetisers for Devil's Dyke (63.5), the undoubted highlight of this section of the Downs. Just before you reach the Dyke, you will clearly see the huge conurbation of Brighton from the Dyke Hotel, and indeed the Dyke area remains a splendid playground for the Brighton populace. The Way passes along a splendid grassy promenade where a fine day will bring out hosts of hang gliders, then begins the dramatic descent alongside the Dyke itself. This is a deep, dry valley with Ice Age origins, and remains a remarkable natural feature, with an array of interesting vegetation.

The Devil's Dyke

Legend has it that the Devil created it in a bid to flood the Weald where Christianity had taken hold, but when he saw a candle being held by a watching woman, he fled, leaving the job unfinished, believing the candle to be the rising sun. Since Sunday is one of the most popular days for visitors to this spot, local church leaders may ruefully reflect that in inadvertently leaving such a remarkable feature in the state he did, the Devil did not do too badly after all in wooing would-be churchgoers away from their weekly observance.

The combination of the Dyke itself and the considerable panorama to its north certainly makes for fine walking, and it is with reluctance that you will drop down to the road at Saddlescombe, only to climb up again almost immediately onto Newtimber Hill. A detour along the road to the left will take you to Poynings. With its fine fourteenth-century flint church, cosy pub, and picturesque assembly of buildings in the shadow of the Downs, it is almost the definitive downland village. Newtimber Hill commands fine views in all directions, and it is followed by a brisk descent to the A23, the busiest road crossing so far, fortunately achieved by means of a bridge. Immediately afterwards comes the pretty village of Pyecombe (66.2), and for once you find yourself passing through a village actually on the route rather than having to detour to reach it. Downland flint is the dominant motif of the village, and there is a lovely twelfth-century church of flint and pebbledash. The village was well known as a centre from which shepherds' crooks were supplied. The Way reaches the busy A273 and turns left alongside it, but you soon cross over it to join a path which heads eastwards away from the road and climbs again, this time alongside a golf course. You then turn sharp left to come within sight of the Clayton Windmills (67.5), better known as Jack and Jill. Jack is a brick tower-mill of 1876, and Jill, a much older lady, is a wooden post-mill of 1821. She came from Dyke Road, Brighton, in about 1850.

Near the windmills, from which there is easy path access to Hassocks and its convenient train station, the Way swings again to the east and for several miles enjoys a glorious high-level promenade, with superb Wealden views to the north. Around this point, you cross into East Sussex. The path maintains a good height, rising slightly to reach Ditchling Beacon (69.3), at 813 ft one of the highest spots on the Way, with panoramic views not only to the Weald but also to the sea. The sprawl of Brighton is still visible, as are the coastal settlements to its east. Ice creams will often be available at the car park, and on Bank Holidays you can derive some smug satisfaction from watching indolent drivers jostling for parking space.

Beyond the car park there is road access to the village of Ditchling, which boasts a largely thirteenth-century church and a wide range of facilities. However, if you decide to make the detour you will have a very long climb back up afterwards. The high-level walk continues, passing Streat Hill with evidence of Bronze Age habitation, and reaching Plumpton Plain above the village of Plumpton, famed for its picturesque racecourse. Then at Blackcap, amidst an abundance of tumuli, the Way turns away from the scarp edge and seems to turn half back on itself, heading initially in a south-westerly direction before swinging south-eastwards over Balmer Down. This is undoubtedly an anticlimax after what has gone before, with restricted views and the path losing height all the time. Moreover, this next section is bitty and you should follow the signposting carefully, for in recent years the Way has been re-routed to take advantage of a footbridge over the monstrously busy A27 road (74.6). In order to meet up with the original route, which crossed the A27 at Newmarket Inn, a tedious stretch beside the dual carriageway follows and it is only when you reach the garage at Newmarket Inn that you can turn away from the A27 and things quieten down. However, you could choose to walk on alongside the A27 into Lewes, the ancient county town of East Sussex. The town contains Norman castle remains and a jumble of medieval streets with a variety of buildings, mostly Georgian and made of local materials. Lewes comes to life on 5 November with one of the most elaborate and impressive bonfire processions in the country, while the wealth of antique shops and both ancient and modern book dealers provide constant delight for the connoisseur and bibliophile.

A27 Crossing to Alfriston (13.6 miles) via Rodmell and Southease

ENJOY: Firle Beacon, Alfriston

The route moves away from the A27 and begins a climb back onto the escarpment, which now faces north-east rather than north. Soon you reach Juggs Road, an ancient route that was used to carry fish to the market at Lewes. As the route proceeds south-eastwards, there are good views all along this stretch to the town, as well as Newhaven and out towards Seaford. The contrast with, say, Heyshott Down and Graffham Down could not be starker, for this area of downland is almost totally exposed and there is an absence of trees throughout this section. Well-defined tracks take you over Swanborough Hill, Iford Hill, Front Hill and Mill Hill above the Ouse valley and its villages of Kingston-near-Lewes, Itford and Rodmell; in due course you descend to this valley, dropping down to a track then turning left along it to reach the unclassified Lewes–Newhaven road. (There is an official alternative route for the latter part of the walk from the A27 to allow walkers to visit Rodmell.)

You turn right onto the road and shortly left, and it is then a short stroll to the pretty village of Southease. Undoubtedly its most interesting feature is its flint church (80.6) complete with round Saxon tower – one of only three in the whole of Sussex. The church, which contains box pews and some thirteenth-century paintings depicting scenes from the life of Christ, is right on the route and its shady churchyard is a lovely place for a rest on a hot day. A short road walk eastwards takes you across the River Ouse and then over the railway line. There is a useful railway halt here, with trains to Lewes and Newhaven, although train times should be checked carefully in advance to avoid a long wait.

You cross the busy A26, the main road linking the port of Newhaven with the A27 trunk road, then have an immediate steep ascent onto Itford Hill. Once the lost height is regained there follows another splendid high-level eastward march on excellent paths, the escarpment now more north-facing again. The ridge walking is easy and satisfying, as the Way passes Beddingham Hill and Firle Plantation, with views out towards Glyndebourne, well known for its festival of opera. The nearby village of Glynde will forever be associated with John Ellman, whose claim to fame is as a first-class sheep breeder of the black-faced Southdown sheep, which can be found grazing along parts of the route. The ridge walk culminates in another of the great summits of the South Downs Way, the 713 ft Firle Beacon, bestrewn with tumuli, and the sight, unusual on this part of the walk: a large clump of trees making up Firle Plantation. As with Ditchling Beacon, the best views are to the north, with Charleston farmhouse immediately ahead. Charleston farmhouse has no dancing connections but was in fact the headquarters of the Bloomsbury Group, the set of influential English writers and philosophers which included Virginia Woolf and Lytton Strachey.

From Firle Beacon the Way continues over Bostal Hill and past the quaintly-named Bopeep Bostal; the curious walker will be reassured to know that 'bostal' in this instance, a term peculiar to the South Downs, means a path up a steep hill. From here it is almost all downhill, the Way passing further tumuli as it drops down to the Cuckmere valley, the last great valley on the South Downs Way. In due course the buildings of Alfriston come into view, and you descend between two patches of woodland and onto a metalled road that leads into the village (88.2). This is one of the biggest settlements actually on the route itself, and it is a fascinating place, with numerous timber-framed, tile-hung and weatherboarded houses, particularly round the square. Several of them house attractive shops and eating places. There are a number of ancient inns in the village; the thirsty traveller who stops at the Star Inn might note that its timbers are ornamented with carvings of beasts, and at one corner of the inn stands what is arguably Alfriston's most celebrated landmark; a large red lion which was once the figurehead of a seventeenth-century Dutch ship. Two other treasures in the village are the fourteenth-century Clergy House, the National Trust's very first acquisition, and the fourteenth-century flint church of St Andrew, known as the Cathedral of the Downs. There is an interesting range of shops, including the marvellous post office offering takeaway teas and hot pies, and another devoted to light music nostalgia. Frank Sinatra and Nat King Cole enthusiasts will find no better collection this side of the Atlantic.

MAIN ROUTE

Alfriston to Eastbourne (10.6 miles) via Westdean, Exceat and Birling Gap

ENJOY: Westdean, Seven Sisters, Beachy Head, Eastbourne

The main route of the Way proceeds across the Cuckmere River then enjoys a delightful stroll southwards along the river bank, which serves as a very pleasant contrast to the high-level walking that characterises so much of the route. The riverside walking ends at Litlington, a pretty village of flint cottages and a charming tea garden. You cross straight over the road here and proceed away from Litlington on a track, rising all the while and passing Charleston Manor, part of which dates back to 1200. Amongst the manor's attractions are a walled garden, a medieval dovecote and one of the biggest tithe barns in the county. Having passed the manor, the Way climbs steeply into a substantial area of beech woodland known as Friston Forest. Soon the Way enters the village of Westdean (91), which is a peaceful and secluded place with a flint-built rectory dating back to the thirteenth century. The part-Norman church of All Saints contains a memorial to Lord Waverley who, as Sir John Anderson, was Home Secretary during the Second World War and introduced the air-raid shelter bearing his name. It is believed that Alfred the Great had a palace here, probably on the site in the village centre where the ruins of the medieval manor and a nearby dovecote are preserved as ancient monuments.

There follows a steep descent south-westwards to the Cuckmere at Exceat Bridge, where you are confronted by the extremely busy A259. Exceat is a major tourist honeypot, boasting a wildlife exhibition and complex, and numerous signposted walks beside the Cuckmere Estuary and back into Friston Forest. Amidst the wealth of signposting, it is quite easy to lose the route of the South Downs Way. It does not follow the wide waterside path on the valley floor, but uses a path a little to the east to meet the valley floor, some way downstream of the A259 crossing. Your arrival at the Cuckmere Estuary is a most exciting moment, signifying that the journey is almost at an end. First, however, you must negotiate the final significant range of hills of the South Downs: the Seven Sisters.

The Seven Sisters consist of a series of dramatic chalk clifftops rising to over 500 ft. The depressions separating each clifftop, or Sister, are the valleys of ancient rivers, formed when the chalk extended further seawards, but later cut off when the sea pounded the chalk away. Even after nearly a hundred weary miles, you will not fail to be thrilled by this magnificent sequence of chalk cliffs, providing superb views both to the sea and inland, and serving as a fitting and splendid culmination to so much hard but satisfying downland walking. Each Sister has a name; from west to east they are Haven Brow, Short Brow, Rough Brow, Brass Point, Flagstaff Point, Baily's Hill and Hill Brow.

Having negotiated the final Sister, you descend to a freak cleft in the South Downs known as Birling Gap (95), near to which is a flight of steep steps that saw use by eighteenth-century smugglers. This is another popular spot for visitors – refreshments may be available – but it can be a frightening place in stormy weather, and coastal erosion has made the houses here particularly vulnerable. The ground rises again, passing the Belle Tout lighthouse, which was operational between 1834 and 1901 and was subsequently turned into a private house; at the time of writing it was a hotel. Coastal erosion recently led to the building being moved, piece by piece, from its original position. Using one of a plethora of available paths, you climb to the last but arguably most famous summit of the South Downs Way. At 534 ft, Beachy Head is one of the highest cliffs on the South Coast, and on a clear day it is possible to see the Isle of Wight and Dungeness in Kent. At the base of the cliff is the distinctive red and white lighthouse, built in 1902 to replace the Belle Tout lighthouse, and capable of sending a beam sixteen miles across the English Channel. In 1999 a portion of cliff fell down hereabouts, and you should take care on the cliff edges as erosion makes further cliff slips very possible.

Beachy Head is an immensely popular spot, and on most days you will not be alone as you stride over the turf and – again with a fair number of paths to choose from – begin the steady descent to the final objective: the town of Eastbourne (98.8). At the foot of the hill the South Downs Way officially ends, and you may then follow the promenade to reach the town centre.

ALTERNATIVE BRIDLE ROUTE

Alfriston to Eastbourne (7.4 miles) via Jevington

ENJOY: Wilmington Long Man, Windover Hill, Jevington

Like the main route, the bridle route crosses the Cuckmere footbridge just beyond Alfriston, then continues eastwards along the track, turns left and enjoys a stroll through the water meadows by the Cuckmere. Soon you reach and cross a metalled road, then join a track that heads south-eastwards, shortly crossing another road. A right turn along this road takes you to the tiny church at Lullington, just 16 ft square with room for over twenty people. Beyond the road the Way, still following a track, proceeds eastwards then south-eastwards, climbing on to Windover Hill. As well as commanding splendid views to the Cuckmere Valley, the Way is within easy reach of that most extraordinary Sussex Downs landmark, the 226 ft high Long Man of Wilmington.

Long Man of Wilmington
Restored in 1874, nobody knows for certain how, or why, it came into existence, but one expert suggests that the figure, holding a staff in each of his outstretched hands, was a 'dodman' holding posts for surveying and establishing ley lines. Another theory is that he represented King Harold of the Saxons, with a spear in each hand. Others claim it represents a pagan god or a medieval pilgrim or even that it has Roman origins.

The South Downs Way passes directly above the Long Man so he cannot be properly appreciated from the path itself. If you wish to get a better view, you would be well advised to detour towards the village of Wilmington itself, which is also worth a visit, with its fourteenth-century Benedictine priory remains and a part-Norman church with an enormous yew tree in the churchyard. Windover Hill is of interest to the historian, for it contains a group of Neolithic flint mines on its south face, and further south of the mines is a well-preserved long barrow, 180 ft long and stretching to 50 ft wide. From the summit of Windover Hill there is then some fine high-level walking before the Way drops down through the Lullington Heath Nature Reserve and along the north-east fringe of Friston Forest to reach the village of Jevington (92). There is a most attractive flint church with a Saxon tower, and there are a number of pretty flint and tiled cottages and a picturesque pub, the Six Bells. From Jevington, the Way rises for the last time and the town of Eastbourne unfolds ahead. Passing Willingdon Hill, from which there are magnificent views to the town of Eastbourne and beyond, the route runs beside a golf course and drops down to Paradise Drive where, for walkers taking this alternative route, the South Downs Way ends (95.6 via bridle route). It now just remains for you to make your way to the centre of Eastbourne. The town, with its three-mile esplanade and fine array of shops, parks and theatres, is a most pleasant place to linger at the end of a long walk, if time is available. Two features of particular interest are the Wish Tower, formerly a Martello tower (coastal defensive fort) and now a coastal defence museum, and the bandstand which contains seats for 3,000 and offers frequent band concerts to delight audiences and passers-by. As you proceed into the town after your long pilgrimage from Winchester, you might like to think that the band's robust rendition of 'When The Saints Go Marching In' is really for you, even though at that precise moment you may feel a more appropriate tune to be 'Show Me The Way To Go Home'.

The North Downs Way

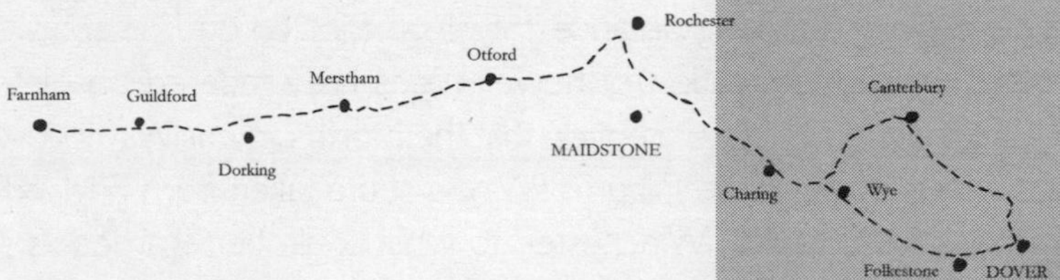

Designation: National trail.
Length: 125 miles (main route) or 130 miles (loop route).
Start: Farnham, Surrey.
Finish: Dover, Kent.
Nature: A walk along the escarpment of the North Downs through Surrey and Kent, with fine views across the Weald and north towards the capital.
Difficulty rating: Moderate.
Average time of completion: 10–11 days.

HIGHLIGHTS OF THIS WALK:

- **St Martha's**
- **Box Hill**
- **Chevening**
- **Canterbury**
- **Dover**

The North Downs Way, opened in 1978, may not be the oldest national trail but its roots lie in pre-history. The ridge of the North Downs (the formation of which I explained in the section describing the South Downs Way) is believed to have formed part of a trading link between the peoples of Surrey and Kent and the Isle of Portland after the retreat of the ice approximately 10,000 years ago. It is even claimed that paths along the North Downs were used by pre-Ice Age hunters some 250,000 years ago. Until Britain was separated from the rest of Europe about 5,000 years ago, people from what is now France and Germany may have gained access to central England by these routes. Since then, it is likely that the routes were used for cattle-droving and long-distance travel on foot or on horseback – routes which the creation of newer roads has rendered obsolete. There is a popular misconception that the North Downs Way follows the same course as the Pilgrims' Way, a route taken from England's former secular capital, Winchester, to what could be regarded as its spiritual capital, Canterbury. Although recognition has been given to the proximity of Canterbury with a loop route which leaves the principal route near Wye and continues to Dover right through the cathedral city, there are considerable differences between them. In any case, the Pilgrims' Way does not have quite the same scenic beauty or historic significance. Not only is it not a properly marked route, but it tends to remain beneath the chalk escarpment rather than climbing onto it as the North Downs Way does, it has probably only been called the Pilgrims' Way since the mid-nineteenth century, and some historians now doubt whether medieval pilgrims actually used it at all!

The nearness of London to the chalk escarpment does undoubtedly have an effect on the character of the route. In contrast to the South Downs Way there are few long uninterrupted stretches of path walking, and it can be fiddly and disjointed. Busy roads and railways run parallel to, and across, the route in many places, creating a constant barrage of noise. Development is so intense that camping is difficult, if not impossible; even the smaller, prettier villages situated on or near the route have expanded through insensitive post-war building so there is little sense of isolation or tranquillity. Virtually the whole route is green belt commuter country, conjuring images not so much of broad vistas of rolling pastures and unspoilt woodland as bowler-hatted *FT* readers scrambling for the last portion of standing-room on the 7.42.

Logistically and technically the North Downs Way is not difficult. Access to amenities is never a problem, as there are so many towns and villages close to the route. There is a fair amount of up-and-down work, with the path rising to nearly 900 ft in places but, save one or two steep climbs, there is nothing that is too arduous. There are ample rewards for modest effort in terms of some superb viewpoints and many attractive stretches of airy downland and beautiful beech-woods. Originally the North Downs were covered with dense woodlands of ash, hornbeam, beech and yew. Much of this has been cleared to expose grazing land, but several pockets of woodland remain, with many lovely flowers including violet, primrose, stitchwort, hazel, honeysuckle and lady orchid; the North Downs is the only area in Britain where the lady orchid is to be found. On the thin, chalky soils of the Downs the walker can also find yellow trefoil, rock rose, hawkbit, pinks and blues of the scabious and knapweed families, and autumn gentian. Birds include the skylark, yellowhammer, wood pigeon, woodpecker, kestrel, chaffinch and grey partridge, and on the ground, you should look out for voles, rabbits, foxes and badgers. In August you may see the beautiful chalkhill blue butterfly on the more exposed grassland, but marbled white butterflies may be seen earlier in the year, especially on the first half of the journey.

Farnham to Newlands Corner (14.4 miles) via Seale and Puttenham

ENJOY: Farnham, Watts Gallery, St Martha's Hill

Farnham, best known as the home of the writer William Cobbett, author of *Rural Rides*, is a very agreeable place to start the journey. Its loveliest street is the elegant Castle Street with its Georgian buildings and almshouses, overshadowed by its splendid red brick Norman castle. It dates from the twelfth century and was the palace of the bishops of Winchester until 1925. The North Downs Way starts rather unceremoniously by a busy road junction of the A31 with the road coming down from the station. It follows eastwards alongside the A31 but then thankfully leaves it by turning right, passing a fine timbered house and ducking underneath the railway, and follows a track into a pleasant meadow, joining a peaceful country road. Detouring along this road for a mile or so brings you to Waverley Abbey, the first Cistercian house in England, dating back to 1128. However, the route turns left off this road onto Compton Way and, crossing the River Wey, passes Moor Park College before climbing steeply away from the valley.

Near the top of the hill, the Way leaves the road, turns left, proceeds across fields and then passes through an area of woodland, broken up only by Crooksbury Road near the end. Emerging from the woods, you turn right onto Sands Road and drop down to Farnham Golf Club where there is a left turn into Blighton Lane. After following this lane briefly, turn right onto a pleasant path which climbs steadily alongside the golf course and, after crossing Binton Lane, proceed along a field edge. There are good views on the right to the wooded Crooksbury Hill and its distinctive mast. The Way passes round the edge of the village of Seale; a detour down the road will bring you to Seale Church, almost entirely rebuilt in the nineteenth century but with some medieval fragments and a pleasant view from the nearby war memorial.

You continue through an area of woodland and then emerge onto pastures with fine views east towards Puttenham Common. The route descends gently to Totford Lane, then, having crossed the lane, enters Puttenham Common and begins climbing again, soon reaching the village of Puttenham (6.6) and proceeding by road down its attractive street. Its church has features dating from the twelfth century and south of the church is Puttenham Priory, a Palladian building dating from 1762. The village lies right below the very busy A31 Farnham–Guildford road, which runs along a narrow 500 ft chalk ridge. As you proceed from Seale to Puttenham the ridge is a constant and attractive feature to your left, and although you may be disappointed that the Way itself does not proceed along it, you would have to concede that the traffic noise would spoil the walk to some extent. The ridge is known as the Hog's Back, and one wonders how many local residents are dying to be asked by walkers or other visitors, 'Do you know the Hog's Back?' so they can reply, 'I didn't know he'd been away!'

From Puttenham the Way crosses the B3000 Compton–Hog's Back road and proceeds along a path past Puttenham golf course and through woodland. You pass underneath the busy and noisy A3 London–Portsmouth road, and soon reach a minor road. The route turns left onto the road and then shortly right onto a sandy lane, but a little further up the road is the Watts Gallery, exhibiting a collection of paintings by the nineteenth-century artist George Frederick Watts, best known for his allegorical works such as *Hope* and *Mammon* but also well known for his portraits of biblical and classical subjects. By detouring down the road in the opposite direction, you will pass by the ornate Watts memorial chapel and into the village of Compton. The church is worth visiting because it contains the only double-deck sanctuary to survive in England. The purpose of the second, 'upstairs' sanctuary is a mystery. The Norman railing, carved from a single piece of wood, is reputedly the oldest architectural wood carving in an English church.

Back on the Way, the route proceeds resolutely eastwards towards Guildford and round the edge of the Loseley Estate and its nature reserve, although views to Loseley House, built in 1562 with stone from Waverley Abbey, are restricted by woodland. The Way proceeds along the northern fringes of the woods, then into more open country past Piccard's Farm and on to the A3100 (11). A detour left along this road takes you into Guildford, a most attractive town with a steep cobbled high street containing many historic buildings, notably the seventeenth-century almshouses and the Angel Hotel which has an old wooden gallery and coaching yard. There is a castle, built by Henry II, of which only the keep survives, and a modern cathedral. The Way, however, goes more or less straight over the A3100, once again crosses the River Wey, and then after crossing the A281 and flirting briefly with the outskirts of the city, it begins the climb to St Martha's Hill. The ascent, initially on the fringes of woodland known as Chantries, continues through woodland to reach the beautiful hilltop church of St Martha, rebuilt in the nineteenth century from a ruin, the original church dating back to 1200. During the climb there are glorious panoramic views of the Surrey countryside. From the church you drop down to a road then climb again to Newlands Corner (14.4). This provides another good viewpoint and, because it is on the A25 Guildford–Dorking road, is a popular stopping-place and picnic area for motorists. The A25, which you cross here, used to be a major arterial road, but with the completion of the M25 is rather quieter and if you have time you may wish to detour alongside it to visit the pretty villages of Albury and Shere. Albury has an attractive park with fine cedar and yew trees, and in the park is a church with a remarkably ornate chapel built by Pugin as a mortuary chapel for Henry Drummond, the owner of the park.

Downs Link Path

On your way from St Martha's Hill to Newlands Corner you meet the Downs Link path. This route runs from Shoreham-by-Sea to Guildford and, as the name implies, forms a link between the escarpments of the North and South Downs. Where long-distance paths overlap, there is always the possibility of overlapping waymarking as well, and thereby the possibility of confusion; a tired walker late in the day following a sequence of beautifully formed arrows may receive an unpleasant surprise when, expecting to arrive in a village that has promised him dinner and a much-needed night's sleep, he is confronted with a signpost indicating that the village is now further away than when he started that morning.

Newlands Corner to Reigate (17.4 miles) via Ranmore Common

ENJOY: Mole Stepping Stones, Box Hill, Colley Hill

After crossing the A25, The Way enters woodland, initially going eastwards as far as the Shere–East Clandon road. After crossing this road and emerging from the woods to pass Hollister Farm, the Way re-enters woodland and follows a broad forest track across Netley Heath and the edge of Hackhurst Downs, then leaves the track and descends steeply in a south-easterly direction to meet a minor road linking the A25 with Effingham. You turn left onto this road, and proceeding north-eastwards, begin climbing again. After briefly following the road, the Way turns right and continues across White Downs through a further area of woodland, although breaks in the woods do allow good views to Dorking and Leith Hill, which at 965 ft is the highest point in Surrey. Eventually the Way reaches a minor road at Ranmore Common (21.7), within sight of an attractively situated church which, like St Martha's Church, is right on the path. Known as the Church on the North Downs Way, it is faced entirely with cobbles.

The Way leaves Ranmore Common by means of a minor road and passes through the Denbies estate, joining a track to begin the descent to the valley. There was a large Italianate house here but it was demolished in 1954, and the estate is now better known for its vineyard, which you pass during you descent. The valley – used by the Romans to take Stane Street to London – was created by the River Mole which has here cut a spectacular gap through the North Downs; Box Hill rises steeply on the other side, and the enjoyment you may feel as you drop downhill will be tempered with dread at the thought of a stiff climb almost immediately afterwards. The descent takes longer than one somehow feels it should, and its beauty is not enhanced by the noise of the busy A24, which runs through the valley. On reaching the valley floor, you meet railway, road and river in close succession, crossing the railway to reach the A24 road. By detouring up the A24 northwards you will reach a station from which trains are available to the pleasant town of Dorking nearby. It will also be possible to view the Burford Bridge Hotel, where Lord Nelson finally separated from Lady Nelson in 1800 and Keats completed *Endymion* in 1818. Thankfully you are spared having to walk across the A24, an underpass having been created instead, and you can proceed safely to the crossing of the Mole.

Mole Stepping Stones

The river crossing may be undertaken by a clearly signposted footbridge, but the more direct and romantic crossing is by means of a set of stepping stones. At times when the river level is higher than normal this crossing may not be feasible and the footbridge will have to be used. Even when the stones are usable, you would be well advised, particularly in wet weather when the stones are already slippery, to check the soles of your boots for accumulations of mud or other alluvial deposit before making the crossing. Few things will be more harmful to the dignity of the intrepid traveller, equipped with all the latest hi-tech gear, than being involuntarily propelled into the murky depths of a Surrey river, particularly if the victim's performance is witnessed by a herd of tittering juveniles on the opposite bank.

There is then a punishing climb from roughly 160 ft to 560 ft in less than half a mile, onto the chalk plateau of Box Hill (23.9). With its sweeping views across the Weald, it is an immensely popular spot, particularly at weekends and holiday times. Thirsty walkers will be well catered for, with ice cream vans sure to be in attendance in summer, and the Boxhills pub, claiming to be the highest pub in Surrey, situated nearby. A stone on the hill marks the spot where one Peter Labellieres was buried upside down; because he thought the 'world is turned topsy-turvy' he believed his body would eventually be righted! The hillside contains lovely woodland, including whitebeam, juniper, yew, oak, birch and the box trees on its flank which gave the hill its name. Box is in fact the densest English wood, and Thomas Bewick, a famous engraver of birds and animals, claimed that one of his blocks, made of the wood, was sound after being used 900,000 times. The Way proceeds eastwards, passing through the woodland of Brockham Hills and losing height all the time, although the views remain good.

You pass along the south edge of Betchworth Quarry and go forward to the B2032, just north of Betchworth which has a useful station on the Guildford–Redhill–Tonbridge line. You turn left onto the B2032, and follow this road round a right-hand and then left-hand bend. When it finally straightens out, the Way turns right off the road through a narrow strip of woodland, left again, uphill and then right once more to follow the side of the Buckland Hills and Juniper Hill. There is thick woodland along the steep slopes to the left, and more open country to the right. Just beyond Juniper Hill there is a sharp left turn, and you rise steeply upwards to the summit of Colley Hill. There then follows an exhilarating high-level walk, first on Colley Hill and then Reigate Hill (31.8), on a good track towards the A217 just north of Reigate. There are superb views both to the north and to the south; the south brings more excellent Wealden panoramas, while to the north you have views right into the heart of London. The great vistas prompted a senior Army officer to build an ornate viewing pavilion here in 1909. Fast, largely level walking takes you forward to the A217, and the possibility of a detour to Reigate, past a motley collection of edifices including a water tower, a fort and, at the time of writing, a cats' home.

Reigate to Oxted (10.2 miles) via Merstham

ENJOY: Gatton Park, Merstham, Oxted Downs

The A217 is crossed by means of a footbridge. You are just a stone's throw from its junction with the M25, and the traffic noise is considerable. You proceed through attractive National Trust-owned woodland, then turn right onto a driveway through Gatton Park. The early nineteenth-century house is now a school, while St Andrew's Church, within its grounds, is of Gothic composition and has what Pevsner describes as one of the best private chapels in the country. Until 1832, despite having just 23 houses, Gatton returned two members to Parliament, making it the most rotten borough but three in the country. It is no wonder that Pevsner describes the town hall, built in 1765 and in which elections for the borough were solemnly held, as a 'very English political joke!' The Way leaves Gatton Park and proceeds gently downhill through fields into Merstham (34). Merstham is a very pretty place, although it has the misfortune to have the M25 run right through its middle; particularly noteworthy is the church of St Katharine, the tower of which dates back to 1220, and a road called Quality Street with attractive old buildings including examples of firestone, brick, half-timbering and tile-hanging.

You cross the M25 and leave Merstham by way of a right turn into Rockshaw Road. The road runs parallel with the M25 which is on the right, and, with the M23 coming in from the left, you could be forgiven for feeling like the jam in a motorway sandwich. Immediately ahead is the interchange of these motorways, and the lover of motorway engineering can obtain a grandstand view of it from the bridge just ahead. The North Downs Way, however, leaves Rockshaw Road just short of the bridge, turns left and passes under the M23, climbing to a triangulation point some 660 ft above sea level, higher than Box Hill. You continue eastwards, crossing a minor road and proceeding to Willey Park Farm where you turn right and follow a track heading south-east. You cross another minor road to join a road that proceeds over White Hill, where there is a good viewpoint, while just south of the path on White Hill is the Iron Age hill fort of War Coppice.

Two roads head off to the left, leading into the commuter town of Caterham, and just after the second turning you leave the road, taking a right turn on a footpath to contour the partially-wooded Gravelly Hill. There are excellent southward views from the hillside before you enter the woods and head in a more north-easterly direction to pick up the crossing of the A22 London–Eastbourne road. Almost immediately after crossing the A22, the Way forks right along a track which proceeds eastwards past Quarry Farm and, after crossing a wide track that leads onto Winders Hill, drops down south-eastwards to meet a minor road. You cross the road, following a track steeply uphill north-eastwards onto the wooded Tandridge Hill and the beautiful National Trust-owned South Hawke, providing splendid views. You then drop down the steep chalk cliffs through the woods, using steps. This is one of the finest moments of the walk so far, if a little unnerving for those with a fear of heights, for you are now crossing over a railway tunnel and, looking straight down, can see the railway emerging from the tunnel far below as it heads towards Oxted. It is a fine combination of natural beauty and man's ingenuity. Once over the tunnel, the Way continues to lose height, proceeding through the woods and into open country, then having passed some limeworks, soon reaches a minor road (42). The Way crosses more or less straight over but by following the road to the right you will reach Oxted, a commuter town with little to see, although the old town contains some old timber-framed cottages, and direct trains to London are available.

Oxted to Wrotham (18.4 miles) via Otford

ENJOY: Titsey Place, Sundridge Hill, Chevening, Otford Mount

Beyond the Oxted road the North Downs Way proceeds eastwards, initially in open country and then alongside the thickly wooded slopes of the Titsey Plantation to the left. You reach a T-junction of paths on the edge of Titsey Park; Titsey Place, within the park, dates back to 1775. At the T-junction you turn left and climb steeply up Pitchfont Lane to the road junction at Botley Hill;

at 882 ft the highest point of the North Downs. At the junction you turn hard right onto the B269, then shortly turn left off it and cut through woodland and open country to the B2024, immediately below Tatsfield. There are some fine views on the Botley–Tatsfield section; indeed, local housebuilders tried to draw Londoners to developments around Tatsfield by saying 'Come to the London Alps!' It has to be said that there are occasions, particularly when rain and mist sweep over the North Downs, on which it is hard to visualise any similarity between these murky heights and sun-drenched, snow-capped peaks of Switzerland and France.

Joining the B2024 briefly, you proceed straight ahead at a three-way junction onto a lane beside the golf course, and a right turn at the next fork takes you onto a drive which goes forward to the A233 Westerham–Biggin Hill road. You have now crossed the border into Kent. Detouring to the right along the A233 brings you to Westerham. Referred to by Daniel Defoe as a 'handsome, well-built market town,' it is indeed an attractive place, and although rather spoilt with modern development, retains some pleasant features including a green, a market square, the part-thirteenth-century church of St Mary, and two fine seventeenth-century buildings; namely Grosvenor House and Quebec House. After crossing the A233 the Way, having lost some height from Botley Hill, climbs up again, through woodland initially and then onto the more open country of Hogtrough Hill.

You continue in a generally north-eastward direction, following firstly a minor road, then field edges, to the 760-ft triangulation point on Sundridge Hill. You then skirt the northern fringes of the beech woodlands at the northern end of Chevening Park, briefly entering the woods themselves at one point, and then begin to veer to the south-east. As you do so, you pass close to the village of Knockholt that lies to your left. The Way continues south-eastwards, dropping steeply downhill into the wide Darent Valley, with magnificent views across Chevening Park, its tree-fringed lake, and the red brick house thought to have been built for Lord Dacre, who died in 1630. At length you reach the B2211 and follow it briefly to the left to reach the A224, turning right onto this road and crossing over the M25. Just to the south-west is the M25 interchange with the M26. The route soon leaves the A224 just short of Dunton Green to turn left onto a minor road and then immediately right, heading north-eastwards across fields and over the main London–Tonbridge railway line. It may make a pleasant change to observe rushing trains rather than rushing vehicles. A glance at the map reveals that this particular stretch of line lies between two of the longest railway tunnels in southern England: the Knockholt and Sevenoaks tunnels (the former running underneath the escarpment of the North Downs).

From the railway the route continues on a well-defined track towards Otford, turning right onto a road and then proceeding eastwards over the River Darent into the village centre (53.7). Otford is a most picturesque place, where even the roundabout comes with pond and weeping willow. Some parts of the church date back to the eleventh century, and the Bull Inn contains a sixteenth-century fireplace. There are also remains of an archbishop's palace, the work of Archbishop Warham and in use from the early sixteenth century. Refreshments should be available in the village, and if so it may be wise to take advantage of them; after a brief walk on the A225 the Way, continuing in the same easterly direction, leaves the road and heads very steeply uphill to Otford Mount, from where there are superb views across the Darent Valley and beyond. The route stays at a good height, crossing a minor road and proceeding round the north edge of woodland within sight of Otford Manor, and above the village of Kemsing. Its church of St Mary is of Norman origin, but contains a remarkable decorated rood screen, Pre-Raphaelite reredos and gold altar canopy. All this was created in the twentieth century by the Gothic revivalist Comper, and described by Simon Jenkins as 'an uncommonly harmonious work of twentieth-century art.'

Back on the Way, you cross another minor road, after which there is a mixture of open and woodland walking, the route still proceeding roughly in an easterly direction, on the top fringes of the escarpment. Then, in Chalk Pit Wood, a more extensive patch of woodland, the Way swings in a southward direction and, crossing a minor road, drops down steeply through cornfields to reach a wide track; the course of the old Pilgrims' Way. Turning left onto the track, it is a straightforward walk eastwards below the escarpment to reach Wrotham (60.4). Once again, you are close to the convergence of two motorways, this time the M26 and M20.

Brass Rubbings

The Way passes round the northern edge of Wrotham, but it is worth detouring to view the charming village centre with its outstanding medieval church, which is particularly rich in brasses and has a remarkable portrait gallery with about fifty figures of five families ranging in date from 1498 to 1615. A brass-rubbing is a most personal and rewarding souvenir of a visit to a church on a national trail, but the hiker, having completed it, would be well advised to post it home. It would be such a pity if rainwater, seeping through his rucksack, soaked his lovingly finished reproduction of Lionel, Duke of Clarence (d.1368) or Roger Mortimer, Earl of March (d.1398), resulting in an indelible imprint on his only dry T-shirt.

Wrotham to Medway Bridge (10.6 miles) via Upper Bush and Cuxton

ENJOY: Coldrum Stones, Holly Hill, Rochester

Leaving Wrotham, the Way crosses the A227 and the M20, and proceeds north-eastwards on a minor road past Hognore Farm then, when the road executes a hairpin bend and starts to descend, the path continues up the hill and into the woods, gaining the upper fringes of the escarpment once more. The Way meets the A227 again but immediately turns right onto a minor road and soon left onto a footpath, staying in the woods as it continues eastwards through Trosley Country Park, immediately south of the sprawling Vigo Village. A detour down the escarpment brings you to the peaceful and isolated Norman church of Trottiscliffe, and half a mile or so to the east are the Coldrum Stones, a megalithic long barrow thought to date back to 2000 BC. Back on the Way, having gained all the height, you promptly lose it again, descending through woodland on the southern fringes of Whitehorse Wood, then climb back up to the top of the escarpment. The views hereabouts are truly magnificent, and this area is justifiably popular with visitors. The Way proceeds northwards up a lane past the 643-ft Holly Hill triangulation point, then when the lane ends it continues north through Greatpark Wood before turning eastwards and then north-eastwards. The going is still predominantly through woodland, broken up by just two patches of open land. Immediately to the east is the less congenial Medway valley, but although the valley is heavily built-up with a number of industrial villages and towns, the woodland of beech, hornbeam and yew hides it from view.

In due course, you reach a crossroads of paths; while a right turn leads shortly down to North Halling in the valley, the Way turns left and follows a course slightly west of north, proceeding downhill through North Wood and onto the hamlet of Upper Bush. Swinging north-eastwards again on a track and then footpath, you arrive at the Cobham–Cuxton road just west of the village of Cuxton. Instead of proceeding into the village, the Way appears to shy away from it, turning left and climbing steeply to cross the railway. The route then executes a rather crude semi-circle round Cuxton, heading north-eastwards initially, dropping steeply and then rising to a thin area of woodland. Superb views now open out across the Medway valley, with your eyes being irresistibly drawn to the Medway bridge, for which you are now heading. Before reaching it, however, you have to drop south-eastwards between two further areas of woodland to complete the circuit of Cuxton, then turn left and proceed beside the busy A228 to reach the junction with the M2 and the all-important Medway crossing. Cuxton, despite being shunned by the path planners, does have some redeeming features, including a hillside church with a Norman nave, and a sixteenth-century gateway which is the only surviving feature of a late fifteenth-century house called Whorne's Place.

The exciting crossing of the Medway may be delayed if you wish to visit nearby Rochester, reached by continuing north-eastwards along the A228. The city contains a twelfth-century, 128 ft high Norman castle keep (the largest in England), several timbered houses, Benedictine priory ruins, traces of the walls of the old Roman settlement of Durobrivae, a seventeenth-century guildhall and a cathedral, built between the twelfth and fifteenth century, which has a magnificent west doorway with highly decorative carving. The cathedral contains the tomb of St William of Perth, who was murdered near Rochester in 1201 during a pilgrimage; after he was buried, a number of miracles were reported to have taken place at his tomb. The city has strong associations with Charles Dickens who spent much of his life in the area, and parts of Rochester appear in his novels *Pickwick Papers*, *Great Expectations* and *The Mystery of Edwin Drood*.

Returning down the A228 to rejoin the Way, your next task will be to cross the Medway, using the left-hand side of the splendid M2 motorway bridge high above the river (71). It is an undeniably exhilarating experience, albeit somewhat alarming for the vertigo-sufferer!

Medway Bridge to Hollingbourne (15.3 miles) via Detling

ENJOY: Kit's Coty House, White Horse Stone, Boxley

Coming off the bridge, you pass to the other side of the M2, turning right just past Nashenden Farm and climbing onto Wouldham

Downs with good views to the Medway valley and the woodlands beyond. The Way then veers south-eastwards over Burham Common to meet the A229 just below Chatham at Blue Bell Hill, the footpath graduating to a narrow metalled road and, soon after Burham Hill Farm, passing the Robin Hood, an isolated but most welcome pub. At Blue Bell Hill the Way, rather than crossing the A229, turns southwards and proceeds along a path parallel with it, swinging west of south to reach Kit's Coty House, a Neolithic burial chamber consisting of three upright stones, 7–8 ft high, surmounted by a capstone nearly 13 ft long. Although their survival over several thousand years is remarkable, their preservation has not been assisted by the graffiti which has been carved on them. Some of the graffiti is in fact well over 100 years old and could therefore be said to have acquired historical interest of its own. However, the iron cage in which the stones are enclosed denies contemporary North Downs Way walkers the opportunity to fascinate future generations of pilgrims with their own suitably apposite inscriptions.

Beyond Kit's Coty House the Way goes on to meet and cross a road junction, then proceeds eastwards, going under the A229. You pass more prehistoric stones, consisting of a single megalith known as the White Horse Stone, and a whole group of fallen sarsen stones – actually the ruined burial chamber of a prehistoric long barrow – known as as the Countless Stones but marked on the map as Little Kit's Coty. These lie on the west side of the A229 underpass, with the White Horse Stone on the east side. Immediately beyond the White Horse Stone you briefly follow a track then turn left and proceed extremely steeply up the escarpment, through beech-woods. Turning right at the top, you go south-eastwards along a path which hugs the border between the woods to the right and open fields to the left. The path takes you virtually all the way to Detling which lies immediately beyond the crossing of the A249 Sittingbourne–Maidstone road. By detouring right at the one minor road crossing on this section, you may descend to reach Boxley, an unspoilt village with a green, pond, and ruins of a twelfth-century Cistercian abbey. Just before the A249 you swing south-westwards to the Pilgrims' Way then south-eastwards to cross the A249 and enter Detling, which is the closest you'll get to Maidstone.

Maidstone
This bustling Medway town, badly affected by flooding in the autumn of 2000, boasts the largest church in Kent (All Saints) as well as a fourteenth-century archbishops' palace. After the introduction of hops from the Continent in the sixteenth century, the town became the centre of the Kentish brewery industry. As you walk through Kent you will see many fine examples of oast houses or kilns which were formerly used for drying newly picked hops.

From Detling you bear left, just east of north, then swing south-eastwards to reach the ruins of Thurnham Castle, described as a typical Norman defensive work, and known to have been occupied by Robert de Thurnham in the latter half of the twelfth century, during the reign of Henry II. You then continue south-eastwards to Hollingbourne, over three minor road crossings, leading respectively to Thurnham with its fine brick and timber Friars Place, Bearsted on the outskirts of Maidstone, and Broad Street. When you reach a fourth road, you turn right along it and descend to Hollingbourne (86.3), turning left at the first crossroads to continue.

I have walked parts of the Detling–Hollingbourne section in glorious autumn sunshine, with splendid views across the Garden of England, but I once walked the whole of it under sullen overcast skies, with continuous mud underfoot; the descents were particularly unpleasant, since it was quite impossible to put one foot in front of another without at least one foot slithering out of control. Muddy footpaths can of course occur on even the simplest stretch of a national trail. Sometimes the mud will cover only part of the path, leaving the walker ample room to pass by without soiling his footwear or his trousers. At other times, however, the mixture of mud and water can be so widespread that the walker is left with an unpalatable choice. He may attempt to chart a parallel course through an uncompromising army of spiteful pathside vegetation which seizes every opportunity it can to wrap itself round him, or deposit stings, thorns or other sharp objects on or through his person; alternatively, he may try to wade through the quagmire, each step accompanied by the very real fear that the leg might emerge from it without a boot or shoe on the other end.

Hollingbourne to Boughton Lees (12.8 miles) via Charing

ENJOY: Pilgrims' Way, Lenham, Charing

Hollingbourne is a very pleasant village of old timber-framed houses, and its church contains a number of fine features, including a chapel with 124 shields round its walls, and a life-size marble effigy of one Lady Elizabeth who died in 1638. The good news is that it also marks the start of a fast, easy stretch of the Way along excellent tracks and paths that follow the line of the old Pilgrims' Way, continuing right up to the commencement of the loop section near Boughton Lees. Although your route stays some way down the escarpment, with no real scenic highlights, the views across Kent are still excellent and, despite the presence of two major roads nearby, there is a pleasantly rural feel and a sense of relief that London suburbia and the industrial Medway valley have been left behind. Ironically, the route does have to pass the big Marley factory complex about three miles beyond Hollingbourne. This stretch runs parallel with three important lines of communication, namely the M20 (motorways are never far away on the North Downs Way), the Maidstone–Ashford railway with several useful stations, and the A20. Three pretty villages lie on the A20 close to the route of the Way along this stretch, and they are all easily reachable from the path using the numerous crossing tracks and roads available. First is Harrietsham, which contains charming seventeenth-century cottages and almshouses, and a church with a beautiful fifteenth-century west tower. Next is Lenham, with its fine square surrounded by medieval houses, a tithe barn, a church with excellent wood carvings, wall paintings, another splendid tower dating back to the fourteenth century, and a floor memorial dedicated to one Mary Honywood who died in 1620 leaving 16 children, 114 grandchildren and 228 great-grandchildren! Another interesting feature in Lenham is a building named Saxon Warriors, so called because of the discovery of a fifteenth-century house inside with foundations that contained three skeletons with swords, daggers and spearheads dating back to the sixth century. Some four miles beyond Lenham is Charing. This again contains several attractive cottages of brick and timber; the sixteenth-century Peirce House in the High Street has fine overhanging gables and close timbers. There is a thirteenth-century church with yet another magnificent tower dating back to about 1500, and the remains of an archbishop's palace that was built here around 1300, and in which Henry VIII stayed in 1520 on his way to Calais.

The Way crosses the A252 at Charing (94.4) – from which it is a short walk to the right, down to the village – then continues along the edge of woodland, still following the Pilgrims' Way, to the hamlet of Dunn Street just above the village of Westwell. It is worth making a detour to visit the village to look at the lovely thirteenth-century flint church, which has a magnificent Gothic stone chancel screen. You enter Eastwell Park, passing right by the lake and also a church which was hit by a bomb during the Second World War and is now a ruin; Eastwell House, though Tudor in appearance, is of twentieth-century origin. The Way reaches the A251 just beyond Eastwell Park at Boughton Lees (99.1) and goes over the main road. This marks the end of an almost continuous south-eastward progression which has persisted since leaving Hollingbourne. Over the road, you follow a minor metalled road north-eastwards towards Boughton Aluph. It is along this road that you must choose whether to follow the coast route to Dover via Wye, proceeding more directly towards your goal along the escarpment, picking your way along a disjointed sequence of often muddy lanes and tracks, the view eventually becoming dominated by the sprawl of Folkestone. Or there is the other route via Chilham and Canterbury, where after taking cream teas by the old village square in Chilham, you can proceed to Canterbury, with its historic cathedral, fine range of shops, theatres, live music, medieval pubs, wine and jazz bars, and restaurants offering choice foods from China, Italy, Spain, Mexico and Thailand. You choose!

COAST ROUTE

Boughton Lees to Etchinghill (13.6 miles) via Wye and Stowting

ENJOY: Wye Downs, Wye Nature Reserve

The coast route leaves the Boughton Lees–Boughton Aluph road fractionally after the loop route does. It bears right, following a path that goes round an orchard, and soon reaches the A28 Ashford–Canterbury road, where it turns left. You briefly follow alongside this busy road, then cross it and proceed through more orchards and fields, crossing the Great Stour to reach Wye (101.4 via coast route). The orchards, which have existed in Kent since Roman times, serve as a reminder of Kent's reputation as the Garden of England; the county's traditionally mild climate has allowed many types of fruit, especially apples, to flourish, and in late summer the trees hereabouts will be groaning with Cox's Orange Pippin, Bramley, Golden Delicious and Worcester Pearmain. Wye is a large and interesting village, with a college that dates back to the mid-fifteenth century, a mostly eighteenth-century church with a massive tower and magnificent Queen Anne chancel, some fine town houses including the early seventeenth-century Old Vicarage House and the timber-framed Yew Trees, and several Georgian buildings.

At a crossroads in the village centre you turn left, then right onto a track that climbs back onto the escarpment, past another orchard and through open land and woodland. An unusual feature on the hillside is the Crown memorial, a large chalk cross cut into the Downs. Having gained the top of the escarpment, the Way turns right and some pleasant high-level walking follows in a south-easterly direction through the Wye and Crundale Nature Reserve. You may be fortunate enough to see badgers or fallow deer hereabouts, whilst plant life includes orchids, wild thyme and cowslips. The Way crosses the minor road connecting Wye with Hastingleigh and continues south-eastwards; then at the Brabourne–Waltham road, you turn right onto it and shortly left, following a metalled lane and then a good track below Hastingleigh. You turn right onto a minor road, and pass a triangulation point, from which there is a tremendous view on a good day.

As the road begins to drop steeply, the route turns left onto a track which contours the hillside for a while, then seems to give up the struggle and plunges down to a minor road. You turn left and follow this road through Stowting (108.1), avoiding the road bearing left to the church, and arrive at a T-junction of roads. You proceed straight over it, joining a footpath and climbing steeply up Cobbs Hill to reach the B2068 road. The Way turns right just before the road and proceeds parallel with it on a field edge, passing two junctions but staying on the right of it. Just past the second junction you cross, turn left onto a path and continue in the same south-easterly direction passing to the north of the village of Postling, following a dry valley. It is easy to detour to Postling, with its church bearing the unusual dedication of St Mary and St Radegund; it has a thirteenth-century tower, some twelfth-century wall painting, and a perfectly preserved dedication stone. The area has associations with the novelist Joseph Conrad, who wrote *Typhoon* and *Lord Jim* here.

You reach another minor road and cross it, but by turning right and following this road it is possible to reach Sandling station, which is on the Ashford–Folkestone railway line. Having crossed the Sandling road, you then rise to and pass the giant masts of Swingfield radio station, still heading south-east, and enjoying excellent views from the hilltop. You arrive at the edge of a wood, where you turn left and drop down to the B2065 just south-east of the village of Etchinghill (112.7). The whole of the rest of the walk beyond Etchinghill overlaps with the Saxon Shore Way, a walk of just over 150 miles between Gravesend and Hastings, round the coasts of Kent and part of East Sussex.

Etchinghill to Dover (12.6 miles) via Creteway Down

ENJOY: Caesar's Hill, The Warren, Shakespeare Cliff, Dover

Crossing the B2065 by Etchinghill, the North Downs Way passes under the disused Canterbury–Lyminge–Folkestone railway and climbs steeply onto an escarpment, heading east then south to meet a minor road just south of the hamlet of Arpinge. You cross the road but stay roughly parallel with it, proceeding alongside first the left and then the right of minor roads heading eastwards, all the time remaining above the steep escarpment. The sprawl of Folkestone, and the sea behind, are now clearly visible below, signifying that journey's end is near, whilst dominating the foreground is the huge terminal for private and haulage traffic for the Eurotunnel. Still close to the road, but following a more winding course, the Way negotiates Castle Hill (also known as Caesar's Hill), passing Iron Age earthworks. You veer north-east to meet the A260 Canterbury–Folkestone road (117.3), then cross it and proceed immediately alongside a minor road heading just south of east along Creteway Down. You pass a triangulation point at 557 ft, and soon afterwards the road and path meet the B2011 (the old A20 Folkestone–Dover road), and the Valiant Sailor pub.

Folkestone

From the Valiant Sailor you have reasonably convenient access to the town of Folkestone. Folkestone, a busy Channel port and seaside resort, is the birthplace of the physician William Harvey and the site of the first nunnery in England, established in AD 630. Although there are some quaint old buildings around the harbour, many of the town's buildings date from the nineteenth century, the resort having developed following the arrival of the railway. Although the Valiant Sailor is as near to the heart of Folkestone as the route gets, it is still quite a long walk from the pub into the town, with a long uphill trudge back to the Way afterwards.

Having crossed the A20, the Way takes a path immediately to the right of the pub, then turns left and, for much of the remaining five miles or so to Dover, continues along the cliffs high above the Channel. Initially you look down on the Warren, a chalk landslip basin rich in fossil remains, tree and scrub growth, and wild flowers. It has been described as one of the great classical landslip areas of the country. You then proceed along the cliffs all the way to Shakespeare Cliff, passing Abbot's Cliff and the old firing ranges at Lydden Spout. These clifftops mark the eastern end of the North Downs escarpment. Down below the cliffs is Samphire Hoe, created by the spoil from the Channel Tunnel construction, on which rye grass and other vegetation has been encouraged to grow. It is now a country park and a very splendid and scenic facility for local people and visitors who come to walk, fish or just relax. The cliff walking is a fine climax to the North Downs Way, with views out to sea which may on a clear day extend to the French coast, although the enjoyment of the walk is undoubtedly marred by the noise on the nearby A20. The Way descends from Shakespeare Cliff to follow an underpass beneath the A20, and emerges in the village of Aycliff. The route turns right onto a metalled road, then shortly left through a housing estate. You climb some steps to reach an area of rough pasture, then follow a narrow but clear path north-eastwards across this pasture, with excellent views to Shakespeare Cliff and out to sea. You keep to the right of the buildings of Dover Young Offender Institution, passing the remains of a twelfth-century Knights Templar church, with its distinctive circular nave. You then turn right into Citadel Road and follow it to a T-junction with the North Military Road. The Way turns left, but by detouring right you reach a viewpoint and car park from which there is a magnificent panoramic view of Dover Harbour. The viewpoint car park provides easy access to the Western Heights; these are earthworks which were enlarged to create a complex network of fortifications to protect the country against threats from France in the nineteenth century.

You follow the North Military Road, ignoring a metalled road signposted for the Drop Redoubt, but soon afterwards you turn right up some steps and head south-eastwards round the edge of part of the old fortifications, with wonderful views to the town and harbour of Dover. The route then swings north-eastwards, dropping steeply down two flights of steep steps, the second of which is the 64 St Martin's Steps. At the bottom you bear right and then left into Adrian Street, turn left up York Street, cross it and proceed via Queen Street and King Street into Market Square, where the North Downs Way ends (125.3). Dover is Britain's nearest point to mainland Europe and, as Roman Dubris, was an important naval base and the starting point of Watling Street. There is a vast amount to see and do in the town; its most interesting feature is probably the Norman castle. The castle has a twelfth-century keep, a Roman beacon dating from AD 50 (one of the oldest Roman buildings in the country), the Saxon church of St Mary in Castro, and an underground network of secret wartime tunnels. These were dug during the Napoleonic war and used as a headquarters to plan the Dunkirk evacuation. Other attractions include the Roman Painted House, which includes some Roman wall paintings, and the White Cliffs Experience, which provides a history of Dover from the Roman times to the Second World War. Despite the construction of the Channel Tunnel, there are still plenty of sea connections to the Continent.

LOOP ROUTE

Boughton Lees to Canterbury (13.1 miles) via Chilham

ENJOY: Godmersham Park, Chilham, Canterbury

The loop route leaves the Boughton Lees–Boughton Aluph road by turning left and follows a footpath across fields to reach Boughton Aluph, with its flint church containing a thirteenth-century chancel and fourteenth-century nave and transepts. Continuing north-eastwards, the route crosses a minor road and passes the buildings of Soakham Farm, then climbs up into woodland. To the right, in the Stour valley, is Godmersham Park with its Georgian mansion which Jane Austen, who was often a guest here, is reputed to have used as the basis for her novel *Mansfield Park*. The Way stays on the fringe of the woodland then drops downhill away from it, heading initially south-east but turning north and joining a track which passes through the hamlet of Mountain Street and into Chilham (105 from Farnham via loop; distances given hereafter are via loop). Chilham is a lovely village, dominated by its castle, which has a Norman keep and a seventeenth-century Jacobean mansion built for Sir Dudley Digges, a high official of James I. There are some magnificent memorials to members of the Digges family in the church, which has a fine fifteenth-century tower with a chequerwork of flint and stone. There are many excellent old half-timbered houses in the village square. The Way proceeds northwards out of Chilham, crossing the A252 Maidstone–Canterbury road and following a metalled road to the village of Old Wives Lees, which is not as quaint or picturesque as it sounds. However, it does have one fine feature, namely North Court Oast, one of a number of old oast houses that have been converted into private dwellings.

You turn right in the village to join a wider metalled road, then when the road bends to the right you continue in a generally north-easterly direction, with a fair bit of up-and-down work. You pass firstly across an orchard, then through a small strip of woodland, emerging into further orchards and going under the railway before joining a track that takes you to Chartham Hatch. This stretch is particularly attractive at apple blossom time, and with hopfields and more old oast houses also in evidence, you do feel very much in the Garden of England. Chartham Hatch is unexciting but Chartham itself, reached by turning right at a minor road junction and detouring southwards, has a lovely thirteenth-century church. The church contains a splendid early fourteenth-century brass dedicated to Sir Robert Septvans, but is best known for its beautiful tracery in the upper parts of the windows.

From Chartham Hatch the Way goes through pleasant woodland, still heading north-east, to reach the A2, passing the Iron Age settlement at Bigbury. It joins a minor road to cross over the A2, then turns right (south-east) and briefly runs parallel with it before resuming the north-easterly progression, dropping to cross a stream and rising to skirt the National Trust viewpoint of Golden Hill. Once over Golden Hill, you pick up a road leading into Harbledown, from which it is a short walk into the centre of Canterbury (112.2). Canterbury is a lively university city, and though many of its historic buildings were destroyed in the Second World War, its magnificent cathedral survives.

Canterbury Cathedral

The first cathedral was built in AD 597, but this has disappeared, and the present cathedral was initiated by Archbishop Lanfranc in 1067. Its finest features are its Norman crypt with exceptionally fine carvings, its twelfth-century choirstalls, and its huge fourteenth-century nave. You will surely want to enjoy these for yourself, particularly if you have travelled from Farnham and like to think that, where the route of the North Downs Way coincides with the Pilgrims' Way, you have been travelling in the steps of the Canterbury pilgrims of long ago. It is unlikely, however, that your desire to identify yourself with your travel-weary forebears will assist in gaining you exemption from the now compulsory and not insubstantial admission charge.

Canturbury to Dover (17.6 miles) via Patrixbourne and Shepherdswell

ENJOY: Patrixbourne, Barham Downs, Waldershare Park, White Cliffs Country Trail

If you are continuing to Dover on the loop route you need to head for St Martin's Church on the A257 Canterbury–Sandwich road, just east of the city centre. By the church, built in AD 560 and one of the oldest in the country, the Way proceeds away from the A257 on a good, wide track in a south-easterly direction, passing through orchards to reach Patrixbourne (115.4). This is a very pretty village with a picturesque group of nineteenth-century cottages built for the tenants of a now vanished estate, and ornately designed in Tudor style. The late-Norman flint church contains some exquisite carvings around its south door. Close by is the chalk stream called Nail Bourne, which dries up during periods of low rainfall. Having joined a minor road to pass through the village centre, the Way turns right onto another minor road by the church and then left, climbing past a patch of woodland onto Barham Downs – once a favourite gathering place of Roman legions – and continuing south-eastwards, roughly parallel with the A2. Shortly afterwards, the Way forks left, then crosses the B2046 and passes through two small settlements; Womenswold and Woolage. Womenswold has a pretty flint church on a grassy mound, surrounded on three sides by eighteenth-century red brick cottages.

Still heading south-east, you pass over Three Barrows Down and through a narrow strip of woodland to cross the Canterbury–Dover railway. By turning sharp left right at the railway crossing you may detour to Barfrestone and its beautiful eleventh-century Norman church of flint and Caen stone. The church boasts some amazingly intricate and perfectly preserved late twelfth-century carvings. The Way picks up a track, still heading south-east, then just beyond Long Lane Farm turns right to proceed in a southerly direction along a path towards Shepherdswell, also known as Sibertswold. You soon cross a road (122.5) and the immediately adjacent East Kent Light Railway. This is actually a preserved fragment of the old East Kent Railway which was one of the least successful ventures of the remarkable railway entrepreneur, Colonel Stephens. Designed to serve what are now disused collieries between Shepherdswell and Richborough (just north of Sandwich), it certainly has its share of tales, some tall, some true. It is reported in that in 1945 a farmer on his way to market to sell his produce, incensed by the failure of a train to stop in response to his hand signal, lay in wait for the train as it returned two and a half hours later, and pelted it with rotten eggs, tomatoes, apples and other items from his compost heap.

From the railway, the Way carries on southwards to meet another road (both these roads lead immediately to Shepherdswell village centre and its railway station on the Canterbury–Dover line) and heads out into the countryside again, apparently aiming straight towards Dover. Unexpectedly, however, you have to swing to the east and then north-east, *away* from your ultimate objective. You cross a minor road just above Coldred at its tiny church of St Pancras, with flint walls and some Saxon features. Soon afterwards you enter the grounds of Waldershare. The park, which contains many fine species of beech, lime and chestnut as well as a huge eighteenth-century Palladian belvedere, is dominated by a Queen Anne brick mansion. The route joins a driveway then, on leaving the park, forks left to pass the church, which contains some splendid monuments. Having crossed over the A256 Dover–Margate road, you pass round the edge of Minacre Farm, crossing two tracks and turning left onto a third to reach a T-junction at the village of Ashley, where you turn right, head downhill and once again proceed south-eastwards on course for Dover. You reach another track by Maydensole Farm, turning right onto the track then bearing left to skirt an area of trees. Once round the woodland, you head in a more southerly direction towards Dover, now on an old Roman road which was built to link Dover with Richborough, where the Romans under Claudius landed in AD 43. The Way overlaps with the White Cliffs Country Trail, which links Dover with Sandwich Bay. You pass through the hamlet of Pineham, now enjoying straightforward walking on a well-defined track, before going under the A2. Soon the track becomes a metalled road which drops down steeply, crossing the Dover–Deal railway. At a T-junction, the Way goes straight over to pass the edge of Connaught Park, and carries on in a straight line to a street that emerges in the town centre of Dover (129.8). If you've regretted your decision not to take the coast route you could celebrate your arrival in Dover with a brisk ascent of the nearby White Cliffs, accessible to the east of the town via the Saxon Shore Way. As you look down on the sea and bustling docks from the magnificent clifftops, you may feel a song in your heart and call to mind Vera Lynn's promise of birds making an appearance over the White Cliffs of Dover tomorrow. Of course if you're on a tight schedule and need to get home that same day, you'll just have to take her word for that.

The Ridgeway Path

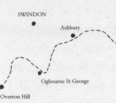

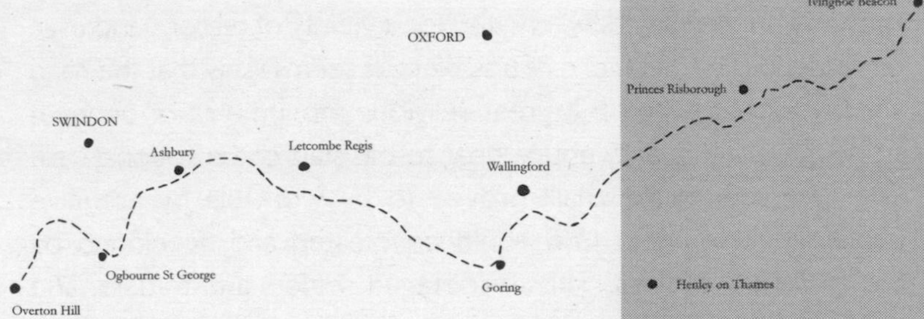

Designation: National trail.
Length: 85.5 miles.
Start: Overton Hill, Wiltshire.
Finish: Ivinghoe Beacon, Buckinghamshire.
Nature: The first half of the walk consists of a journey along ancient downland tracks through the heart of Wiltshire and Oxfordshire. The second half, whilst following further old tracks, incorporates a wider variety of paths and landscapes of the Chiltern Hills.
Difficulty rating: Easy.
Average time of completion: 5–7 days.

HIGHLIGHTS OF THIS WALK:

- **Avebury**
- **West Kennett Long Barrow**
- **Wayland's Smithy**
- **Grim's Ditch**
- **Coombe Hill**

A walk along the Ridgeway Path is also a walk back to pre-history. The Ridgeway Path as we know it today formed part of an old road with Bronze Age origins known as the Great Ridgeway which linked Lyme Regis in Dorset with Hunstanton in Norfolk, the route serving as a drove road, a trading route, and a convenient track for invaders. Parts of the Great Ridgeway were absorbed into routes such as the Wessex Ridgeway, the Ridgeway, the Icknield Way and the Peddars Way, created for a variety of reasons and uses by subsequent generations of travellers. It seems likely that the road already existed when the great religious monuments of unhewn stone were set up at Avebury, near to the start of the national trail. The light soils of the chalk proved to be workable by primitive implements, which in turn could be created and developed by the availability of flints. This encouraged settlers and traders, and explains the large number of burials and fortifications on the route. The idea of a long-distance path which incorporated sections of the Great Ridgeway, offering the walker a combination of well-defined upland tracks, fine scenery, and many historic sites and monuments, was first suggested in 1947 and the official route opened in 1973.

As has been stated above, it is a path of two halves. The western half, following the old Ridgeway, passes along seemingly endless broad tracks, often deeply rutted and used by horse riders as well as walkers, through open, rolling countryside with few habitations close at hand. The eastern half, using parts of the Icknield Way and passing through the Chiltern Hills, does have some stretches of a similar nature but these are punctuated by areas of woodland and housing, with a feeling of being rather closer to civilisation, and many of the paths are narrow and suitable only for walkers. However, the Chilterns offer some extremely pleasant scenery and a rich variety of trees and plants. Although the beech is prominent, there is also much oak and ash amongst the woodland, and the area is also noted for its wealth of orchids and rare gentians. If you are particularly fortunate you may also spot an edible dormouse, a species that is more common to the Chilterns than anywhere else in the country; fat dormice were eaten by the Romans, hence their alternative name.

Technically, the Ridgeway Path poses no special demands for the walker; climbs and descents are always fairly gentle and the most gruelling ascent is literally within 100 yd of the finish. However, one should not be complacent, for the exposed sections on the first half of the walk could render the ill-equipped walker quite vulnerable in wet weather, and heavy rain may also turn many sections into mudbaths. I made the mistake of thinking that trainers would be adequate footwear for a traverse of the Ridgeway at the end of a particularly soggy May, and limped home sporting a pair of feet that looked as if they had been processed through the office shredder.

Overton Hill to Ashbury (20 miles) via Ogbourne St George and Fox Hill

ENJOY: Avebury, Barbury Castle, Smeathe's Ridge, Liddington Castle, Wayland's Smithy

Most walkers arriving by public transport to tackle the Ridgeway will get off the bus at Avebury, and indeed this village is deserving of inspection by all eastbound walkers before the pilgrimage begins. Its stone circle is the largest monument of its kind in the country, and goes back 4,000 years, certainly earlier than the main phase in the building of Stonehenge. It consists of a circular bank and adjacent ditch, and on the inside of the ditch is a collection of over 100 standing sarsen stones (sarsen meaning 'saracen', or foreign to the indigenous chalk, being a kind of prehistoric sandstone), some weighing up to 50 tons. It is believed that the circle represented a religious or social centre for the primitive farming communities drawn to the downs of Wessex. The village also boasts a large thatched barn and a part-Saxon church, containing Norman aisles and a fine Norman tub-font. The walk from Avebury to the start of the route goes past the site of a 50 ft wide avenue of megaliths, and then through West Kennett. This village is most famous for its long barrow which dates back to 2500 BC; it is notable for its exceptional size (350 ft long and up to 80 ft wide), and contains several burial chambers where large numbers of skeletons have been discovered.

An unpleasant walk eastwards alongside the busy A4 brings you to Overton Hill – the site of further stone circles – and the official start of the route. Immediately, as you join a wide track that strikes out northwards into open downland, the scene is set for the next 42 miles, with open downland track walking, some distance away from villages or towns, predominating over those miles. Overton Down and nearby Fyfield Down bring more sarsen stones once believed to be old pagan monuments but subsequently realised to be the weathered-down remains of a layer of rock which once covered the chalk. In fact, the stone has been a useful source of building material in the area. Having proceeded a fraction east of north to pass Avebury Down (walkers coming from Avebury can cheat slightly by joining the Ridgeway here instead of Overton Hill) and Monkton Down, the track then swings in a more north-easterly direction over Hackpen Hill. The views are extensive and totally unspoilt. You cross the Broad Hinton–Marlborough road, and after passing three tidy pockets of woodland you reach Uffcott Down and drop slightly to reach another road crossing. Immediately beyond is the first highlight of the walk itself, Barbury Castle, a huge Iron Age circular hill fort commanding spectacular views. The route continues through the large car park and past toilet facilities, serving visitors not only to the fort but the country park which has also been created around this important prehistoric site. In 1985, workmen digging a new pipeline hereabouts uncovered a body dating back to AD 300 which, tests showed, came from a Romano-British farming community. They christened the body Eric (Early Remains In Chalk) but later the body had to be re-christened Erica when it was found to be that of a female!

Beyond the car park the track continues, but very soon there is a turn to the left onto a much less well-defined track. You should avoid the temptation to continue along the broader one, on pain of going severely off course. The reward for leaving this better-defined track is a splendid march along Smeathe's Ridge, a true ridge route with the ground falling steeply away on either side. This is an ancient route which was used when the lower path across the plain was too wet. You avoid the apparently laborious climb to Coombe Down but turn left onto another comparatively thin track through the pasture, dropping down to join a wider track and then a metalled road. You turn right onto it but when the road shortly bends left, the route goes straight on along an unmetalled lane. By detouring along the road you arrive at the pretty village of Ogbourne St George (9), which contains a seventeenth-century manor house built on the site of a twelfth-century Benedictine priory. The lane bypasses the village, heading south, but in due course the route takes a left turn off it, descending to cross the River Og and then passing through the extremely picturesque hamlet of Southend with its red brick half-timbered and thatched cottages.

Having scurried straight over the busy A345, the attractive town of Marlborough lying just a few miles to the south, you then follow a lane uphill, passing beneath the abutments of an old railway bridge. You turn left onto another lane, still climbing out of the Og valley, until you reach a crossroads of paths where you turn left and proceed onto Round Hill Downs, having now regained the height lost since Smeathe's Ridge. Soon the track reaches a metalled road, turning left onto it and following it to a crossroads, going straight over; beyond the crossroads, the track becomes unmetalled again and heads resolutely northwards, still climbing. The walking on this section is quite exposed and the only real shelter is to be found in a clump of trees lying immediately to the right of the path.

The route now turns left off the main track, initially descends and then climbs to pass over Liddington Hill, just to the right of Liddington Castle. The castle dates from the Iron Age but seems to have been used until the Anglo-Saxon period, while Liddington Hill is one of the highest points on the national trail. The walking is exhilarating and it is a shame when the track begins to descend quite steeply to reach a metalled road. The route turns left onto this road and shortly right onto another, and there follows a desperately tedious tramp along this busy highway, which passes over the M4 and continues to the hamlet of Fox Hill (16.5). Here, at least, is the comforting sight of a pub right on the route. Shortly after passing the pub, you turn right off the road onto a track. This is the start of an almost unbroken 23 miles or so in which the national trail proceeds along broad upland tracks, first in a north-easterly and then a south-easterly direction, the route well signposted and carrying no possibilities of going astray. Having left the metalled road just beyond Fox Hill, the track climbs gently and then continues pleasantly above the pretty villages of Bishopstone, Idstone and Ashbury, moving into Oxfordshire as it does so. Ashbury boasts pretty chalk-built cottages – the church of St Mary is built of chalk and brown stone – and Idstone is a hamlet of chalk, sarsen and brick with two fine old farmhouses. Just beyond the road leading down to Ashbury (20), and only a short stroll away from the route, is Wayland's Smithy, a chambered Neolithic tomb or long barrow, built in about 2800 BC.

Wayland's Smithy

Excavations in 1919 and 1920 revealed eight Stone Age skeletons and one possibly Iron Age or Romano-British burial, but subsequently an earlier Stone Age barrow was found within the larger one, with fourteen further graves. The tomb is named after Wayland the Smith, who actually figures in Scandinavian mythology as a manufacturer of invincible weapons; legend says he lived in the cave on the site and re-shod overnight the horses of those who left money in payment.

Ashbury to Streatley (22 miles) via Ridgeway Centre

ENJOY: Uffington White Horse, Segsbury, Scutchamer Knob, East Ilsley

This is a long section but could be broken at the Ridgeway Centre and you could couple a stay here with a detour to the nearby town of Wantage. Soon after Ashbury and Wayland's Smithy, the route crosses a metalled road leading to Compton Beauchamp. In this village is Compton House, a Georgian mansion, and a church which contains many twentieth-century additions, including reredos, font cover and chapel screens, all designed by Martin Travers. Beyond the Compton Beauchamp turning, you rise quite steeply to pass White Horse Hill above Uffington. It is worth pausing at this Iron Age site; although the earthworks are unimpressive, the view from the escarpment, which requires a short detour, is magnificent. The White Horse itself is generally thought to have been cut into the chalk scarp in the first century AD, although other possibilities are that King Alfred commissioned it to celebrate his victory over the Danes in the ninth century or that it was cut as a tribute to Hengist, the Saxon leader, who had a white horse on his standard. Slight anticlimax follows as the track drops down again, although the views remain excellent. As you now head south-east, the unmistakeable sight of Didcot Power Station looms large in the distance. This will rarely be out of sight for the next few hours, although the sight of this is more than made up for by the lovely views across huge areas of unspoilt Oxfordshire countryside. Soon a road is signposted that leads off to Kingston Lisle with its Georgian mansion and Blowing Stone, which legend states was used by King Alfred to summon his troops. The next significant road crossing is close to the attractive woodland of Sparsholt Firs, and there then follows a stretch of lovely open walking past the summit of Hackpen Hill. From here you get good views to the thatched village of Letcombe Bassett, whose church of St Michael contains a Norman chancel, while also near the route hereabouts are the impressive earthworks of the Iron Age fort of Segsbury.

The route continues over the A338 (28) where a detour to the left brings you to the Ridgeway Centre, offering accommodation and a reminder of the great diversity of users of this route. You may indeed be grateful for the generous width of the path when you are passed – as I was along this section one fine Bank Holiday weekend morning – by motorcyclists, motorists, cyclists, joggers and horseriders. This is definitely horse country, with numerous gallops marked on the map close to and sometimes adjoining the route. The problem for walkers along much of this section is the excessive use of the track by wheeled transport which, although much resurfacing has been done, has created several badly rutted sections. You will often be forced to choose between walking a grassy tightrope or preferring to chart a course through one of the channels, the latter becoming impracticable in very wet or muddy conditions.

Before continuing you may wish to consider detouring along the A338 to the historic town of Wantage, the birthplace of King Alfred, a couple of miles beyond the Ridgeway Centre; the next crossing, also with the possibility of a detour to Wantage, is the B4494, and after this is one of the more distinctive landmarks on this section, the tall monument to the soldier and sometime Baron of Wantage, Robert Loyd-Lindsay. Beyond the monument the track is wide, and the walking remains easy as you pass Ridgeway Down, Ardington Down and East Ginge Down. Just beyond East Ginge Down is the triangulation point of Cuckhamsley Hill, nearby to which, to the right of the track, is the green mound known as Scutchamer Knob, a Saxon long barrow or burial mound. Its colourful name is believed to have been derived from the Saxon king Cwicchelm who died in AD 593.

Very shortly you cross another metalled road due south of East Hendred, and the track continues over East Hendred Down and onwards to Bury Down. You are now walking through Berkshire. The sprawls of Harwell, with its atomic energy station, and Didcot, with its power station, are clearly visible to the left, and another eyesore comes into view, namely the A34 dual carriageway. The Ridgeway negotiates this by means of an underpass, but if the prevailing westerly wind is blowing, the traffic noise will continue to be heard for a good mile or two beyond. The route heads resolutely south-east over Several Down and Compton Downs; a right turn off the route on Several Down provides a detour to East Ilsley. This pretty village has a Georgian hall, a pond, the seventeenth-century Kennet House, an early thirteenth-century church, and numerous stables, providing a reminder that East Ilsley has traditionally been an important base for racehorse training. Continuing along the route onto Compton Downs, you join a concrete drive, but soon turn left off it and head temporarily north-eastwards before continuing due east and then returning to a south-easterly course. As you continue over Blewbury Down and Roden Downs, the going can be very muddy. Beyond Roden Downs you begin to descend, and you find yourself looking down to the lush green valley of Streatley Warren immediately to the right, with the Thames valley to be seen just a short way ahead.

At length you reach a metalled road, then follow it eastwards for just over a mile past Thurle Grange to the A417; at the end of a hard day's walk, it can seem a very long and tedious stretch. The route turns right onto the A417 and right again onto the A329, which leads into Streatley (42) with its Georgian houses and nineteenth-century malt-house. To continue the Ridgeway Path, you will turn left in the village onto the B4009, and proceed over the Thames into Goring. You may feel a touch of the London bus syndrome here, reflecting it to be somewhat ironic that you should have to walk 42 miles without passing through a single settlement of any size to reach two almost adjacent to each other, each offering a wide range of amenities including (at the time of writing) a youth hostel in Streatley.

Youth Hostels

The original ethos of youth hostels – to provide reasonable but low-budget accommodation to young people who might otherwise be unable to afford to get out and enjoy the countryside – has been somewhat eroded by the extension of facilities with consequent price increases, and their availability to motorists and others who have not arrived by their own steam, although it is fair to say that many hostels, particularly the remoter ones, have striven to retain their character and special atmosphere. Whatever the future for youth hostelling in this country, it is a fair bet that all walkers, even those who can now afford to sleep in luxury hotels during their walking holidays, will treasure their memories of youth hostel life. They might nostalgically recall the surly warden standing balefully by the locked door, only deigning to open it at 5 p.m. precisely to admit the queue of thirty that for the last 35 minutes had been standing in the pouring rain outside; the all-pervading smell of dirty, sweaty feet in every corner of the building; the competition for space and utensils in the members' kitchen with a party of eight non-English speaking teenagers attempting to make a beef stroganoff with rice for 16 people; the loudmouth monopolising the commonroom conversation with his intrepid boasts about the mountains, rapids, jungles and seas he had successfully and contemptuously mastered; the night's sleep in the dormitory punctuated by nine distinctive types of snoring that proceeded on a rota basis throughout the hours of darkness; and, before escape was allowed next morning, the traditional hosteller's duty of sweeping a passageway with a broom that was so full of dust, dirt and fluff that after 20 minutes' feverish activity the floor was three times as dirty as it had been at the beginning.

Streatley to Watlington (15 miles) via Nuffield and Swyncombe

ENJOY: South Stoke, North Stoke, Grim's Ditch, Swyncombe Park

Soon after crossing the Thames you turn left, just bypassing the centre of Goring, a pleasant town with more amenities than Streatley and containing a twelfth-century church and the attractive old Miller of Mansfield Hotel. The route, now back in Oxfordshire, passes along a mixture of suburban roads and paths which proceed gently northwards to the pretty village of South Stoke with a partly thirteenth-century church. A left turn in the village takes you to the riverside, and there follows a delightful stretch of two miles or so along the east bank of the Thames, providing some contrast to the quite remote downland walking that has gone before. The riverside path passes under the main London–Bristol railway line, Brunel's fine bridge carrying the railway not only over your route but over the Thames at this point. The route then joins a path that is set a little way back from the river, and proceeds to North Stoke. It goes right past the extraordinarily attractive church, which contains fourteenth-century wall paintings and a Jacobean pulpit, and follows along the main street, the route continuing in the same (northerly) direction to enter Mongewell Park and pass Carmel College. Just before reaching a busy road and bridleway underpass, you turn right to follow a path that runs roughly parallel with the road. You cross over the road and immediately join the course of an old earthwork known as Grim's Ditch.

Grim's Ditch

Parts of this earthwork reach a height of six feet from the top of the dyke to the bottom of the ditch. Its purpose is unclear but it may have been a tribal boundary or, like Offa's Dyke, a boundary line between kingdoms. Although the latter explanation would be consistent with Saxon or Danish origins, there is also a possibility that the earthworks formed a sort of prehistoric network associated with the Ridgeway hill forts. Grim, incidentally, is another word for the Nordic god Odin.

From Mongewell Park to Nuffield, a distance of four miles, the path proceeds in an almost straight easterly line alongside the tree-lined remains of the ditch. To begin with it is like going through a narrow tunnel of woodland with open fields on each side, although the strip of woodland widens as progress is made. It is lovely, relaxing walking, and it is almost a shame to bear left and climb up away from the ditch to reach a metalled road and the village of Nuffield (52). The route turns right onto the road and then left opposite the partly Norman church, in the churchyard of which the car magnate and philanthropist William Morris is buried. Having taken the left turn, you are soon following a perilous path across a golf course; numbered posts mark the way but do little to indicate from which direction the danger of low-flying golf balls lurks. One would suppose that golfers themselves would be equally wary of passing hikers, particularly as there is nothing in the laws of the game that specifically tells a player what to do when his ball lodges itself in a walker's cagoule hood.

If you have survived the golf course you must then cross the busy A423, and there follows a short but very pleasant woodland walk and a confident march across open fields, bisected by a narrow strip of woodland. Beyond lie the buildings of Ewelme Park, a mock-Elizabethan house. The route passes just to the right of this, then bears right, passing round a field edge and then dipping quite steeply downhill through beautiful woodland, with the lovely Swyncombe Park on the right. This is indeed a most refreshing interlude between the bouts of pounding, wide tracks. At the foot of the hill the route emerges from the woods, turning right onto a lane which passes the nineteenth-century Swyncombe House and its pretty Norman church of St Botolph, built partially of flint. The lane meets the Ewelme–Cookley Green road and you cross over it, joining a very attractive path that heads downhill with fine views to the woodland of Swyncombe Downs up ahead.

Having dipped down, the path rises to enter the woods and then gradually drops through patchier woodland to reach a much wider track at the foot of the slope. You turn right onto this track and follow it eastwards. This is part of the Icknield Way; thought to be named after the Iceni tribe, it is probably pre-Roman, having been a trading route from Norfolk to the South West, and tending to follow a line at a slight distance from the Chiltern Hills rather than along the top of the escarpment. You must follow it north-eastwards for several miles, with the wooded slopes of the Chilterns as a constant companion to your right, and good views across more open countryside to your left. The track is broken up by a number of road crossings, all providing the opportunity of a detour to visit a village or small town to the left, most of which are well signposted from the route. Of all of them, Watlington (57) offers the widest range of amenities, and is worth visiting for its handsome Georgian houses and thatched cottages, and a fine seventeenth-century town hall. It may provide a welcome break from the track, which can get intolerably muddy, and as you flounder along waterlogged sections, desperately trying to find alternatives, you may well have to remain philosophical and keep your spirits high by a brisk refrain of the song of the bold hippopotamus with his call to wallow in glorious mud.

Watlington to Wendover (17 miles) via Princes Risborough

ENJOY: Bledlow, Chequers, Coombe Hill

Beyond Watlington you plough on past Shirburn, Lewknor, Aston Rowant, Kingston Blount, Crowell and Chinnor. There is a somewhat unwelcome intrusion just past the Lewknor crossing – namely the M40 – but in due course peace reigns again and you can continue to enjoy lovely views to the Chiltern escarpment. Many of the villages beyond Watlington are worth detouring to visit: Shirburn has a castle dating back to the late fourteenth century, Lewknor boasts a part-thirteenth-century church with many fine memorials, the church of Aston Rowant has a Norman nave, Crowell boasts the fine seventeenth-century Elwood House, and the church in Chinnor contains a truncated effigy of a knight in chain-mail, although the landscape round Chinnor is somewhat disfigured by a cement works. Beyond Chinnor, at the hamlet of Hempton

Wainhill, you should watch carefully for a right turn beside a house, but by detouring straight ahead you can reach the pretty village of Bledlow which has many attractive herringbone brick cottages, the seventeenth-century Red Lion Inn and a remarkable church. It contains a twelfth-century font, fragments of medieval wall paintings, and much thirteenth-century work. Restoration appears minimal; as Simon Jenkins writes in his book *England's Thousand Best Churches*, 'Everything needs attention, but has mercifully failed to get it.' Having turned right at Hempton Wainhill, you climb into the woods above Bledlow, passing close to the seventeenth-century Bledlow Cross, a well-known local landmark which lies to the right on Wain Hill. As the route continues as a good path through the woods, care should be taken to branch off right rather than follow the Upper Icknield Way downhill again; the correct route, now in Buckinghamshire, heads south-east through open country, maintaining the height gained.

After crossing a road, you proceed through fields, heading south-eastwards on to Lodge Hill, a most satisfying viewpoint. Following an all-too-brief walk across the hilltop, the route, now swinging to the north-east, drops down to a metalled road, crosses it and proceeds through open country past a cottage and alongside a golf course. You cross a railway line and, after a brief climb, pass over a railway tunnel. Shortly after the second line is crossed, the route reaches a metalled road, turns right onto it and then left to follow the busy A4010 northwards. Just as you reach the houses of Princes Risborough you turn right into a lane, returning to the Upper Icknield Way, and there follows a somewhat tedious trudge north-eastwards round the edge of the town. At length the metalled Brimmers Road is reached, giving quick access to the amenities of Princes Risborough (68). The town is not unattractive, with many timbered and thatched cottages, a seventeenth-century manor house and a brick market house with arcades and crowned with a wooden cupola.

The route goes straight across Brimmers Road and continues along a lane, shortly turning right onto a path which climbs steeply up onto Whiteleaf Hill. It heads directly for a metalled road, but at the last minute swings left and proceeds into woodland to meet another road. You turn right onto it, then shortly left, proceeding northwards and passing close to Whiteleaf Cross which, like Bledlow Cross, is believed to date back to the seventeenth century. You bear right into the very attractive Giles Wood, and drop steeply downhill to reach a road at the hamlet of Lower Cadsden, the charms of which are infinitely enhanced by a route-side pub. You turn left onto the road and pass the pub, then soon turn right and climb again up onto Pulpit Hill. In good weather this is lovely open walking, and it is hard to believe London is so close (less than an hour by train). The route avoids the thick woodland further up the slopes of Pulpit Hill but swings gently north-east and then south-east, keeping the woods to the right and heading towards the Chequers estate. Dropping slightly, along a path which can be extremely heavy-going owing to the clay soil underfoot, the route crosses the driveway leading to Chequers. Looking to the left as you cross, you will observe the sixteenth-century mansion for which Lord Lee of Fareham created a trust in 1917 enabling it to be used by British Prime Ministers. It remains the PM's country residence to this day. Michael Marriott remarked, 'There can be few countries in the world where foot-travellers may approach so close to the residence of the national leader.' Don't expect him to be available to receive your petition in support of mandatory mudscraping equipment at two mile intervals along the route, though.

After crossing the driveway, you soon reach a metalled road which you go over, entering woodland almost immediately on the opposite side. Clearly defined, albeit often muddy, tracks take you northwards and uphill to reach a metalled road – confusingly, this area is described on maps as another Lodge Hill – onto which you turn right and soon left, still heading north. You pass through another patch of woodland, but soon the route emerges onto the upper slopes of Coombe Hill, the highest and one of the best viewpoints in the Chilterns and indeed on the Ridgeway Path, with good views to the nearby town of Wendover and a magnificent panorama of the Vale of Aylesbury. The route passes a distinctive monument dedicated to the men of Buckinghamshire who died in the Boer War, then swings to the north-east and begins a lovely descent by means of an excellent path which proceeds unerringly towards Wendover along the wooded slopes of Bacombe Hill. At the foot of the hill, you turn right onto the B4010 then proceed over the bypass and the railway and enter the little town of Wendover (74), which boasts an excellent range of amenities. Besides the early fourteenth-century church of St Mary, there are a number of attractive old buildings, some of which are timber-framed. One of the most impressive is the Red Lion; Oliver Cromwell stayed here in 1642 and the room where he slept is kept much as it was in his time. The walker nearing the end of his Ridgeway Path pilgrimage may wonder what future generations would think if his own lodgings in the town were left for posterity in this way, with the bagful of banana skin and orange peel from his previous day's packed lunch, his discarded leaky water bottle, half a dozen used pieces of sticking plaster and a pair of socks with more holes and a riper smell than a pound of Swiss cheese.

Wendover to Ivinghoe Beacon (11.5 miles) via Wigginton and Tring

ENJOY: Aldbury, Ivinghoe Beacon

Shortly before Wendover's main street curves to the left, you turn right onto an attractive metalled path, which continues beside a stream and arrives at a road near the church. You turn left onto the road and continue along it to a crossroads, going straight over onto Hogtrough Lane. You head steadily uphill along the lane going south-east, but in due course you reach an area of woodland and bear left, initially heading just south of east and then swinging resolutely north-east through Hale Wood on Cock's Hill. This is quite delightful, if potentially very muddy, woodland walking along a comparatively narrow path. At length the surface becomes rather wider and firmer, providing quick walking as far as a metalled road. Crossing straight over, the route continues as a narrow path through the woods, but soon meets a deep gully into which it is necessary to descend before turning right and proceeding along its stony floor, climbing quite steeply. This is tough walking, but the gradient eases and you soon reach another metalled road, near the hamlet of Chivery. The route crosses the road and heads north-east across fields to pass a prominent mast, arriving at a metalled road, turning left onto it and then almost immediately bearing right into Pavis Wood.

There follows another pretty woodland walk along a well-defined track, heading north-east. Reaching a road as it negotiates a sharp bend, the route joins the road, heading just north of east and, effectively, going straight ahead. The walk from here to Wigginton is tedious, one has to say. The road walk continues through the unremarkable village of Hastoe, then just after a road leads off to the left, heading for Tring, the Ridgeway Path turns left and proceeds north-eastwards along a track, heading for Wigginton. A little way to the south, and running roughly parallel with the route, is the line of Grim's Ditch. You may sense some anticlimax along this section, which is in no way relieved as, just before Wigginton (80), the route bears left off the track and follows a narrow path which keeps a field and woodland to the left, and the houses of Wigginton to the right. The path, as in Hale Wood, can be insufferably muddy. The Wigginton–Tring road is reached and crossed, and more mud may be encountered as the route heads eastwards to round the south edge of Langton Wood. The route, now passing briefly through Hertfordshire before returning to Buckinghamshire, turns north-eastwards and heads downhill to cross the A41(M) by means of a bridge. Shortly after this bridge crossing you arrive at the old A41, turning right to follow it briefly, then leaving it by turning left onto a well-defined track that heads north-eastwards in a virtually straight line, proceeding downhill and keeping the grounds of Pendley Manor to the left. Arriving at a metalled road, you turn left onto it and reach a T-junction where you turn right. By detouring left here, you can follow the road to the pleasant small town of Tring, which boasts a park that was formerly the home of the Rothschild family, and a zoological museum which is part of the British Museum's natural history section. Having turned right at the T-junction, the route crosses over the Grand Union Canal and goes forward to Tring Station. Tempting though it may be to stop here and pick up a train homewards, there are still a few miles to go. It's likely that you'll find yourself back here having trudged on to the end of the route and then sought the nearest public transport – the biggest winners in the choice of route are the local minicab drivers.

Soon after the station a metalled road leads off to the left, and soon after this the route itself makes a left turn onto a track, but by detouring straight ahead along the road you reach the charming village of Aldbury with its triangular green, duckpond, part-thirteenth-century church and timber-framed cottages. Having turned left onto the track, the route turns left again almost at once, proceeding along a well-defined track that heads north-westwards. Soon turning right, the route climbs up into attractive woodland, emerging onto the grassy slopes of Pitstone Hill, although the views are undoubtedly marred by the quarries and works to the left. The ultimate objective, Ivinghoe Beacon, can now be seen clearly ahead. Lovely, airy walking follows, as you head north-eastwards and dip down to cross the Ivinghoe–Aldbury road, from which you proceed on a good path up onto Steps Hill, entering an area of patchy woodland. Swinging in a more northerly direction, the route now drops, quite steeply in places, to meet another road, and after crossing this, you have a choice of paths which lead unerringly northwards to the 756 ft summit of Ivinghoe Beacon (85.5).

The final climb is the steepest on the whole of the national trail, but the reward is a magnificent view in all directions, not least to the village of Ivinghoe and the splendidly restored seventeenth-century windmill near Pitstone. The hilltop is not without historic interest; it is one of several beacon points that were established in the area during the reign of Elizabeth I to summon men in case of invasion from Spain, and there are barrows nearby dating back to the Bronze Age and beyond. It is however, some way back to civilisation. The nearest village with reasonable amenities is Ivinghoe; this is worth visiting in any event, with its part-fourteenth-century church, the Old Brewery House which dates back 200 years, and the King's Head, an inn dating back nearly half a century. But after making your weary way there, you couldn't be blamed for forsaking its delights in order to get back to home comforts. And maybe to see if there is any known cure for Scutchamer Knob.

The Thames Path

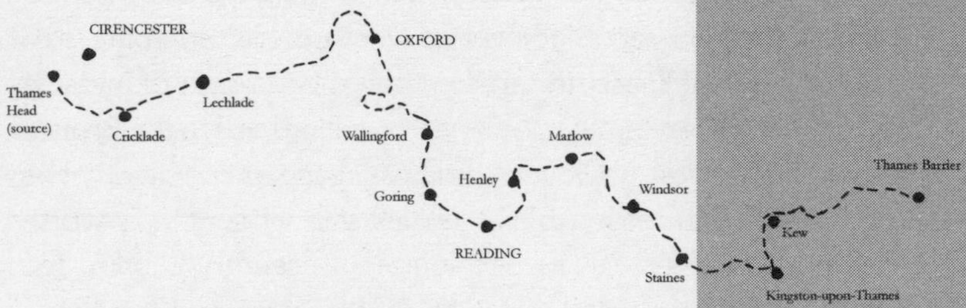

Designation: National trail.
Length: 184.5 miles via the right bank route, 185.5 miles via the left bank route.
Start: Source of the Thames, near Kemble, Gloucestershire.
Finish: The Thames Flood Barrier, Charlton, London Borough of Greenwich.
Nature: A walk beside the river Thames from source to estuary.
Difficulty rating: Easy.
Average time of completion: 12–14 days.

HIGHLIGHTS OF THIS WALK:

- **Lechlade**
- **Oxford**
- **Henley**
- **Marlow**
- **Hampton Court Palace**
- **Richmond**
- **London**

Walking the Thames Path has two principal attractions. Firstly, it is a charming walk which progresses through some of England's loveliest and gentlest countryside and then proceeds through the fascinating heart of its capital. Secondly, the completion of the walk will allow the traveller to boast that he has followed England's longest and best-known river from source to estuary – from a few dribbles in a Gloucestershire field, to a wide band of water of immense historical, industrial and economic importance. Its bends and loops, its tributary streams and its weirs and locks combine to provide endless interest for the walker. The waters are cleaner than they have been for at least a century, and provide a home to many species of bird and fish, including salmon, which once again successfully navigate what used to be one of the prime salmon rivers in Europe. The walker may also appreciate the rich variety of wildlife and plant life by the water, including water meadows resplendent with buttercups, meadowsweet and clover, and woodlands that are rich with oak, ash and beech. There are many other things for the hiker to enjoy. There is the tremendous range of rivercraft, from rowing boats to luxury cruisers. There are the beautiful towns and villages close to or right by the river, many of which repay a full day's exploration. Finally there are the contrasts, from swathes of unspoilt Oxfordshire countryside to the huge monoliths of central London. Your watering-hole may one day consist of a tranquil rural hotel formerly beloved of ladies and gentlemen of leisure wishing to take some rarefied country air, and on another could be a dockland pub such as the Prospect of Whitby at Wapping, where our aristocratic forebears would have blenched at the sight of bare-knuckle brawls and cockfighting.

In an age of intensive urban development, it may surprise the walker to learn that the river can be followed along most of its length. The reason can perhaps be traced to the creation in the late eighteenth century of a towpath alongside the river between Lechlade (about 20 miles downstream) and south-west London. Historically, the canal system played a crucial role in the transportation of goods and materials around the country, and towpaths were required alongside the canals to enable men and horses to tow the barges prior to the advent of motor transport. There were, of course, obstacles, but where these arose the towpath simply switched to the opposite bank, with navigation ferries being used to facilitate the switch. It was the closure of these ferries, following the decline of water transport, which provided the biggest difficulties for the powers-that-be in establishing a continuous riverside recreational path. Other difficulties have arisen where (surprisingly rarely) access to the towpath has had to be suspended for development or security reasons, or where no towpath has ever existed – as is the case between the source and Lechlade, and from Putney onwards. Notwithstanding the difficulties, the route is an extremely satisfying one. The continual switching from one bank to the other in order to adhere to the towpath where possible adds to the variety and helps to provide fresh perspectives of riverside scenes. In London one is given the choice of following either riverbank. It has to be said that the second half of the walk, with many places of scenic and historic interest, is more interesting than the first, where, especially in wet or muddy conditions, the incessant tramping through featureless water meadows could become monotonous. However, the remoter sections do offer peace and solitude, well away from centres of population, busy roads and tourist traps. The path is well signposted and route finding is never a problem. Planning to walk the path is easy as well; public transport links are so good that the walk can easily be tackled in day trips and weekend breaks, and weather conditions will rarely be so bad as to preclude walking on it, whatever the time of year.

Source to Cricklade (12.3 miles) via Ashton Keynes

ENJOY: Somerford Keynes, Cotswold Water Park, Cricklade

The start of the route is, fittingly enough, at the source of the Thames, marked by an inscibed stone, and a short distance from the village of Kemble where there is a convenient railway station. The walk south-eastwards from the source stone to the A429, forming the first mile of the route, is a most peculiar one. Unless the weather conditions are exceptional, you will see no water at all on this section; it will simply be a tramp through a couple of fields indistinguishable from any other that you have seen from the window of your train, coach or car en route to the start. Near the A429, however, a shallow channel to your left suggests something more encouraging, and closer inspection may reveal a few token dribbles of water. Once over the A429 and heading south-eastwards towards Parker's Bridge, you may see the channel beginning to fill as a result of underground springs pushing water to above ground level.

The channel is lost as the route turns left onto the road at Parker's Bridge and enters the small Cotswold village of Ewen, turning right in the village down a lane heading for Poole Keynes. Soon, however, the route turns left onto a track heading south-eastwards towards Upper Mill Farm, and you are reunited with the infant Thames, in the form of a moderate flow of water. From here to Neigh Bridge, past Upper Mill Farm and Old Mill Farm, the route continues alongside this modest stream, keeping it to the right. At Old Mill Farm it is possible to detour to the left to visit the village of Somerford Keynes, where All Saints Church has an Anglo-Saxon doorway on the north side. The building is thought to be the remains of a church built around AD 685.

At Neigh Bridge the Cotswold Water Park is reached; the route turns left onto a metalled road and shortly right into a lane which proceeds south-eastwards and then eastwards towards Ashton Keynes. The course of the Thames is lost once more, this time amongst a profusion of lakes which are the result of flooded gravel workings. Continuing eastwards, the route enters Ashton Keynes (7) where the infant river does become visible again and makes for a picturesque sight at the bottom of Church Walk by Brook House and Ashton Mill. The route passes right through the village, heading eastwards towards Kentend Farm. The village contains a seventeenth-century pub, some ancient crosses, a number of fine Cotswold houses, a manor house also dating from the seventeenth century and Holy Cross Church, which has a Norman chancel arch. Students of Pevsner's *Buildings of England* series will wish to make a masochistic beeline for the Gothic-style school of 1870, which Pevsner describes as 'truly horrible.'

Having left Ashton Keynes behind, the route heads resolutely south-eastwards to a point just north of Waterhay Bridge, then follows a serpentine course heading vaguely north-eastwards past a further grouping of old gravel workings that are now lakes. At length the route, having lost the Thames once more, meets it again and proceeds briefly beside it; near Hailstone Hill you forsake the river again, striking out north-westwards to join the course of an old railway. Turning right onto it, the route follows it and then, on reaching the river, turns left to resume its Thames-side course. The Thames is now noticeably wider than it was round Ewen and Somerford Keynes. There follows a pleasant, if sometimes rather muddy, walk through water meadows to the edge of Cricklade where you cross the river and proceed through fields to a road which is in fact the top end of Cricklade's main street (12.3). Cricklade, the first town on the route and the only town in Wiltshire that lies on the Thames, is a useful stopping point for refreshment and accommodation. There is evidence that this was once a Roman town, lying as it does within a square earthwork enclosure near to the point where the Roman road from Silchester to Cirencester crossed the Thames. The town has two fine churches, the Norman church of St Mary and, better still, St Sampson. This has a splendid turreted tower built by the Duke of Northumberland around the Reformation, and some excellent carved heraldic work inside. Cricklade's wide main street has several good seventeenth- and eighteenth-century houses, one of the best of which is Robert Jenner's School, founded in 1651. It's good to be able to stop for a drink and shake off some of the mud. There's no doubt that the Thames Path can often be extremely muddy, with a tendency for the local soil to stick to one's boots. You may reflect grimly that there is no real need to take any photographs of the countryside hereabouts as you will be bringing most of it home with you.

Cricklade to Lechlade (10.9 miles) via Castle Eaton

ENJOY: Castle Eaton, Kempsford, Inglesham, Lechlade

The national trail, having reached the top end of the main street, turns right along it briefly and then leaves it, following a lane that leads back to the Thames and joining an excellent riverside path. Soon you pass underneath the horribly busy A419 road, but the traffic noise subsides as progress is made and you now enjoy a tranquil riverside walk north-eastwards to Castle Eaton along the right bank. Castle Eaton (16.5) is a lovely spot; thirsty walkers will doubtless appreciate the Georgian red brick Red Lion Inn, and the church is worth visiting too, with an idyllic riverside setting and a sumptuous Jacobean pulpit inside. The route leaves the village on the Hannington road, soon turning left onto a metalled road to Blackford Farm, then turns sharp left to pick up the river again and follow a riverside path as far as Hannington Bridge. Here it is worth making a detour to the left to visit Kempsford, a charming village of seventeenth- and eighteenth-century cottages, some thatched, and the delightful church of St Mary with a preserved Norman ashlar nave dating back to 1120. Those deciding not to make the detour can still enjoy a captivating view across the river and adjacent meadows to the church tower. Back on the route, you have to forsake the river for a good part of the walk to Inglesham, turning right onto the road at Hannington Bridge and soon left onto a track that runs eastwards, parallel to the Thames eastwards as far as Sterts Farm but some distance from it. There are good views to the attractive town of Highworth on its hill to the right, but this walking is muddy and unexciting.

Ever since the path officially opened it has been anticipated that a right of way would be available that returned you to the Thames in the region of Sterts Farm and followed the river direct to Inglesham. At the time of writing, however, you must continue eastwards to Upper Inglesham, turning left onto the A361 and then first left down to the tiny village of Inglesham. The route passes right beside the tiny thirteenth-century church which, with its Jacobean box pews and wall paintings, is well worth a visit. The Thames is then followed all the way from Inglesham to Lechlade along the right bank (from now on, the expressions 'right bank' and 'left bank' will be used to denote, respectively, the right-hand side and left-hand side of the river facing downstream). Just beyond Inglesham there is a roundhouse to be seen on the opposite bank; this was one of a number of lock-keepers' quarters on the now disused Thames and Severn Canal, which met the Thames here. By now the Thames, though still not the broad sweep of water which will in due course accommodate rowing crews and luxury cruisers, is beginning to look more recognisable as a major waterway.

Lechlade, reached by a most pleasant walk from Inglesham with the ever-maturing river to the left and broad meadows to the right, is a key point on the route. It is the highest navigable point on the Thames for cabin cruisers but, more crucially for the walker, it is here that the towpath starts; it continues all the way to Putney Bridge, one hundred and fifty miles downstream. The advent of the towpath heralds an end to the rather 'bitty' walking that has been experienced so far, and from now on the going is generally better defined and more comfortable. Lechlade (23.2) is an obvious place to stop for rest and refreshment. Access to the town is over the river by means of Halfpenny Bridge, so called because of the amount of the toll at one time. This most attractive town, containing a number of Georgian houses, takes its name from the river Leach, one of the Thames' tributaries. It has a fine church, St Lawrence, notable firstly for its carving on the tower exterior, depicting a magnificent monster holding a sword, and secondly for the roof bosses, which form what has been described as a 'gallery of domestic and religious activity.' Many of Lechlade's buildings have become antique shops and any guidebook writer should hesitate before recommending a particular eating place or store to replenish his rucksack for fear that, before the ink is dry on the page, that establishment will be similarly converted and its proprietor, instead of offering chocolate bars and filled rolls to the hungry walker, can provide him with little more to sustain him on his journey than fading pine bookcases, vulgar porcelain figurines and mangy tiger-skin rugs.

Lechlade to Newbridge (17.1 miles) via Radcot

ENJOY: St John's Bridge, Kelmscot, Tadpole Bridge

Leaving Lechlade, it is a fairly short walk along the right bank to St John's Bridge. At nearby St John's Lock, the first of 47 locks on the Thames, there is a nineteenth-century statue of Old Father Thames. This was formerly placed at the source of the river but certainly enjoys more admirers in its present position. Shortly beyond St John's Bridge the path switches to the left bank and stays there for the next six miles, passing into Oxfordshire. Besides the river itself, a number of features are worthy of note along this stretch. These include some concrete pillboxes, which were part of a Second World War defensive system, and the small riverside communities of Buscot, Eaton Hastings and Kelmscot. Kelmscot boasts an impressive gabled Elizabethan manor house backing onto the river. The poet William Morris lived here; he came here in 1871 and when he started his private printing works in Hammersmith in 1891 he called it the Kelmscott [sic] Press. At the far end of the village is St George's Church, which contains a thirteenth-century gabled bell-cote and a Norman nave, and in a corner of the churchyard is the lichen-covered tomb of the Morris family. The manor house is now a Morris museum, with several rooms decorated, appropriately enough, in Morris wallpaper. Buscot and Eaton Hastings are over the river but there is a charming view to the old church at Eaton Hastings, nestling in a small clump of trees. The path arrives at Radcot Bridge (29.8) and switches back to the right bank. The triple-arched Radcot Bridge, believed to have been completed by the fourteenth century, is the oldest bridge on the Thames. It was the site of a battle in 1387 and again in the English Civil War when its capture by Parliament forced the Royalists to abandon Oxford. The four miles beyond Radcot Bridge feel very remote, with no settlements of any significance and just tiny pockets of sturdy woodland to offset the starkness of the surrounding fields. You pass Rushey Lock and soon reach Tadpole Bridge, beside which is the Trout Inn.

The route uses Tadpole Bridge to switch to the left bank and then enters Chimney Meadows Nature Reserve, an area of lovely riverside woodland. This makes an undeniably pleasant change from the open meadows, although the woodland is but a long narrow strip, extending only a short distance from the river. The route keeps to the left bank beyond Tenfoot Bridge, switching to the right bank at the Shifford lock cut. Lock cuts are short, straight channels of water which have been created at pronounced bends in the river, providing a short cut for river craft. Beyond Shifford lock cut it is straightforward, albeit featureless, walking along the right bank to Newbridge (40.3). Despite the name, the fine four-arched bridge which carries the A415 over the Thames here is certainly not new; it is thought to have been completed by the fourteenth century. There is another riverside pub here, the Rose Revived. Pubs will always be something of a lottery for the long-distance walker. Although many route-side pubs are aware of the number of walkers likely to wish to use them, and cater sympathetically and welcomingly for them, there are always exceptions. At one extreme will be the 'spit and sawdust' establishment where one is fortunate to obtain as much as a packet of crisps with one's pint, never mind a cheese roll or a ham sandwich. At the other extreme will be the more exclusive establishments where cagoule-clad hikers are welcomed with less than open arms, and will find even one of the less expensive starters swallowing up two entire days' food budget.

Newbridge to Oxford (14 miles) via Swinford and Eynsham

ENJOY: Stanton Harcourt, King's Weir, Oxford

Newbridge is situated on the busy A415 Witney–Abingdon road. You must cross it and return to the left bank, continuing through pleasant but unremarkable water meadows. You pass Northmoor Lock and reach the pretty hamlet of Bablock Hythe with its little church and attractive pub. Here the towpath switches to the right bank, but the Thames Path is unable to do likewise, there being no permanent crossing point nearby. With no right of way available on the left bank, the route is forced to forsake the river for a spell, turning left to follow a road and then right along unexciting farm tracks through fields. There are good views eastwards to the high ground of wooded Wytham Hill, and a detour to the left before the path turns riverwards takes you to the fine village of Stanton Harcourt. The village is famous for Wesley's Cottage north of the church, so named because John and Charles Wesley, together with their sister, used to visit the vicar there. The other noteworthy feature of the village is Pope's Tower, one of the few remaining parts of a once impressive manor, and the original home of the Harcourt family. It was here that, in 1718, Alexander Pope completed the fifth volume of his translation of *The Iliad*. The route meets the river again shortly before Pinkhill Lock. There is a weir bridge which allows for a return to the right bank and an uneventful two-mile walk through the meadows to Swinford (48.1), with its eighteenth-century toll bridge carrying the B4044. There is a good opportunity to replenish supplies at Eynsham, a short walk up the road to the left; the town is an attractive one with a 20 ft-high fourteenth-century cross, and an arcaded hall in its square.

From now on civilisation will never be far away and the sense of remoteness rather disappears. Oxford is now approaching, and not only its suburbs but its busy approach roads will become a constant feature until you reach the city in another six miles. Beyond Swinford the route stays on the right bank, hugging the base of Wytham Hill and the woodland which clothes it. Once past Wytham Hill, water meadows again take over, and the only feature of note until the A34 bridge is King's Weir. There are one or two pronounced bends in the river on this section, and time lost by earlier stops and detours can be made up by taking short cuts across the open meadows without fear of losing the route. Such a strategy, though having much to recommend it, may backfire on the more thin-skinned walkers who, sitting in the pub that evening recounting their adventures to others, may be roundly accused of cheating.

The Thames Path passes beneath the very busy and noisy A34 and continues towards Oxford. Walkers studying their maps will note that the Thames has an alternative name around the city, the rather more poetical Isis. Just after the A34 bridge are the ruins of the twelfth-century Godstow Abbey; Rosamund, the mistress of Henry II, was educated here. A bridge over the river just before the ruins takes you to the popular and picturesque Trout Inn, originally a hospice, and the attractive scene is further enhanced by the presence of a delightful weir. By turning right rather than left over the bridge to the Trout, you can detour to the outstandingly attractive village of Wytham, which contains a turreted sixteenth-century abbey and fine thatched grey stone houses. The Thames Path continues along the right bank from Godstow; despite the A34 to the right and the suburbs of Oxford to the left, the immediate surroundings initially remain free from habitation and noise. The huge green expanse of Port Meadow opens up on the opposite bank with the Summertown district of Oxford visible beyond and, as further progress is made, Oxford's housing seems to become more and more intrusive. The route switches to the left bank at

Medley Bridge, just past the hamlet and pub at Binsey, and it is a short walk from here to Osney Bridge (54.3).

This is the closest the Thames Path gets to the centre of Oxford, and the best place to leave the route and enjoy the city. Whole books have been written about its treasures, but any visitor's itinerary should include the twelfth-century Christ Church cathedral, the smallest in England, Wren's Sheldonian Theatre, the seventeenth-century Bodleian Library and the eighteenth-century Radcliffe Camera, reckoned to be one of the finest examples of English Baroque architecture.

University of Oxford
A university is reckoned to have existed in Oxford since the twelfth century, and many of the colleges for which Oxford is famous, including Corpus Christi, Magdalen, Christ Church, Trinity and St John's, date back to the fifteenth and sixteenth centuries. Walkers fortunate enough to be in the city during vacations may well get the chance to enter the quadrangles and sometimes even the buildings of the colleges.

Oxford to Culham (12.1 miles) via Abingdon

ENJOY: Sandford-on-Thames, Abingdon, Culham

The route switches again to the right bank and proceeds tantalisingly round the edge of the city, not quite close enough to witness its treasures at first hand. Beyond the heavily built-up Osney and Grandpont districts, things open out a little. Christ Church meadows can be viewed across the water, as can St Mary's Church at Iffley a little further downstream, reckoned to be one of the best preserved twelfth-century village churches in England with magnificent exterior carving. It is certainly worth making a detour over the nearby weir to see it. Continuing on the right bank, the Thames Path goes under another very busy highway, the A423, and on to Sandford-on-Thames. The lock here has the greatest fall of water on the Thames, and there is a charming lockside pub called the King's Arms. Once out of Sandford, the route moves into more open country and swings to the south-west, thereby becoming significantly exposed to the prevailing wind for the first time. A lane leads to Radley, famous for its public school; there is also a useful railway station here. Meanwhile the Thames Path, continuing on the right bank, proceeds pleasantly but uneventfully towards Abingdon (64.2). You should, however, look out for the splendid eighteenth-century Nuneham House across the river.

There is a switch to the left bank by means of a crossing over the foamy waters of Abingdon Weir, and after a pleasant walk through the meadows the town of Abingdon itself is reached. There is much of interest here, including the remains of a Benedictine abbey founded in 675, the Long Alley almshouses built in 1446, and the seventeenth-century County Hall, reckoned to be one of the finest in the country. It was built when Abingdon, now in Oxfordshire, was the county town of Berkshire. On leaving Abingdon the Thames swings southwards, with the route still on the left bank. The massive funnels of Didcot power station now come into view and will rarely be out of sight for the next few miles. The river swings eastwards, passing Culham to the left. Culham (66.4) is a delightful village with a manor house, parts of which date back to the fifteenth century, and gabled dovecote. Its setting, slightly back from the river, is enchanting. There is a railway station but this is some way beyond the village on a busy main road. If time allows, Sutton Courtenay, on the opposite bank but easily reachable from Culham, is another attractive village to visit, with medieval houses, a Norman church and a seventeenth-century manor. The novelist George Orwell is buried here.

The extent of the Thames' meanders is underlined by the fact that, although this section is twelve miles long, Culham is actually just six miles from Oxford as the crow flies. And as you look back at your endeavours over the last couple of days, you may note that the Thames at Abingdon, prior to its confluence with the Ock just south of the town centre, flows for a while in a westerly direction, seemingly *away* from the sea and your final destination. Even more to your consternation, you may note that you are only nine miles or so by road from Newbridge, which you passed on the Thames Path some *twenty-five* miles back!

Culham to Cholsey (14.5 miles) via Wallingford

ENJOY: Wittenham Clumps, Dorchester-on-Thames, Shillingford, Wallingford

The Thames Path runs in a south-easterly direction for a while, the walking enlivened only by the imposing spire of Appleford church on the opposite bank. There follows a large loop, the route swinging north-east to Clifton Hampden. This village, with its half-timbered and thatched cottages, is a real joy; Pevsner describes the church, perched on a cliff, as having a theatrical quality both in position and manner of restoration. The restorer, Gilbert Scott, was also responsible for rebuilding the bridge in Gothic style in 1864. The Thames Path uses Scott's bridge, a fine arched brick-built structure, to switch to the right bank, then begins to loop south-eastwards and continues in that direction to Little Wittenham. There are views over the river to the sumptuous houses and manicured lawns of Burcot. Immediately ahead are the twin Sinodun Hills, site of a Celtic camp and hill fort dating back to 1500 BC, and Wittenham Clumps, a wooded hill with fine views from the summit which stretch to the Vale of the White Horse, although before these hills are reached the Thames Path switches to the left bank at Day's Lock. Nonetheless, a detour to climb the hills may be a welcome antidote for the walker tiring of tramping along the flat. The route continues along the left bank with good views to the attractive Little Wittenham Wood on the opposite bank. Close by to your left is Dorchester-on-Thames, a village which used to be a city;

the cobbled street contains many timber-framed and brick-built houses, and there is a seventeenth-century coaching inn, the White Hart. Undoubtedly the finest treasure in the village, however, is the abbey. It is 200 ft long and boasts a twelfth-century lead font and three magnificent fourteenth-century chancel windows.

The towpath soon switches again to the right bank, but in the absence of a crossing point the Thames Path walker has to abandon the river for a short while and endure a rather unpleasant piece of roadwalking along the A423. It is with relief that you soon turn right at a crossroads and come down to the pretty village of Shillingford. Its most interesting feature is a thatched boathouse, but there is a fine bridge beside a plush riverside hotel. Rejoining the Thames and remaining on the left bank, the route continues past a large marina at Benson. It then crosses the rushing waters of the weir by Benson Lock to switch to the right bank, and follows a straight course slightly west of south through the meadows to reach the market town of Wallingford (77.7). Wallingford was an important Royalist stronghold in the English Civil War. It has fine Georgian houses and its seventeenth-century town hall, standing on stone pillars, contains several portraits by Gainsborough. Of just as much interest to the tired traveller is the fact that the town has ample facilities for refreshment and accommodation.

The route continues on the right bank beyond Wallingford, offering very pleasant walking through meadows dotted with pockets of woodland. There are views over the river to the lovely Mongewell Park and its college, and the romantic ruin of the small Norman church of St John the Baptist. Three miles downstream from Wallingford, you come to Cholsey (80.9) where there is a railway station, although it is a long way from the river. The sight of boat owners relaxing in their vessels or putting out onto the serene sunlit water must sow at least momentary regret in the mind of the passing walker that ten years ago he passed up the opportunity for traineeship in investment banking in favour of shelf-filling at Asda.

Cholsey to Reading (15 miles) via Goring, Pangbourne and Tilehurst

ENJOY: Goring, Pangbourne, Mapledurham

Beyond Cholsey you continue along the right bank, but as you approach Moulsford you are forced away from the river to follow the A329 into the village, with its picturesquely-named Beetle and Wedge pub. Near the pub the towpath returns, the route descends to the river, and it is then straightforward walking to Streatley, the meadows giving way to pleasant woodland just beyond Cleeve Lock. Streatley is a tidy village with Georgian houses, nineteenth-century malt-house, and a fine view of the Thames valley from nearby Streatley Hill. From here the Thames Path leads over the river to its twin village, Goring (84.8); as you cross, you can enjoy a fine view back to the riverside Swan Hotel. There is a brief overlap here with the Ridgeway Path, a rare instance of where two national trails follow the same route.

Goring, the site of a twelfth-century Augustinian priory, contains some fine buildings including a church which contains much Norman work. The area around Goring Lock and its associated weirs is particularly attractive. From Goring to Pangbourne the Thames Path initially follows the towpath along the left bank, passing underneath a fine Brunel railway bridge of robust red brick. The main London to Bristol railway line runs close to the route for several miles hereabouts, and the noise of trains will be a constant feature on this section. Shortly after the bridge, the towpath switches to the right bank but the Thames Path remains on the left bank, and climbs into Hartslock Wood. There follows a fine high-level promenade above the river, before the route turns away from the Thames and flirts briefly with the edges of the Chiltern Hills. The steep descent and uphill climb which follows is something of a culture shock after so much strolling on the flat. The route continues along a driveway through the woods before descending to the lovely village of

Whitchurch, turning right onto the B471 and briefly following this road as far as the toll bridge, where there is a lock and weir with an impressive cascade. From the bridge there is a lovely view back to Whitchurch with its church and mill. Immediately across the bridge you join the towpath on the right bank, but detouring straight on takes you to Pangbourne (89) which deserves a visit. Kenneth Grahame, author of *The Wind In The Willows*, lived here, and there are many fine seventeenth- and eighteenth-century houses in the village.

The route strikes out into the meadows again, with good views over the water to the Tudor splendour of Hardwick House. Between here and Reading the Thames Path sticks to the right bank, the river here forming a border between Berkshire and Oxfordshire. On the opposite bank is the beautiful secluded hamlet of Mapledurham, almost hidden amongst woodland, with seventeenth-century almshouses, a fourteenth-century church and a great sixteenth-century mansion where Elizabeth I was a guest. The towpath does in fact follow the left bank past the village, but there is nowhere for you to cross and no easy means of access nearby; instead you are forced to continue through a trim but characterless housing estate before gratefully descending to the river again at Tilehurst (92.5) and picking up the towpath once more. Despite the presence of housing nearby, there is still a rural feel to the walking, particularly across the river, but as Caversham Bridge comes within sight the residential and industrial buildings of Reading become more concentrated, and soon the towpath converts itself into an urban leisure facility for townsfolk. The importance of the river to the town's leisure industry is further emphasised at Caversham Bridge where there is a big rowing clubhouse, plush hotel and smart riverside pub. A short walk across a working quayside brings you to Reading Bridge (95.9), with the town's multifarious facilities just minutes away.

Reading, which was badly bombed during the Second World War, is hardly a beautiful place; it is a busy industrial and university town noted for the manufacture of biscuits, as well as brewing, engineering, printing and electronics. For obvious reasons, boats and boating also play an important part in the town's economy. Henry I lies buried in the remains of the town's twelfth-century Benedictine abbey, and Oscar Wilde spent two years in the town's jail in the 1890s. Reading is also a key railway junction and its very busy railway station provides direct trains to all parts of the country. Its platforms, especially in winter or at night, are not noted for their warmth and, unless there are no other waiting facilities available, will find favour only amongst walkers who are shortly going into polar expedition training.

Reading to Marlow (17.6 miles) via Shiplake and Henley-on-Thames

ENJOY: Sonning, Henley-on-Thames, Medmenham Abbey, Bisham Abbey, Marlow

As the Thames Path proceeds Londonwards from Reading Bridge along the right bank, the scene is hardly enticing, and is only partially mitigated by the green of King's Meadow to your immediate right. The huge gas-holders, the modern Tesco supermarket and the roar of the high-speed trains on the Reading–London line do little to enhance the beauty of the Thames at this point. The highlight of the walk out of Reading's urban sprawl is the crossing of the Kennet, one of the principal tributaries of the Thames. The route stays on the right bank and, having left Reading behind, proceeds through pleasanter meadows to reach Sonning and its immaculately kept lock. Sonning, where once a bishop's palace existed, is a very pretty place, boasting three inns and a beautiful eleven-arched red brick bridge over the river. There follows a switch to the left bank and some quite delectable walking on the border between Oxfordshire and Berkshire, the Chilterns providing a fine backcloth to the combination of lush meadows and woodland adjoining the river. You continue along the left bank past Shiplake College and its extensive grounds, temporarily leaving the riverside to make your way into the pretty village of Lower Shiplake (102.6) with a useful station on a single track line. The route follows a lane out of Lower Shiplake, coming down to the riverside beyond Bolney Court, and a broad stretch of meadow takes you forward to Marsh Lock, negotiated by means of a wooden causeway. On each side of the bank there are huge, luxurious dwellings, whose back gardens lead directly down to the homeowners' boats on the river itself.

Having passed Marsh Lock there is then a straightforward walk into Henley-on-Thames (104.8). The town has many good timbered houses, including the fourteenth-century Chantry House, and many elegant Georgian houses on its main street. Henley is of course most famous for its June/July Royal Regatta, a rowing festival that has been held here since 1839, although only since 1998 have professionals been allowed to compete. There is a fine five-arched bridge across the river here, built in 1786, which the Thames Path crosses to switch to the right bank before continuing on through the meadows. The river is wide and straight here, and with the absence of locks and weirs is very popular boating country. One most interesting feature on this section is Temple Island, a fishing lodge topped by an Italianate cupola on an island in the river. Just beyond Temple Island on the opposite bank is the gleaming white mansion of Greenlands, built for Viscount Hambleden, better known as W. H. Smith.

The river curls from a north-easterly to a south-easterly direction, passing Hambleden lock and weir by Mill End, where there is a white weatherboarded mill whose records go back to Domesday. The turbulent waters of the weir claimed the life of a bargeman in 1753. Shortly beyond the mill there is a brief towpath switch; in the absence of a crossing the Thames Path temporarily leaves the river, now separating Berkshire from Buckinghamshire, turning right along a road into Aston to pass the conveniently-sited Flowerpot Inn. It then turns left along a path and proceeds slightly above the river past the magnificent red brick Culham Court, before descending to rejoin the river and towpath, and passing Medmenham Abbey on the opposite bank.

Medmenham Abbey

This was formerly a Cistercian house but the present Gothic building is largely late nineteenth-century. As river travellers proceed peacefully upstream, the timeless scene causing them to nostalgically recall a more civilised and quieter age, they may conveniently care to forget that the Abbey was leased to Sir Francis Dashwood in the eighteenth century, who used it to hold meetings of a club reputedly known as the Hellfire Club. Members met once or twice a week to devote their time to black magic rites and other dubious pursuits, and many statues with pornographic inscriptions found their way into the Abbey. Meetings of the Club were held in a chapel decorated with an indecent ceiling painting, and there was a temple with an entrance formed to resemble female genitalia! The pornographic detail has since been removed, so don't bother to make a detour to see it.

The Thames Path continues along the right bank past Hurley, an attractive village with two tithe barns and a twelfth-century inn, and passes over the lock island. It is always a delight to view the locks with their immaculately kept gardens, as well as their nameboards, which give each an identity and character of their own. It is also fascinating – if one has the time – to watch a boat negotiate a lock before proceeding on its way. Shortly after Hurley the route uses a splendid bridge, built in 1989, to switch to the left bank; until 1953 the switch was accomplished with the aid of a ferry. From here you continue past Temple Lock through the meadows. Over the river there are the magnificent buildings of Bisham Abbey, where the England international football squad regularly meet to prepare for matches and tournaments, and the riverside Bisham Church. Despite it being inaccessible across the river, you can still enjoy viewing its restored Norman round-headed windows, steep gables and embattled tower.

Soon afterwards the route reaches Marlow (113.5), a picture-postcard town with elegant Georgian houses, a huge riverside church with a soaring spire, Marlow Place, thought to have been built in 1720 for the Prince of Wales, and the exclusive Compleat Angler Hotel. It has other famous associations: Mary Shelley wrote the Gothic novel *Frankenstein* here, and the remarkable iron suspension bridge, completed in September 1832, was the work of William Tierney Clark, who is better known for his bridge in Hungary linking Buda and Pest.

Marlow to Runnymede (18.2 miles) via Maidenhead

ENJOY: Cookham, Cliveden, Bray, Boveney, Windsor, Eton, Runnymede

Beyond Marlow the route initially remains on the left bank and, having passed the Marlow lock and weir, proceeds pleasantly through meadows to Bourne End, which hosts a chandlery and a vast profusion of rivercraft. The route crosses with the towpath to the right bank and passes the village of Cookham, which boasts a splendid nineteenth-century bridge as well as pretty red brick cottages around a green. The painter Stanley Spencer (1891–1959) lived here and his painting of the Last Supper hangs in the part-twelfth-century church. Below the bridge there are a number of boathouses, one of which is the office of the Keeper of the Royal Swans. Also, just downstream of Cookham, is Formosa Island, the largest island in the Thames; it contains the remains of an eighteenth-century house surrounded by 50 acres of green woodland.

The Thames Path regrettably has to leave the riverside just before Cookham Bridge, passing through the village itself, crossing the A4155 and then following a minor road back to the right bank. Patience, however, is rewarded, for the return to the river brings views to the Cliveden Estate and its glorious beech-woods which drop right down to the water. As you continue beside the river again, you can look back to Cliveden House. Built in 1851, this was once owned by the Astors and was a meeting place of politicians and international celebrities known as the Cliveden Set before the Second World War. It is now only a short stroll downstream to Maidenhead (121.1), past the picturesque and popular Boulter's Lock. Maidenhead is not as charming as many towns on the Thames, but you will note two fine bridges: the seven-arched road bridge, completed in 1777, and a railway bridge designed by Brunel, containing the flattest and widest brick arches in the world. From the railway station there are main-line trains to Reading and London. If you are returning to Reading by train, having hiked these 25 miles in one or more days, you may be surprised to find it is much shorter as the crow flies and just 15 minutes away by train. You would do well not to get too absorbed in your slumbers or your newspaper for fear you will find that you have missed Reading altogether and will not be stopping again until Bristol Parkway.

The Thames Path uses the road bridge to switch to the left bank from Berkshire into Buckinghamshire and then passes under Brunel's bridge. It is then a pleasant walk along the left bank through the meadows all the way to Windsor, with the open expanse of Thames Field to the left. Just before passing underneath the M4, you pass Bray lock and can see the village of Bray over the river to the right; the village has a large church and is famous for its sixteenth-century turncoat vicar, Simon Alleyn, who lived through four reigns and adjusted his religious attitude to suit each of them. Half a mile downstream from Bray is Monkey Island, on which is a hotel that incorporates part of an eighteenth-century fishing lodge built for the Third Duke of Marlborough. For a while the peace of the river is somewhat shattered by the noise of the nearby M4, but tranquillity is restored by the time Boveney is reached.

As you approach Boveney the route passes the fine lawns of private riverside houses that were built in Edwardian times for the earliest 'commuters'. There are also fine views of the Victorian Gothic splendour of Oakley Court across the river. Boveney is a beguiling spot with its lock and tiny riverside chapel, which was actually built from rubble and contains some Norman work. Just beyond Boveney the path returns to Berkshire, leaving Buckinghamshire for the last time, and Windsor Castle can now be seen across the meadows. Soon after passing underneath the A332, you climb away from the riverbank and up to Eton High Street (127.8). The route bears right across the bridge which links Eton with Windsor, and then switches to the right bank to continue on its way. However, few walkers will resist the temptation to explore these two towns: Eton with its quaint old High Street and college, founded in 1440 by Henry VI, and Windsor with its magnificent royal castle founded by William the Conqueror and including the stunning Perpendicular Gothic architecture of St George's Chapel.

The route continues on the right bank to Victoria Bridge, following the towpath, then has to leave it and switch to the left bank to bypass a private area of castle grounds. After a short riverside walk it is then necessary to join a road through Datchet. Although its green lawns and gracious houses provide a pleasant interlude, it is hoped to re-route the Thames Path away from the road as far as Albert Bridge. At Albert Bridge the road arrives at the river, and you cross the bridge here to return to the towpath and continue along the right bank. There is then lovely walking past Ham Bridge and Old Windsor Lock; to pass Ham Island the Thames Path follows a lock cut rather than an extravagant loop made by the river. Then, after passing round the back of Old Windsor and its popular Bells of Ouseley pub, you reach the meadows of Runnymede (131.7) and proceed past the Magna Carta memorial, a domed classical temple built by the American Bar Association. Behind the memorial, and guarded by Lutyens' gatehouses, stands a splendid expanse of inclined parkland dotted with trees. In the park there are further memorials, one of which commemorates 20,000 airmen who died in the Second World War. An island in the river at this point is appropriately enough named Magna Carta Island, for King John sealed the first draft of the Magna Carta at this spot. This is of course a magnet for visitors from home and abroad; even the walker with little historical knowledge will here permit himself a superior smile at the hopefully apocryphal story of the touring couple who reached it at lunchtime and upon seeing a sign indicating 'Magna Carta signed 1215' remarked, 'What a pity. We must have just missed it!'

Runnymede to Teddington (20.7 miles) via Staines and Walton-on-Thames

ENJOY: Chertsey Bridge, Shepperton, Hampton Court Palace

Beyond Runnymede you pass underneath the vast M25 bridges, thus getting a tangible indication of your progress towards the capital, and then proceed beside an ugly industrial estate, while close by to the left is a vast profusion of reservoirs and lakes. Soon you enter Surrey and arrive at Staines, where the route switches to the left bank. Staines (136) has little to interest the walker or tourist, although the nineteenth-century town hall has been converted into an impressive arts centre and may be worth a quick visit. The route progresses out of Staines along a path interspersed with a section of road, but all the way to Laleham the journey is distinctly urban in character with houses and flats immediately beside you throughout. Unusually for a national trail, many of the waymarks along the route contain mileage signs. There is little along this section to capture your attention, with the exception of Penton Hook lock. Penton Hook is in fact a huge loop of the river, and the land round which the loop threads has become an island; hence the Thames Path does not attempt to follow the loop, but cuts round the top of it. To the south-west there are more lakes, the popular Thorpe Park being situated on an island in the middle of one of them. Just beyond Penton Hook the village of Laleham appears to your left, and at last the housing thins out as the path continues through

Laleham Park. However the stillness is again shattered, this time by the M3. Soon after passing under the motorway bridge, the route reaches Chertsey Bridge, a graceful seven-arched structure, and by detouring right across the bridge you can visit the town of Chertsey itself. It is an unremarkable commuter town but does have one interesting feature, namely the curfew bell in the church. This commemorates Blanche Herriot, who at the time of the Wars of the Roses, knowing her lover was to be executed at curfew, climbed the church tower and hung on to the clapper until he was reprieved!

The section beyond Chertsey Bridge through Chertsey Meads provides the last stretch of open meadow walking on the whole route. Continuing along the left bank, it twists and turns with the river and passes through a further built up area on the north-western fringe of Weybridge, and goes on to Shepperton. The river Wey meets the Thames at this point. There are houses on both sides of the river and in the absence of bridges or ferries, the only way from one house to another across the water is by private boat. The variety of rivercraft on this section of the Thames is huge, ranging from small motorboats and rowing boats to pleasure cruisers; from houseboats gaily decorated with lines of clean washing, to rather sad-looking barges sitting in bankside decay and neglect. At the confluence of the Wey and the Thames just south of Shepperton (141.5), an area dotted with small channels and islands, the Thames Path makes use of a ferry for the only time on the route; assistance needs to be summoned by means of a bell. Any delay in engaging the service of the ferryman, who is likely to be found in the nearby boating accessory shop, is compensated for by a lovely crossing over a breathtakingly beautiful piece of water, with trees all around. When the ferry is not operational, there is an alternative route away from the river and through the old village of Shepperton with its fine church of St Nicholas dominating a little square of red brick houses off the village street. This route then returns to the main Path at

Walton Bridge by means of field-edge and roadside walking. If the ferry is available, the ferry crossing will take you to Desborough Cut, which the Thames Path follows in preference to the serpentine course taken by the old Thames channel round the Shepperton Loops. The Cut, completed in 1935, has a pleasantly rural feel with fields to the right, but at Walton Bridge beside Walton-on-Thames, where the Cut effectively ends, the urban theme returns. Walton-on-Thames is an unexciting commuter town, and the five miles from here to Hampton Court on the right bank provide but few highlights. That notwithstanding, this section of route is extremely popular with walkers and fishermen and cyclists. Early on there are the picturesque Sunbury and Molesey locks and a view over the river to Sunbury and its church which has a tower and cupola. Beyond Sunbury, the Molesey Reservoirs are situated to the right, and there is a large waterworks across the river. It is not thrilling stuff. Things do improve with the advent of Hurst Park; across the river there are views to Bushy Park and the church at Hampton, close to which is the actor David Garrick's domed temple, built to house a statue of Shakespeare, and soon the magnificent Hampton Court Palace comes into view. There is now a switch to the left bank, using the bridge (designed by Lutyens in 1933) carrying the A308, and the entrance to Hampton Court Palace (147.6) is just over that bridge.

Hampton Court Palace

Unless you are in a tearing hurry, a visit to the palace must not be missed. Created by Cardinal Wolsey in 1514 and beloved of Henry VIII, it contains some of the finest examples of Tudor architecture and of Christopher Wren's work. Of particular interest are Anne Boleyn's Gateway, surmounted by a splendid astronomical clock made for Henry VIII, the Great Hall with its hammer beam roof, and of course the Maze, naturally not to be recommended if you have lost your bearings once too often today already.

The Thames Path continues with a delightful walk along the left bank to Kingston-upon-Thames, with the open expanse of Hampton Park to the left and, by contrast, the built-up areas of Thames Ditton and Surbiton to the right. Kingston, a Royal Borough, is a huge, sprawling place and has for centuries been a key river crossing; although the present bridge was opened in 1828, a bridge existed here in the thirteenth century. Seven Saxon kings were crowned at Kingston and their coronation stone is preserved here. The route uses the bridge to switch to the right bank and proceeds downstream to Teddington Lock (152.4), the last lock on the Thames. The weir here marks the beginning – or end – of the tidal section of the Thames. Of note on this section are the massive weeping willow trees on the opposite bank. From Teddington Lock to Greenwich, three miles from the end of the trail, a waymarked Thames Path route exists along the full length of both the right and left banks. You may choose to switch from one to another at will, or stick to one and avoid crossing the river at any time. Of course you may opt to walk *to* Greenwich on one bank, and then return *from* Greenwich using the other, a laudable objective indeed for the walker who wishes to maximise his knowledge of the river. I shall give itineraries for both right and left bank routes.

RIGHT BANK

Teddington to Putney (11.6 miles) via Barnes

ENJOY: Ham House, Petersham, Kew

The right bank route stays by the river and there is a positively rural feel about the immediate surroundings as Richmond is approached; there are good views ahead to the natural platform of Richmond Hill, on which Joshua Reynolds once lived. The route passes seventeenth-century Ham House, close to Petersham, a charming village with fine seventeenth- and eighteenth-century houses and a splendid old church with high box pews and galleries. Soon you reach Richmond itself (155.8), another Royal borough and containing much fine Palladian architecture. Particularly noteworthy is Maids of Honour Row that was built to house the ladies of the court during the reign of George I. Staying right beside the river, the route continues through the Old Deer Park, past a golf course and on to the 368-acre Royal Botanic Gardens, known popularly as Kew Gardens. These were founded in 1759 and contain a collection of over 25,000 living plant species and many noble buildings including the nineteenth-century Palm House and the eighteenth-century Chinese Pagoda. A recent addition is the Princess of Wales Conservatory, a futuristic building for plants from ten different climatic zones.

Beyond Kew Gardens is Kew Bridge, and beyond that is rather nondescript urban walking as far as Chiswick Bridge. There is now a definite sense of being in London surburbia. Beyond Chiswick Bridge you can marvel at the architectural contrast between a fine blue-washed Georgian house and, almost adjacent, the vast grey pile that was once Mortlake brewery. From here it is a short walk to Barnes, with impressive Regency riverside terraces, and the home of composer Gustav Holst for a time. Beyond Barnes are the playing-fields of St Paul's public school and then the blatant Victorian extravagance of Hammersmith Bridge with its remarkable turrets of gilt and green, designed by Sir Joseph Bazalgette, chief engineer of the Board of Works, and built in 1887. Just beyond the bridge you pass the Harrods Furniture Depository with its twin cupolas – a useful landmark for Boat Race commentators – then proceed past a cluster of lakes and on to the busy London suburb of Putney. Putney Bridge (164) is the starting point for the Oxford vs Cambridge boat race, and although boating eights can be seen at many places on the Thames and at any time of year, they are particularly noticeable downstream of Teddington, with no locks or weirs to interrupt their progress. Walkers may be entertained by the stentorian tones of their coaches, yelling encouragement at the crews from the banks. Putney is a very popular place for crews to begin and end their activity, and on busy days, when competitive boating is in progress, the towpath hereabouts will be alive with all the hallmarks of the British at play: wet-suited oarsmen, ambulancemen, curious spectators, refreshment vans, and signs threatening summary execution for anyone silly enough to as much as think about stopping their car in a controlled zone.

LEFT BANK

Teddington to Putney (14.1 miles) via Chiswick

ENJOY: Strawberry Hill, Eel Pie Island, Syon Park, Strand on the Green, Chiswick, Hammersmith

The left bank route, having crossed the bridge at Teddington Lock, has to follow the A310 road through Teddington itself to Strawberry Hill, notable for a Gothic Revival villa, built between 1750 and 1776 for the author Horace Walpole. After the briefest flirtation with the river, the route proceeds through the centre of Twickenham and then down to the Thames again where the true riverside walking recommences. Twickenham contains some impressive seventeenth- and eighteenth-century houses, a pub delightfully named the Barmy Arms, and views to an island with another lovely name, Eel Pie Island – so called because it was a popular spot for Victorians who enjoyed their *ale* and pies there! More open country is reached and the route passes Marble Hill, an eighteenth-century white villa.

Having passed St Margarets to the left and Richmond (156.3) over the bridge, you reach Isleworth. The highlight here is the eighteenth-century London Apprentice inn, although there are many other fine houses in the old village area close to the river. The Thames Path leaves the river and enters Syon Park, with a good view to Syon House, a remodelled Tudor building topped by a stone lion, with grounds laid out in the eighteenth century by Capability Brown. Catherine Howard was a prisoner at Syon House before her execution, and the park is also the site of an English Civil War battle in 1642. Between Syon Park and Kew Bridge the walking is fiddly as Brentford, a market town and former county town of Middlesex, is negotiated, the only real highlight being a brief brush with the Grand Union Canal, which meets the Thames here. The walking improves once you have passed Kew Bridge and reach Strand on the Green, a marvellously preserved row of old riverside houses and pubs.

The walk on past Grove Park to Chiswick Bridge is unremarkable, but beyond Chiswick Bridge you reach the open fields of Duke's Meadows and there are good views across to the river to the cheerful waterside scene at Barnes. The route negotiates a new riverside development then enjoys a very pleasant road walk through the older, more 'villagey' parts of Chiswick and its neighbour Hammersmith, with fine seventeenth- and eighteenth-century houses and impressive Georgian architecture. The riverside Chiswick Mall includes Kelmscott House, built around 1780, and once the home of William Morris; you may recall Kelmscot village near Lechlade earlier in the walk and its strong associations with Morris. Also in Chiswick is the seventeenth-century Hogarth's House, for fifteen years the summer home of the artist William Hogarth. Many of Hammersmith's finest riverside houses are to be found on Hammersmith Terrace, with a number of eighteenth-century houses, inns (The Dove being one of the most interesting) and boathouses.

Beyond Hammersmith Terrace, the Thames Path itself returns to the riverside and after passing Joseph Bazalgette's remarkable bridge it is a straightforward riverside walk to Putney Bridge (166.5). To the left lies Fulham Palace, described as one of the best medieval sites in London, with buildings dating from the fifteenth century. It was the residence of the Bishops of London from the twelfth century until as recently as 1973. The only slight deviation of the Thames Path from the river is at Craven Cottage, home of Fulham Football Club. The Thames Path is the only national trail that goes directly past a Premier

League ground, and therefore the only occasion on which you may find yourself mingling, not with fellow hikers or casual strollers, but football supporters. Walkers with a dislike of large crowds may indeed prefer to avoid this section of the walk at a time when supporters are arriving or leaving a game, particularly if they have inadvertently attired themselves in the club colours of the away side.

RIGHT BANK: Putney to Greenwich (16.3 miles) via Battersea, Westminster Bridge and Bermondsey

ENJOY: Albert Bridge, Battersea Power Station, Lambeth Palace, London Eye, Tate Gallery, Millennium Bridge, *HMS Belfast*, Greenwich

There is no towpath downstream of Putney, so the walking becomes more fiddly on both banks. From Putney Bridge the right bank route leaves the Thames almost immediately and follows along streets before returning to the river with Wandsworth Park to the right. Soon, though, the route loses the river again and proceeds through Wandsworth. This part of London was made famous for hats in the eighteenth century by the influx of Huguenot refugees, who were skilled hatters, and the brewing industry has been important here since the sixteenth century. Wandsworth also has a prison, built in 1857. Any thought of picturesque rurality has now gone; this is an uncompromising urban landscape of sprawling concrete, relieved only by parks and gardens. The route returns to the river briefly and passes Wandsworth Bridge, then leaves the river and follows roads, including a section of the A3205, towards Battersea. There is then a more sustained section of riverside walking which includes a fine riverside housing development and an eighteenth-century church. The path passes Battersea Bridge and, shortly afterwards, Albert Bridge. Built in 1873, it is a riot of gold, green and pink, but it is also weak; a notice warns marching troops to break step before crossing!

Beyond Albert Bridge there is pleasant riverside walking past Battersea Park, which houses an impressive 100 ft high 'peace pagoda'. At Chelsea Bridge you leave the river and follow a road beside the park, passing a smart athletics track, then endure a messy walk back to the river beside traffic-choked roads, including another section of the A3205, and passing underneath the main railway lines into Victoria. There are two features of interest on this otherwise rather grim section: firstly Battersea power station, designed by Giles Gilbert Scott and built in the 1930s, closed in 1983 and redeveloped with a view to reuse as a leisure complex, and secondly the Battersea Dogs and Cats Home, which was opened in 1860. The Path goes right past the home, and the sound of the dogs can easily be heard from the pavement. It is a relief to get back to the river at Nine Elms, close to the New Covent Garden Market, for it is now straightforward riverside walking via the Albert Embankment all the way to Hungerford Bridge. You pass two bridges, Vauxhall Bridge and Lambeth Bridge, but the undoubted highlight of this section is Lambeth Palace, home of the Archbishops of Canterbury for the past 750 years. It was begun in the thirteenth century and has been added to many times, its best building being the Great Hall of 1660. The march to Westminster Bridge (172) and on past the former Greater London Council buildings, through Jubilee Gardens to Hungerford Bridge, is particularly satisfying. In Jubilee Gardens is the magnificent London Eye, its rotating capsules giving superb views across London and up and down the river. With the Houses of Parliament and Big Ben to be seen across the river, there is a definite feeling of having arrived in the heart of the capital. All human life is to be seen accompanying the walker along these walkways, from the sad tramps and beggars surveying the ground for discarded portions of takeaway meals to wealthy men-about-town striding confidently ahead, their glances pavementwards confined to checks for scuff marks on their new Gucci shoes.

From Hungerford Bridge the right bank walk stays with the river virtually all the way to Tower Bridge. It continues past the Royal

Festival Hall and Waterloo Bridge, beyond which is the National Theatre, built in 1976. Next comes the exuberant Gabriel's Wharf plaza, the Oxo Tower, which houses modern shops, eateries and offices, and the ornate Blackfriars Bridge, which opened in 1869. Between here and Southwark Bridge there are three features of particular interest. The most notable is the thatched, timber-framed reconstruction of the Globe Theatre; built by Shakespeare and others in 1599, it burned down in 1613 and was rebuilt in 1995. The other very exciting features of note hereabouts are the former Bankside Power Station, which has been converted into the Tate Modern art gallery, and the Millennium Bridge, providing easy pedestrian access to St Paul's Cathedral. The route moves slightly away from the river to pass along the narrow Clink Street, site of the medieval Winchester Palace of which but a few traces remain. After the airy riverside promenading it is quite a shock to be walking along this narrow lane with forbidding old stone buildings rising up on each side, one of which is a former jail that is now a museum. Before returning to the waterside, the route passes within sight of Southwark Cathedral; dating back to 1220, it is the earliest Gothic church in London. Nearby is London Bridge and the station of the same name. Beyond London Bridge the route returns to the riverside, passing a large new office and shopping complex, and then the warship *HMS Belfast*, which saw service in the Second World War and the Korean War and is now open to the public. Just beyond *HMS Belfast* is Tower Bridge (174.5). Built between 1886 and 1894, with bascules that weigh 1200 tons each, it is the last bridge over the Thames that walkers will see on the Thames Path.

After Tower Bridge the character of the route along the right bank changes. The busy tourist areas are now left behind and you see a different, albeit equally fascinating, side of London, and tangible reminders of its immense importance as a busy port. Although the warehouses and wharves still remain, they are now unused and empty, with bigger ships demanding deeper water and better facilities.

From the ashes of a dead industry has a risen a phoenix in the form of massive development. The following stretch through Bermondsey and Rotherhithe, where the Thames swings southwards, sees you following long-established riverside walks, roads set slightly back from the river with closely-packed housing on either side, or new walkways which have been incorporated into the modern complexes. One moment you will pass a brand new block of luxury flats, and the next you will meet reminders of an earlier age, in the form of cobbled streets, cosy pubs and, at one point, a pumphouse which was built in 1930 to control Surrey Docks' water level. Efforts have been made to create some rurality amidst the concrete; there is now a nature park at Rotherhithe with pond and trees, and nearby there is a working city farm with a good variety of animals. The route runs right through the farm when it is open.

Soon after the old Surrey Docks, the right bank path moves well away from the river, and there is an uninspiring trudge through Deptford, with traffic noise, largely absent for many miles, returning with a vengeance. Francis Drake was knighted at Deptford and Peter the Great of Russia studied shipbuilding here, but apart from the old church of St Nicholas there is little to fire the imagination and it is a relief to return to the river at Greenwich (180.3). Greenwich is at the bottom of a distinctive loop of the Thames, which owes its familiarity not so much to the field trips organised so painstakingly by geography teachers but the designers of the opening titles of *EastEnders*.

LEFT BANK

Putney to Greenwich (15.8 miles) via Chelsea and Westminster

ENJOY: Cheyne Walk, Houses of Parliament, St Katharine Docks, Great Eastern Pier

The left bank route also leaves the river immediately at Putney Bridge and makes an extravagant arc round Hurlingham Park, which includes the Hurlingham Club and associated sports facilities. You stay with the river past Wandsworth Bridge, alongside wharves which are reminders of former days when the Thames was of considerably greater commercial importance, and then pass a big retail park which is another indicator of our changing world. After leaving the riverside and following roads to Sands End, you reach Chelsea Harbour, a marina with plush vessels surrounded by magnificent new buildings. During the rest of the journey you will see many more exciting modern waterside complexes, sitting cheek by jowl with rundown, often derelict areas that cry out for redevelopment. At the end of Lots Road you reach Cheyne Walk, and from here the route follows the river all the way to the Houses of Parliament. The fine embankments on both sides of the river were the work of Joseph Bazalgette, creator of Hammersmith Bridge (see above). Cheyne Walk contains many fine early eighteenth-century houses; their inhabitants have included the novelists George Eliot and Henry James, and the poet and painter Dante Gabriel Rossetti.

The route follows the Chelsea Embankment past the magnificent Albert Bridge and then the Royal Hospital and its grounds, where the annual Chelsea Flower Show is held. The Hospital, built by Wren and founded in 1682 by Charles II for invalid and veteran soldiers, is lodged in by several hundred Army pensioners today; they are a distinctive sight with their scarlet frock coats. Also of interest nearby is the Chelsea Physic Garden for botanical research, established in the seventeenth century. After proceeding past Chelsea Bridge, you continue alongside Grosvenor Road and Millbank, passing the tiny Pimlico Gardens and the colourful and ornate Vauxhall Bridge. Between Vauxhall Bridge and Lambeth Bridge is the Tate Gallery; opened in 1897, it contains collections of the work of J. M. W. Turner and William Blake.

Beyond Lambeth Bridge the route passes through gardens to reach the Houses of Parliament. Parts of the present Gothic-style building, designed by Sir Charles Barry and A. W. Pugin, go back to the mid-nineteenth-century, but the House of Commons was destroyed in an air raid in 1941 and has been rebuilt to its old character. Big Ben, which many erroneously believe to be the clock towering above the Houses of Parliament (it is in fact the bell which chimes every 15 minutes) was named after Sir Benjamin Hall, First Commissioner of Works at the time the bell was cast at Whitechapel Bell Foundry in 1858. Westminster Bridge (173.5) lies immediately beyond; the bridge was the work of Thomas Page in the nineteenth-century, and the large statue on the bank here, completed in 1902, is of Boudicca, Queen of the Iceni. The route continues to Hungerford Bridge along the Victoria Embankment, past Westminster Pier where, as at many other spots nearby, river trips are available. Hungerford Bridge on the left bank is the closest that you get on the Thames Path to the West End and its unrivalled eating and shopping facilities. With several miles still to walk, and only limited rucksack space, it might be seen as a little unwise for the hiker to embark on a spending spree in Piccadilly or Oxford Street, but if he is beginning to feel the effects of his walk from rural Gloucestershire, has a few pounds to spare, and wishes to impress present or prospective hiking partners, he could not be blamed for making a detour to Fortnum and Mason in search of their own-brand English Breakfast Tea and Foot Embrocation Cream.

From Hungerford Bridge, the left bank walk proceeds alongside the river past Cleopatra's Needle, an ancient Egyptian granite obelisk that was moved to England in 1878. After Waterloo Bridge the route continues past the eighteenth-century Somerset House, once the general register office for births, marriages and deaths. It remains by the river past the impressive *HMS President* and Blackfriars Bridge as far as the Millennium Bridge, then continues to Tower Bridge past Southwark Bridge and London Bridge following close to the river, although a brief diversion may be necessary if the container crane is at work on Walbrook Wharf. Apart from St Paul's Cathedral, well signposted and easily reached from the Thames

Path, and the fine old church of St Magnus the Martyr, which is right on the route, there is not the variety of attractions that exist on the right bank, although the new high-rise office buildings and luxury flats may be of interest to students of modern architecture. There are, however, good views to the multifarious attractions on the right bank. At length you reach the Tower of London, home of the Crown Jewels and site of the imprisonment and execution of Thomas More, the Duke of Monmouth, two wives of Henry VIII, and many others. Tower Bridge (176.8) lies immediately beyond, and after that comes St Katherine Docks, one of many rejuvenated areas of London dockland. This is particularly rewarding for the visitor, with Thomas Telford's huge warehouses being converted to shops, restaurants, and pubs; the waterside theme is maintained through the presence of ships of both ancient and modern design, with traditional sailing ships sitting alongside massive luxury cruisers. The character of the route changes now, and the tourists are largely left behind as you proceed along Wapping High Street. As on the right bank, modern development sits alongside often rundown and derelict old buildings, although along cobbled streets there are many pretty old houses and pubs, notably the Prospect of Whitby. Wapping, like the Tower, also saw executions, being the site of the execution docks; Captain Kidd was one of those executed here for crimes on the high seas.

The route passes into Shadwell, where the northern end of the Rotherhithe Tunnel is situated, and follows a road named Narrow Street. There is more modern development here, including luxury flats with balconies looking down on the carefully redeveloped and refurbished waterfronts, and more new property, adjoining unappealing mudflats, is being built all the time. As in Wapping, there are many houses of character, including some fine Georgian red brick buildings. Beyond Shadwell, the river begins its loop down to Greenwich. The area of land within the loop is known as the Isle of Dogs, formerly notable for its shipbuilding. You begin right by the river but soon are forced onto Westferry Road, which takes you round the edge of Millwall towards Greenwich. At length you reach the Greenwich foot tunnel (182.3) and use it to cross the river and be reunited with the right bank route for the first time since Teddington Lock. You leave Westferry Road for a pleasant foray into John McDougal Gardens, return to the road briefly and then leave it to pass Burrell's Wharf. This is a splendid, one might say Italianate, development; nearby is the Great Eastern Pier, a reminder that Brunel's famous *Great Eastern* ship was launched from the Isle of Dogs in 1858. You continue beside or close to the river all the way to Greenwich, past the Ferry House pub, to arrive at the tunnel and the end of your left bank walk.

Greenwich to Thames Barrier (4.2 miles) past O_2 Arena

ENJOY: O_2 Arena, Thames Barrier

There is much to see in Greenwich, most notably the National Maritime Museum, designed by Wren in 1694 as a naval hospital and later housing the Royal Naval College. Also of interest is Queen's House, designed by Inigo Jones in 1637 and the first Palladian-style building in England, and, in Greenwich Park, the building which formerly housed the Royal Observatory, founded in 1675 by Charles II. The zero line of longitude passes right through it, although the observatory itself has since moved to Cambridge. For lovers of old ships the focal point of Greenwich will be the *Cutty Sark*; built in 1869 and one of the great tea-clippers, it is now preserved as a museum. *Gipsy Moth*, in which Francis Chichester circumnavigated the world in 1966–7, is also here. The Thames Path follows the right bank out of Greenwich beside the river, past some working river wharves, and continues slightly west of north before curling round the O_2 Arena and proceeding south-eastwards. There is a short cut which takes you over the A102 just before that road plunges into the Blackwall Tunnel, and past the

O_2 Arena on the left. Designed by the Richard Rogers Partnership, it opened on 31 December 1999 as the Millennium Dome and in its opening months housed a variety of exhibitions combining education and leisure, although it was constantly plagued by well-publicised financial troubles. However, as the O_2 Arena it is now flourishing as an arts and exhibition centre. Covering an area of nearly 20 acres, and at 164 ft high, the arena is certainly well worth a detour for a closer look.

Returning to the Thames Path, there is just a mile or so of riverside walking to go, with the Barrier – the end of the route – in sight. To reach it involves a rather dismal trudge through a bleak landscape, with big industrial estates and works dominating the scene. The 1,706 ft long Barrier, completed in 1982 is, however, a most impressive climax to the walk. While its stainless steel hoods shoot from the water like sea monsters from a sci-fi movie, the flood gates remain submerged and are rotated into position when exceptionally high tides are expected. In its first fourteen years this happened over two hundred times. You pass underneath the control centre to arrive at the magnificent mural on the wall of the subway depicting the river from source to finish (184.5 via right bank route, 185.5 via left bank route). Nearby you can also find a spotlessly clean and friendly cafe, with a very good information centre, from which it is only a short walk to Charlton station to commence the homeward journey. The river itself carries on for some 25–30 miles and you may express some sadness that the route does not in fact extend all the way to the mouth of the river, thereby giving you a complete overview of the Thames from start to finish. However, a closer look at the map may quickly persuade you that the Countryside Commission were wise not to trouble your blistered feet any further.

The Peddars Way and Norfolk Coast Path

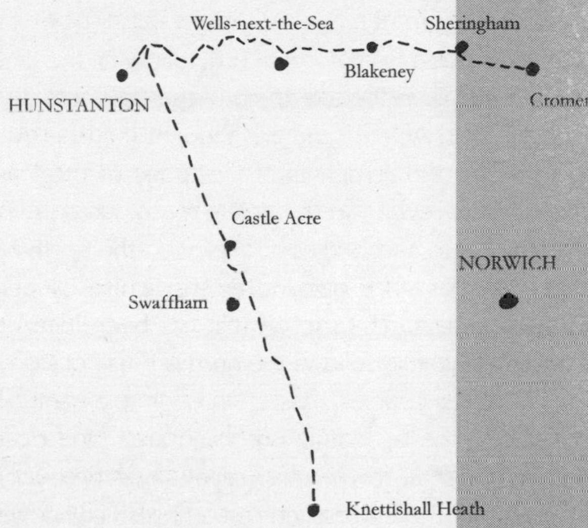

Designation: National trail.
Length: 95 miles.
Start: Knettishall Heath, Suffolk.
Finish: Cromer, Norfolk.
Nature: A largely level walk along a stretch of old Roman road, and then a section of Norfolk Coast Path. The Peddars Way section makes up the first half of the walk, the Norfolk Coast Path the second. The two sections join at Holme-next-the-Sea, just outside Hunstanton.
Difficulty rating: Easy.
Average time of completion: 7 days.

HIGHLIGHTS OF THIS WALK:

- **Brettenham Heath**
- **Castle Acre**
- **Hunstanton**
- **Scolt Head Island**
- **Wells-next-the-Sea**
- **Blakeney**
- **Cley next the Sea**

This national trail, opened by the Prince of Wales in 1986, is a very undemanding route, and arguably the easiest national trail to complete, especially if taken in short stages. Any hills are very gentle – the path rarely climbs more than 300 ft above sea level – and there are no technical demands on the walker. This is one of the driest parts of the country, and you will be unfortunate to meet bad weather, especially in summer.

The Peddars Way was a Roman road, built following the extensive Romanisation of Norfolk in the aftermath of the unsuccessful revolt inspired by Boudicca in AD 61, and it is thought that the Way was initially used to police the remnants of the tribes of the Iceni that remained following the revolt. The complete route linked the Roman garrison in Colchester to anchorages or a ferry on the north Norfolk coast, and the Way has since enjoyed extensive use by peasants, pilgrims and many others. The section that has been incorporated into the national trail faithfully follows the northern half of the original route for much of its course, passing through pleasant Norfolk countryside including the fascinating Breckland area, and close to a number of villages and small towns which repay a brief detour or stop. However, there is not the endless interest and scenic variety which other national trails provide. Moreover, you may be disappointed not to be able to follow the whole Way from Colchester, which would near enough have created a coast to coast route. As it is, you are left, for the Peddars Way section at any rate, with a path which it has been suggested rather unkindly, 'starts in the middle of nowhere, ends in the middle of nowhere, and goes nowhere in between!'

However, the attraction of the Norfolk Coast Path section of the walk, which starts at Hunstanton, is beyond doubt. The Norfolk coast is one of the richest areas in Britain for viewing seabirds at all times of year, and its salt marshes provide a great diversity of plant life. There are also many attractive coastal villages and towns with fine old buildings and some particularly interesting churches. The going, along the flat for most of the way, is largely very easy, although there is one tough stretch of walking on soft sand dunes, and another on shingle.

Knettishall Heath to Little Cressingham (14.7 miles) via Stonebridge, Thompson

ENJOY: Breckland, Thompson Water, Shakers' Furze

The start of the route, by a minor road at Knettishall Heath in Suffolk, is right in the heart of Breckland, some distance from Thetford, the nearest town, and a taxi journey may be required. Some drivers, perhaps walkers themselves, will express great interest, and may suggest detours to off-route sights as well as good eateries and pubs. Others will remark, 'Rather you than me' and refer smugly to the fact that this is their last job before their shift ends and they will shortly be heading home for a hearty breakfast and a few hours' kip. On a cold, wet, windy day it will indeed be a hardy walker who is not tempted to ask the driver if he might join him.

Breckland

The route for this first section passes right through Breckland, literally 'patches of exhausted land'. Due to overgrazing, the shallow soil of this area was nutrient-poor as long ago as the Middle Ages and farmers moved to richer pastures, leaving a waste of exposed sandy heathland on which conifer forests were planted to stabilise the soil and act as windbreaks. The area has now become a haven for wildlife and plant life. The heaths are now home in summer to 90 per cent of Britain's stone curlews; other feathered inhabitants of Breckland at various times of year include the ringed plover, tree pipit and woodlark. A great range of butterflies populate the area, red deer can be seen in the forest, and you may also spot a brown hare. Breckland was the last mainland stronghold of the red squirrel, but the species is now almost extinct in this area and it will be a fortunate walker indeed who finds one. There are many species of wild flowers and plants which are very rare elsewhere, such as the Spanish catchfly, spring speedwell and grape hyacinth.

You begin by heading north through pretty woodland, but almost immediately turn north-east to cross the Little Ouse and enter Norfolk, then proceed resolutely in a north-westerly direction across classic Breckland countryside. Soon the Way crosses the A1066 Thetford–Diss road, but by turning left down the road you reach Brettenham Church, lying on the edge of the picturesque Shadwell Park. This was an important crossing point of the River Thet, and a Roman village existed here between the first and fourth century AD. The Peddars Way crosses the Thet further east and continues north-west along good paths, with forestry dominating the views to your right, and the wide expanse of Brettenham Heath visible to your left. You then cross two important thoroughfares, namely the very busy A11 London–Norwich road and then the Thetford–Norwich railway. The route proceeds through the forest of Roudham Heath and then continues through more open country to Stonebridge, on the A1075 Thetford–Watton road. Stonebridge itself (6.5) is uninteresting, though the enthusiast of old railways will doubtless appreciate the robust brickwork of an old bridge on the now disused Thetford–Watton line. Just to the west of Stonebridge is East Wretham, beyond which is Wretham Park. This contains some fine reed-fringed lakes, which vary in levels as the water rises from the underlying chalk; dry one season, dark and deep the next. Beyond Stonebridge, forestry becomes even more dominant as the route heads north-westwards towards Little Cressingham. Initially you follow a metalled road, then proceed on a stony track through extensive woodland, with much of the surrounding countryside owned by the Ministry of Defence. At length you reach another attractive lake, Thompson Water, which was created by damming a tributary of the River Wissey nearby. On a dry, warm morning you may see roe deer from the nearby woodlands taking a drink here.

By turning right just beyond Thompson Water it is possible to reach the village of Thompson, which has a pretty church of knapped flint dating back to the early fourteenth century. Beyond

Thompson Water the route passes through a lovely pine wood known as Shakers' Furze, then skirts Merton Wood and Merton Park. The park, populated by horses and geese, contains an interesting church including a Jacobean two-decker pulpit and a splendid font with angel wings. The little town of Watton lies beyond to the north-east. The national trail, however, moves away to the north-west and out of Breckland into more open farmland. You join a farm track to reach the B1108 and then turn left to follow a path running parallel with that road as far as Little Cressingham; it is worth taking a short detour to the right off this path to inspect the round-towered Threxton Church, which has a fine porch and excellent thirteenth-century north arcade. The most noteworthy feature of Little Cressingham (14.7) is a set of four bowl barrows over 200 ft in diameter, one of which was found to contain an early Bronze Age Wessex burial; Great Cressingham, two miles to the north-west and off the route, has a church with a particularly good roof and chancel, and nearby there is an old priory and a fragment of a sumptuous sixteenth-century brick house.

Little Cressingham to Castle Acre (11.7 miles) via North Pickenham

ENJOY: Swaffham, Palgrave Hall

The twelve miles of the Peddars Way from Little Cressingham to Castle Acre, still heading north-west, sees an almost exclusive reliance on metalled roads which, whilst allowing fast and easy progress, can be tiring on the feet. You climb gently to Caundle Common and then maintain a parallel course with the River Wissey, passing close to the neo-Georgian Pickenham Hall which lies immediately to your left as you cross the B1077 at South Pickenham. Soon afterwards the route turns left onto another minor road that crosses the Wissey and passes through North Pickenham. The winding course of this road from Little Cressingham contrasts with the dead-straight walking that has characterised much of what you have done so far, but when the metalled road out of North Pickenham reaches a crossroads you go straight on over, and the walking becomes straight and true once more. This is known as Procession Lane, the name derived from the ancient custom of beating the bounds. Historically, beating the bounds meant marking parish boundaries by walking round them and striking certain points with rods. However, any illusions of having been transported to a more leisurely age are shattered when you reach the A47 Kings Lynn–Norwich trunk road, with the possibility of a detour to the attractive town of Swaffham. Features of note in the town include the church of St Peter and St Paul with its squadron of 88 flying angels in its roof, a huge marketplace with an eighteenth-century market cross, and a rotunda built by Horace Walpole.

The route now uses a combination of winding track and metalled road to head on towards Castle Acre. The only real highlight of this walk is Palgrave Hall, situated close to the site of the medieval village of Great Palgrave of which there is now no trace. Easy walking beyond Palgrave Hall takes you to Castle Acre itself (26.4). The village, enclosed by earthworks of a castle built by the son-in-law of William the Conqueror, has a good range of amenities and a number of interesting features. Arguably the most notable is the ruin of Cluniac Priory, in a lovely setting amongst well-kept lawns. The west front of the priory church contains one of Britain's finest surviving tiers of Norman arcading, and one of the prior's rooms is still intact and contains a small museum. The village contains several other attractive old buildings, many of flint; particularly noteworthy is the Ostrich Inn, with its huge fireplaces and beamed ceilings. The church of St James has a superb font cover and an ornate pulpit which incorporates painted panels of saints in deep blues, reds and golds, with texts emanating from their mouths. It has an early Gothic door, the opening of which may have been high enough for a knight in full armour to ride into the sanctuary for a blessing before a battle, without having to go to the trouble of dismounting. Simon Jenkins described it as the world's first drive-in church!

Castle Acre to Fring (14 miles) via Great Massingham

ENJOY: Harpley Church, Harpley Common, Houghton Hall estate

For the 18 miles or so from Castle Acre to Ringstead (which lies just a couple of miles from the end of the Peddars Way section) the route continues north-westwards through unspectacular but pleasant rolling countryside, tending to bypass places of habitation. As it sticks faithfully to the old Roman road virtually throughout, the walking is straightforward and easy. Immediately after leaving Castle Acre there is a stretch of walking of some three miles either on, or beside, a metalled road. At a triangulation point signifying one of the highest points of the route – still only 302 ft! – the metalled section ends and from here right up to Ringstead the walking is on good farm tracks, the only contact with motorised traffic occurring at the infrequent road crossings. Soon after forsaking tarmac for the farm track, the route crosses three roads in close succession, beginning with the B1145 Kings Lynn–Aylsham road, while detouring right down the second or third one brings you to Great Massingham. This is a very pretty village with a large pond, an attractive church with a fine porch and fourteenth-century font, and further facilities for rest and refreshment.

Back on the route, the next major crossing is at Harpley Dams (33.7) on the A148 Kings Lynn–Fakenham road just west of Harpley. It is worth following the busy road to this village to inspect its church, a superb work of decorated Gothic craftsmanship, with some splendid bench-end carvings depicting bears, monkeys, mythical beasts and bishops. The gentlest of inclines takes you onto Harpley Common, dotted with tumuli. At the next road crossing, a detour along the road to the left will take you to Anmer, which as well as a fourteenth-century church contains a hall with a late Georgian brick façade, while east of the village there is a fine bell barrow. You then cross the B1153 Gayton–Brancaster road, enjoying fine views to the beautiful woods of the Houghton Hall estate. There is a splendidly remote feel to the walking hereabouts, with colour being provided in the summer by the profusion of poppies and rosebay willowherb. Continue on to pass close by the village of Fring (40.4), which has a pretty woodland setting and an imposing church tower. One other feature to look out for, over to the right, is the restored brick tower mill near the village of Great Bircham, a name evoking images of a fictional prep school featured in a children's comic paper in less politically correct times.

Fring to Thornham (14.2 miles) via Hunstanton

ENJOY: Ringstead, Hunstanton, Gore Point

Beyond Fring the feeling of remoteness begins to disappear, with more houses and hamlets dotted around the countryside. You cross the B1454 just east of the village of Sedgeford, and pass right by the Sedgeford Magazine, which looks rather like an old chapel but is in fact thought to have been built as an armoury or powder store shortly before the English Civil War. The route crosses a stretch of dismantled railway, which once linked Hunstanton with Wells-next-the-Sea, and continues on to Ringstead. The village, the first community of any size actually on the route since Castle Acre, has one or two interesting features, including the tower of the ruined church of St Peter within the garden of a Georgian house, and a brick tower mill. The village also had a good range of facilities at the time of writing and you may be fortunate enough to find a cup of tea, a much-needed reward for pounding the tracks.

For walkers doing the whole national trail, Ringstead is a major watershed in the route, marking the end of the 'lonely' part of the walk and the entry into an area that is immensely popular with both casual day visitors and holidaymakers; from now until Cromer, other people will never be far away. After a moderate climb out of the village on a metalled road, there is the exciting sight of the sea for the first time. The route leaves the metalled road just beyond the mill to follow a path down to the busy A149 north Norfolk coast road, then after crossing that, a metalled road is followed to Seagate (46.4), just to the west of Holme-next-the-Sea. Here the Peddars Way part of the walk ends and you meet the Norfolk Coast Path. However, to turn *right* along the Coast Path eastwards towards Cromer – the ultimate objective – would mean missing the initial stretch of the Norfolk Coast Path, which has actually started at Hunstanton, two miles to the left. A solution which may appeal to you will be to use a bus or taxi from here to Hunstanton, and then begin the Norfolk Coast Path from there. However, neither form of motorised transport can be guaranteed to be available when required, unless you have been particularly well-organised with planning. The chances are that in the time taken and the money spent in procuring the services of GetUThere Cab Hire, you could have proceeded to Hunstanton under your own steam and enjoyed a relaxing three-course meal on a verandah overlooking the sea, followed by a session at Giovanni's Foot Masseur next door.

Hunstanton is a pleasant seaside town with an essentially Victorian atmosphere and wide sandy beaches, and in the summer it becomes packed with holidaymakers. Centuries of erosion have undermined the cliffs near the town, revealing multicoloured layers of rock in stripes of red and white chalk and a form of brown sandstone known as carr stone. The town is unusual in being the only East Anglian coastal town to face west, looking out to the Wash. The Wash itself is interesting, being the second largest area of intertidal mudflats in Great Britain and home to rich communities of starfish and molluscs as well as a breeding colony of common seals. The area attracts a great number of birds, including brent geese, curlew, dunlin and knot, of which huge numbers congregate in winter. Indeed, much of the Norfolk coast is a birdwatcher's paradise.

The start of the Norfolk Coast Path is indicated by a helpful national trail information board close to some ornamental gardens on the seafront. The journey begins with a pleasant walk along a wide greensward, but after passing the coastguard lookout and St Edmund's Point you have a punishing tramp over the dunes past Old Hunstanton to the vicinity of Seagate. Here you reach the join with the Peddars Way (51.1, assuming you walk into and then back out of Hunstanton; all mileages hereafter are based on this assumption) and the route then continues through the Gore Point nature reserve to the north of Holme, by means of a boardwalk laid across the dunes. Between the dunes are pools, known as slacks, which host many marsh-loving plants, most notably the marsh helleborine. Natterjack toads can be found in the marram tussocks and on the edge of the woodland on the reserve you can observe flycatchers and redstarts, whilst the early summer brings green hairstreak butterflies on the gorse and brambles.

You leave the boardwalk to follow the sea defence bank into Thornham (54.6). Progress may well be slow along this stretch in summer, not because of the difficulty of the terrain, but the constant need to give way to flip-flop-clad parents who, out for their post-Sunday lunch stroll, will feel a twinge of envy and nostalgia if they recall undertaking similar exploits themselves, before their turn came to attempt to coax screaming offspring to walk any more than 200 yd from the family car.

Thornham to Wells-next-the-Sea (16.7 miles) via Brancaster, Burnham Overy Staithe, Holkham

ENJOY: Scolt Head Island, Holkham Nature Reserve, Holkham Hall

Thornham is a fine village with a busy harbour, three pubs, a Georgian hall, a large Iron Age earthwork and a partially thirteenth-century church with a very wide high nave. There is no coastal path available between Thornham and Brancaster, so rather than following the main A149 road through Titchwell the route heads inland, climbing south-eastwards away from Thornham on a metalled road, using farm tracks to progress east and turning left to drop to Brancaster on another metalled road. The sea is clearly visible but it is a shame to miss out on the RSPB reserve at Titchwell, which contains a wide range of species including bearded tits, marsh harriers, godwits and avocets. A detour to the reserve is recommended when the A149 is reached at Brancaster (58.6), a pleasant village with a fourteenth-century church. There is then a straightforward boardwalked route beside Brancaster Marsh to Brancaster Staithe, where refreshments should be available. The route then follows a path parallel with the A149 between the buildings of Brancaster Staithe and the marshes as far as Burnham Deepdale. From there you follow the sea bank, with creeks, marshes and dunes all around. This is superb bird-watching country. To your left is Scolt Head Island, a National Trust-owned nature reserve which is home to thousands of nesting Sandwich terns, as well as gannets, skuas and oystercatchers; it may be possible to join a boat trip to the island from Brancaster Staithe. Even from the Coast Path itself, you should look out for red-throated divers, wigeons, teals, grey plovers, sanderlings and snipes.

The route reaches the A149 again by a windmill, and it is then a short walk north-eastwards alongside the A149 to Burnham Overy Staithe (64.6). This is a large village, popular with holidaymakers, and the closest you get to Burnham Thorpe, where Lord Nelson was born in 1758. Beyond Burnham Overy Staithe the route heads out again to the marshes between the A149 and the sea, initially following a good boardwalk. However, this soon gives out and there follows a weary trudge over the sand dunes across part of the extensive Holkham Nature Reserve, with woodland to the right and Holkham Bay to the left. The Reserve contains salt marshes which include a rich diversity of special plants, including sea lavender, sea pea and sea heath. No doubt to your relief, you leave the dry sands at Holkham Gap and enter the woodland. There is a road hereabouts leading to Holkham village and the eighteenth-century Palladian Holkham Hall, which contains an impressive art collection. You pick up a firmer path on the south side of the woods, and at Abraham's Bosom Lake you join a road which proceeds south in a straight line to reach the seaside town of Wells-next-the-Sea (71.3). Famous for its sprat and whelk trade, Wells is the only port on the north Norfolk coast to have a usable harbour, and from the cheerful quayside you can observe a variety of sea-going vessels.

From Wells the route follows a good path just inland of the Wells and Warham salt marshes; in the winter it is worth looking across the marshes for wintering wild pink-footed and brent geese. Not far off the route near Wells is the village of Stiffkey, with its sixteenth-century flint-built hall, while on nearby Warborough Hill there is an Iron Age barrow. One of the vicars of Stiffkey, Harold Davidson, was known as the 'prostitutes' parson' because of his frequent forays to Soho. The village is also well-known for Stewkey Blues, which are in fact cockles; this may come as something of a disappointment to the overnight visitor who, having seen their availability advertised in the village, might have believed them to be a band providing a night's entertainment at the village pub.

Wells-next-the-Sea to Cley-next-the-Sea (10.4 miles) via Morston, Blakeney

ENJOY: Blakeney, Blakeney Eye, Cley next the Sea

You proceed beside the marshes, passing the village of Morston with a church that boasts a thirteenth-century west tower, and continue on to Blakeney (78.8). This is a beautiful brick and flint village with some fine buildings, including the Georgian Red House on the quay and the old Guildhall, which has a fourteenth-century undercroft. Its waterfront is crowded with yachts and cruisers; now that the estuary has silted up, the village is no longer viable as a commercial port and only small pleasure boats can sail up the channel. It has a fine church with two towers, one of which is over 100 ft high and is a prominent landmark for miles around. Between the village and the sea lies Blakeney Point, another National Trust owned nature reserve and reachable only by boat from Blakeney, but accessible on foot from Cley next the Sea beyond the river Glaven. The Point is a breeding-ground for oystercatchers, terns and gulls, and in the summer you can see flowering sea holly and the yellow-horned poppy. The route continues by the area of marshes and creeks known as Blakeney Eye – with a similar area known as Cley Eye across the Glaven – then follows alongside the Glaven to reach Cley (81.7). The whole walk from Blakeney to Cley is fascinating at any time of year. The winter brings the twite, snow bunting and shore lark, the summer may see ringed plovers and marsh harriers, and in the autumn you may get sightings of rare migrants such as bluethroat, wryneck and warbler.

Cley next the Sea

Cley, like Blakeney, is a most attractive village with flint built houses and an early eighteenth-century windmill. There is a fine church, largely rebuilt in the fourteenth century, containing many interesting nave arch carvings including a musician, a lion chewing on a bone, and St George fighting what Simon Jenkins says looks like a 'domesticated village dragon.' The village, despite being called Cley next the Sea, is locally pronounced 'Cly' and has not really been 'next the sea' since the seventeenth century, when land reclamation left it one mile inland.

Cley next the Sea to Cromer (13.3 miles) via Weybourne, Sheringham

ENJOY: Skelding Hill, Sheringham, Beacon Hill, Cromer

Beyond Cley, an easy walk along the sea bank across the marsh takes you to Cley Eye. The Coast Path turns right at Cley Eye and proceeds along a shingle path. The trudge through the shingle is even harder work than the sand dunes at Holkham. If you have just enjoyed Cley church, you may wryly reflect that St George's resolve and commitment might well have been tested far more had the devil thrown a shingle bank across his path to saintly glory.

At Gramborough Hill, just beyond Salthouse, the going gets marginally better. A brief climb onto the hill gives excellent views back to Cley and Blakeney, and also to the sea, of which there have been precious few uninterrupted views since leaving Hunstanton. Shingle then alternates with welcome sections of springy turf until the Coast Path reaches the car park at Weybourne Hope (86.9). In the Second World War the coastline here saw an extensive military presence because of its easy accessibility for large ships and thereby the possibility of invasion. The nearby village of Weybourne contains the ruins of a thirteenth-century Augustinian priory, of which a remarkably large central tower remains. There follows some cliffwalking, culminating in Skelding Hill, alongside Sheringham golf course. The hill provides the most arduous climb of the walk so far, but you are well rewarded with good views to the sea, the nearby town of Sheringham and perhaps steam locomotives on the preserved Sheringham–Weybourne–Holt railway. Walking the cliffs is a rare treat after the low-level coastal walking that has characterised the Norfolk Coast Path so far, but erosion is a serious problem and diversions round cracks in the cliff are likely. The Coast Path descends to reach the cheerful resort of Sheringham (90). Famous for its seafood, the town is a popular resort with a good sandy beach and promenade, while All Saints church has a west tower built in around 1300.

Beyond Sheringham, you must move inland for the final section to Cromer. Having emerged from the town you take a right turn directly away from the sea, crossing the railway and A149. You then pass the ruins of the thirteenth-century Beeston Priory, bear left and then head right, just east of Beeston Regis, making for an area of woodland. There is then a climb through the woods to Beacon Hill, the highest point in Norfolk – all of 328 ft above sea level! Beacon Hill is the site of a Roman encampment, and indeed reminders of the country's Roman occupation might revive memories of the tramp up the Peddars Way, which may already seem a long way back. After crossing Sandy Lane, which leads down to West Runton and the sea, the route heads north-eastwards and then eastwards towards Cromer, initially through woodland and then into more open country below East Runton. The national trail passes under the Norwich–Cromer railway by means of a fine arched brick bridge, and then continues along a good track to reach the A148. You turn left to reach Cromer and the end of the national trail (95).

Cromer is a lively coastal town with a pier, lifeboat station and good sandy beaches, and is famed for its fishing, especially for crabs. Its narrow streets of old houses twist round the church of St Peter and St Paul which boasts the highest church tower in Norfolk at 160 ft. To reach the pier, which marks the end of the route, you bear left into Beach Road beyond the station and cross Runton Road to reach the sea front, going forward to the pier. It's certainly a more impressive and less remote finish to the national trail than the start at Knettishall. But don't expect the Cromer Town Band to be standing on ceremony to serenade your crossing the finishing line. You'll have to content yourself with a celebratory crab butty.

The Cotswold Way

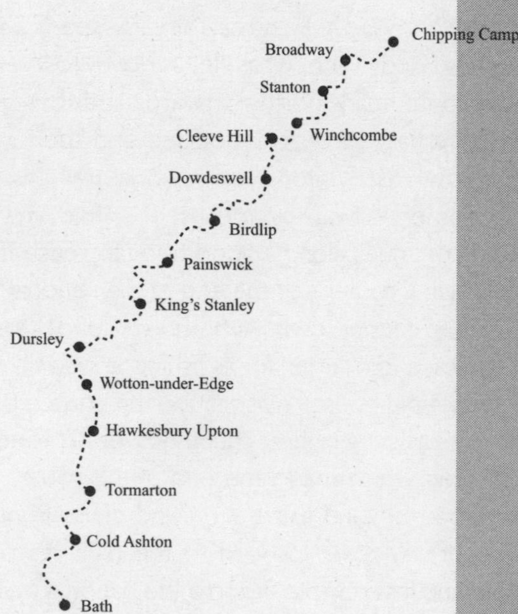

Designation: National trail.
Length: 102 miles.
Start: Bath, Bath and North East Somerset.
Finish: Chipping Campden, Gloucestershire.
Nature: An up and down journey along the Cotswold escarpment with fantastic views, pretty villages and towns, and many historical features of interest.
Difficulty rating: moderate, strenuous in places.
Average time of completion: 7–8 days.

HIGHLIGHTS OF THIS WALK:

- **Bath**
- **Stinchcombe Hill**
- **Cam Peak/Long Down**
- **Painswick**
- **Cleeve Hill**
- **Belas Knap**
- **Stanton**
- **Broadway/ Broadway Tower**
- **Chipping Campden**

The Cotswold Way

Who could resist it? A gentle stroll across countryside that is often stunningly attractive and largely undemanding, beginning in one of the most beautiful cities in England and ending in a town for which the expression 'chocolate box' might have been invented and where the biggest dilemma for the walker at journey's end is the choice of tearoom. The Cotswold Way certainly looks, on paper, to be one of those national trails that are a genuine pleasure to be walked, with no significant logistical challenges to overcome and requiring no superhuman levels of fitness or navigational expertise. The route follows the range of limestone hills known as the Cotswolds running from Bath to Chipping Campden, averaging 600 ft in height and peaking at Cleeve Cloud which stands 1086 ft above sea level, and on its way seeks out some of the area's loveliest viewpoints and settlements. The region is certainly very rich in beautiful towns and villages, products of the golden age between the fourteenth and sixteenth centuries when the woollen industry of Flemish weavers was at its peak.

It is indeed surprising that having been waymarked from end to end as a recognised 'name' path for decades, and enjoyed huge popularity throughout that time, it only acquired national trail status in 2007. Yet for all its good points, some walkers may be disappointed that the route never seems to enter the heart of this lovely region of England, shunning such Cotswold gems as Bibury, Stow, Northleach, the Slaughters, Bourton-on-the-Water or Cirencester. Moreover, the walking can be fiddly, with few sections where the walker can really get into his/her stride and enjoy lengths of uninterrupted ridge-top marching which is a characteristic of long stretches of the Ridgeway Path or the South Downs Way. And there are disadvantages of having such a great city as Bath to start from: with sufficient interesting buildings, shops, restaurants and cafes to keep any visitor happy for a fortnight, one wonders who in their right mind would want to shoulder a hefty pack and start trudging away from it.

You would certainly have to be in a great rush to give the splendours of Bath a miss before starting out. The city's history began in 44 AD when it became an important Roman settlement known as Aquae Sulis or 'the waters of Sul', a Celtic goddess. The warm mineral springs for which the city has been famous since those times originate in the eastern Mendips, collecting mineral salts on the way and reaching the surface again in the city. The city prospered throughout the Middle Ages, then early in the eighteenth century Dr William Oliver built a bath here for the treatment of gout; his name has become immortalised with the creation of the Bath Oliver biscuit! The development of Bath as a showpiece of Georgian architecture was largely attributable to John Wood who settled here in 1727, while the establishment of the city as a centre for high society owed much to the dandy Beau Nash, who brought the elite of London to the baths as well as the balls and assemblies that made the city a byword for fashion and elegance and helped inspire the work of many novelists including Tobias Smollett and Jane Austen. In the centre of the city stand the Roman baths, which count among the best-preserved Roman remains anywhere in Britain, while nearby are the seventeenth-century abbey and eighteenth-century Pump Room. The whole city is packed with excellent Georgian buildings, among the most noteworthy of which are those forming the Circus, designed by John Wood, and Royal Crescent, designed by his son; the Crescent, together with the Circus and its link road, form a giant question mark. The river Avon flows through the city and over the river is built the magnificent Pulteney Bridge, designed by Robert Adam in 1771, with a row of shops built immediately above the bridge. Today thousands of visitors come to enjoy the city and sample the spring waters, which in terms of their therapeutic quality more than make up for their taste.

Bath to Tormarton (16 miles) via Weston and Cold Ashton

ENJOY: Bath, Little Down Hill Fort, Granville Monument, Dyrham Park

You begin your pilgrimage from Bath by way of the Circus, Royal Crescent and Royal Victoria Park, then head north-westwards quite steeply uphill beside a municipal golf course. Bearing left into Sion Hill and continuing via Summerhill Road, you then find yourself losing much of the precious height already gained, using footpaths to descend south-westwards to the pretty village of Weston; although it looks like a suburb of Bath, it has a distinctive character and identity and a very attractive church. Leaving Weston by heading south-westwards uphill along Anchor Road, you bear right, climbing up a steep grass slope to the triangulation point at Penn Hill, then continue north-westwards to join a clear bridleway that takes you to another triangulation point at Kelston Round Hill, nearly 700 ft above sea level. Now swinging just east of north, you proceed via a plantation to the superb viewpoint at Prospect Stile, then, keeping Bath Racecourse to your right, you swing north-westwards, following the escarpment edge to reach Little Down Hill Fort, an Iron Age site with single ditch and low earth ramparts. The Way initially skirts the south-eastern edge of the fort then turns due west through the middle of it – this is as far west as the Cotswold Way will go – before swinging north-east, descending and joining a track.

Following beside Lansdown golf course and keeping an area of woodland to your left, you head eastwards then swing north-westwards, going forward to yet another triangulation point at Hanging Hill. Now veering east, you continue along the hilltop to the Grenville Monument, which commemorates a bloody battle in the English Civil War in July 1643 as a result of which Sir Bevil Grenville, commander of the Royalist troops, was killed. From the monument, you head briefly southwards then more resolutely north-eastwards across a very picturesque pastoral landscape, passing just to the east of the hamlet of Lower Hamswell and skirting the left side of a pond; continuing north-eastwards past Hill Farm, you join Greenway Lane and follow it uphill to the busy A46, which you cross. Immediately to the other side of the A46 crossing is the pretty hilltop village of Cold Ashton, which boasts a fine gabled sixteenth-century manor and superb views to the surrounding countryside. It was inside the manor that Sir Bevil Grenville, having been taken there after the battle commemorated by the Grenville monument, lost his life.

The Way swings north in the village, passing the small village church and arriving at the busy A420 and a welcome pub. You cross the A420 then head north-westwards, almost immediately crossing back over the A46 at the hamlet of Pennsylvania where, if the pub by the A420 didn't satisfy you, you will find another! You head north-westwards, crossing a minor road and entering Dyrham Wood, descending to a stream and now heading just east of north; emerging from the wood you now proceed through more open countryside to reach the pretty village of Dyrham with its mellow stone cottages. You pass through the eastern edge of the village, keeping to your right the village church and Dyrham Park, a baroque-style house built between 1691 and 1702 by William Blaythwayt, who served both James II and William III as Secretary of State for War. Surrounded by an ancient deer park, it is one of the National Trust's finest properties, and deserves a visit just for its tapestries, gardens and orangery, where mimosa and grapefruit as well as oranges are grown; film buffs may recognise it as the setting for Darlington Hall in the 1993 motion picture *The Remains of the Day*. You turn in a more easterly direction to follow the park's boundary wall, then go sharply left (northwards) initially along a road to a T-junction, just west of which is Hinton Hill Fort, site of a battle in 577 AD between the Saxons and ancient Britons.

You continue northwards along a footpath from the T-junction, swinging eastwards to pass a triangulation point and arrive back at the A46 again; already you and this busy trunk road are becoming good friends and you're likely to see it again before the day is out! Continue beyond the A46 in a direction just south of east, then veer north-east to Lower Lapdown Farm beyond which you walk eastwards parallel with the M4, soon turning left to cross the motorway. Having crossed the motorway, you almost immediately reach Tormarton (16), which brings the possibility of refreshments. The sight of cars thundering far beneath you may cause you to reflect soberly on the hectic and petrol-driven rat race to which so many in our society have succumbed, and cause you to long for a greater spirit of ecofriendliness amongst your fellow human beings. Or it may make you wish you were sitting in the luxurious comfort of one of them, speeding in leather-upholstered seats towards a four-course meal in town instead of forcing your thirty pound pack and blister-encrusted feet onwards at a steady half a mile per hour with your only remaining rations consisting of a half-eaten pack of swiss roll.

Tormarton to Wotton-under-Edge (16 miles) via Old Sodbury and Hawkesbury Upton

ENJOY: Dodington House, Sodbury Hill Fort, Horton Court, Wotton-under Edge

Tormarton is a pretty village with a fine Norman church, the exterior of which is decorated with gargoyles, and which the Way makes effectively a detour to visit. You leave the village in a north-westerly direction, using footpaths to arrive at – you've guessed it – the A46 yet again; once more you call to mind the ancient wisdom of the Green Cross Code and lunge across it, then, continuing north-westwards, pass through a narrow strip of woodland to enter the attractive meadow scenery of Dodington Park. Away to the left is the square-shaped Dodington House, a Palladian building that was designed and commenced around 1795 by James Wyatt and completed in 1813, and with grounds that were laid out by Capability Brown in 1764. You cross the drive leading to the house and proceed to a road at the hamlet Coomb's End, bearing right along the road then left, north-westwards, along a path and then a road into Old Sodbury, the logical first overnight stop for strong walkers doing the Way in one go.

The Way continues north from Old Sodbury to Little Sodbury via Sodbury Hill Fort, which is Iron Age in origin but was utilised subsequently by both the Romans and the Saxons. Having rejoined a road, you pass through Little Sodbury, noteworthy for its fifteenth-century manor house once lived in by the Christian martyr William Tyndale, who attained fame by translating the Bible into English. The village church has an unusual dedication to St Adeline. Beyond the village you proceed north-eastwards across fields, crossing a road just east of the village of Horton, then continue via an Iron Age fort commanding lovely views to Horton Court, which is owned by the National Trust. Some parts of this building date back to 1180, making it one of the country's oldest inhabited buildings. Now you head north-east towards Hawkesbury Upton, initially along a field path parallel with Highfield Lane and then up Bath Lane; you share your route briefly here with that of the Monarch's Way which links Worcester with Shoreham-by-Sea in West Sussex, based on the route taken by Charles II after his defeat at Worcester in 1651. In due course you reach the north-west fringe of Hawkesbury Upton which, one has to say, sounds more inviting than it is, as it has little of real historical interest. From Hawkesbury Upton you follow the road north-westwards, soon passing the 120 ft-high Somerset Monument which commemorates General Lord Somerset, who served at the battle of Waterloo. You then swing north-eastwards, leaving the road to enjoy some woodland walking and a descent to the Kilcott valley.

On reaching Lower Kilcott you turn north-westwards again, following a lane towards the village of Hillesley and passing the pretty Kilcott Mill; forsaking the lane, you continue north-westwards through fields to reach the village of Alderley, hitting the village street, such as it is, by the village church. If you were pushed for time you could simply follow the road all the way to Wotton-under-Edge (32), the next major staging post of your walk, but the Way itself strikes out north-eastwards, passes over the stream coming from the intriguingly named Ozleworth Bottom, and then continues north-westwards over fields to the village of Wortley where a number of cloth mills were once situated. There's another opportunity for you here to stroll to Wotton-under-Edge by road, but the Way has other ideas, taking you north-eastwards uphill through woodland to the top of the escarpment, and going forward to join a track. Enjoy the lovely views while you can, for you then turn sharply north-west and drop down very steeply, skirting the hamlet of Coombe and finally veering just south of west to arrive in Wotton-under-Edge.

Wotton-under-Edge is an old market town with some fine old buildings including a fourteenth-century school, seventeenth-century almshouses and a church which dates back to the fourteenth or fifteenth century; the church has some excellent brasses and an eighteenth-century organ which was built for St Martin in the Fields and played by the composer Handel when George I attended services there. In Orchard Street is a house where Isaac Pitman devised his famous system of shorthand in the nineteenth century, providing the basis for a splendid question in a How Well Do You Know Britain trivia quiz, as budding Magnús Magnússons or Chris Tarrants enquire of their victim what boon to overworked secretaries originated in Wotton-under-Edge. With no points whatever for anybody believing it to be a cure for Ozleworth Bottom.

Wotton-under-Edge to King's Stanley (14 miles) via Dursley

ENJOY: Wotton Hill, Tyndale Monument, Stinchcombe Hill, Cam Long Down, Hetty Pegler's Tump

This section is crammed with scenic highlights. Indeed, within a few minutes of wiping from your lips the last traces of marmalade from your full English breakfast, which you will certainly need today, you are climbing steeply north-westwards onto Wotton Hill, providing the first of many panoramas of this section. On the hill is the Jubilee Plantation, containing trees planted in honour of Queen Victoria's Golden Jubilee and the accession of Queen Elizabeth II. Continuing north-westwards you pass through a beautiful area of woodland, going beside an Iron Age hill fort called the Brackenbury Ditches, then, emerging from the woods, you proceed across open country to the magnificent viewpoint of Nibley Knoll, dominated by the Tyndale Monument. The monument, standing over 100 ft high, was erected in 1866 in honour of William Tyndale (see Little Sodbury above), and provides a fantastic landmark enabling you to monitor your progress and confirm bearings for many miles beyond.

There follows a short, sharp descent to North Nibley, the site of the last battle in England between private armies (the earls of Warwick and of Berkeley) in 1470; it boasts a house, Nibley House, originating in the seventeenth century, and a fifteenth-century church. You cross the B4060, continuing north-westwards along a road leading towards the church, then soon bear right and now head just east of north through trees to find yourself back at the B4060 again. You continue just north of east, with Stancombe Park to your left, and Dursley, the next settlement of any size, a short way to your right; it is easy enough to short-cut to it if you're pushed for time or if the weather is bad, but in fact the Way swings dramatically westwards and climbs onto Stinchcombe Hill, a fantastic viewpoint from which it may be possible to view the Malverns and the Brecon Beacons. The Way goes round the complete plateau of Stinchcombe Hill, past Drakestone Point (with a topograph which may assist you to locate places of interest) and beside the golf course, which must be one of the prettiest places to play golf in the west of England.

Now turning eastwards, the Way passes the clubhouse and descends through woodland to Dursley (39) where there is ample opportunity for refreshment and accommodation; Dursley, literally

'Deorsige's clearing', was a centre of woollen cloth manufacture from the fifteenth century, and boasts an early eighteenth-century Market House with bell turret and niche containing a statue of Queen Anne. J. K. Rowling chose it as the surname of Harry Potter's mean-spirited aunt and uncle Petunia and Vernon, but one hopes this is no reflection on the authors' opinion of the town!

You leave Dursley and head north-eastwards across meadows, ascending steeply to Cam Peak and Cam Long Down; there are superb views from these hills, with Dursley in the foreground and, further afield, the river Severn and the Forest of Dean. Moving off Cam Long Down, which in shape is not dissimilar to a loaf of bread, you now proceed just south of east, dropping down but then rising beyond Hodgecombe Farm to the edge of Uleybury Hill Fort, which dates back to the Iron Age. It boasts impressive earth ramparts and ditch and made most advantageous use of the escarpment for defensive purposes. The B4066 road is straight ahead of you here, but the Way swings left and now returns to a north-easterly progression, following an undulating course and returning to the B4066 at the quaintly-named Hetty Pegler's Tump. Named after a seventeenth century owner of the land, this mound is a Neolithic long barrow, 140 ft in length and 90 ft wide. Now proceeding roughly parallel with the B4066, you continue through the trees onto Frocester Hill, yet another splendid viewpoint, where you can look back with satisfaction on the Tyndale Monument visited some hours back; from there you carry on along the escarpment to Nympsfield Long Barrow, another Neolithic construction which dates back to 2800 BC and which was used for burials.

From the long barrow you proceed into Stanley Wood and on into the woodlands below Pen Hill, swinging northwards and descending to enter the village of Middleyard, beyond which you head north-westwards across the meadows to the neighbouring village of King's Stanley (46), skirting the eastern edge of the village and passing Stanley Mill, a five-storey building constructed in 1811 but now disused. Proceeding northwards, follow the road to cross, in quick succession, the A419, the Stroudwater Canal which dates back to 1779 and the Stroud–Gloucester railway. An alternative route skirts the north-eastern fringes of the woodland of Pen Hill, emerging onto Selsley Common and proceeding north-eastwards across the common to reach a road, passing All Saints Church with windows by Rossetti and Morris. You go forward to Selsley then strike out north-westwards, downhill and across the A419, swinging westwards to follow beside the canal and go forward to meet the main route at Ryeford. This is as close as you'll get to the bustling town of Stroud and its accommodation opportunities. Beware, though, of booking accommodation without checking just how far off the route it is: what seems like a simple fingernail's width on the map in the comfort of your home may turn out to be a soul-destroying trudge after a sweaty day's walking, especially when the last bus of the day to your chosen night spot was seen disappearing over the horizon 20 seconds before you reached the bus stop.

King's Stanley to Birdlip (16 miles) via Painswick

ENJOY: Haresfield Beacon, Painswick, Painswick Beacon, Cooper's Hill, Witcombe

Heading generally north-eastwards, you have some rather fiddly field walking as far as the hamlet of Westrip, after which a walk through the delightfully-named Three Bears Wood takes you onto Maiden Hill and round the edge of the village of Randwick into the beautiful Standish Wood. Now veering north-westwards and then slightly south-westwards, you reach a magnificent viewpoint with topograph; having enjoyed fine views of the Vale of Gloucester, you continue north-westwards, losing a little height but quickly regaining it and going forward to Ring Hill and Haresfield Beacon, where another great panorama awaits. Ring Hill once housed an Iron Age hill fort which was later populated by the Romans, while Haresfield

Beacon is one of the highlights of the whole walk with views to the Severn and Forest of Dean, as well as to the city of Gloucester and your new-formed acquaintances Cam Long Down and Tyndale Monument. You now head in a more easterly direction, following along a wooded hillside and going first just north of east then just south of east to Scottsquar Hill; you cross the A4173 road just south of the village of Edge then follow the meadows north-eastwards to arrive at Painswick (55).

Painswick

Arguably the most famous aspect of Painswick is the parish churchyard, in which there are over 100 clipped yews of all shapes and sizes, some of which date back to the early nineteenth century; traditionally there were only 99 trees, and it used to be said that every time the hundredth was planted, it was removed by the devil. The church has a particularly fine peal of bells, housed in a tower that is topped by a spire that rises to 172 ft, while the assembly of table and pedestal stone tombs in the churchyard, dating back to the eighteenth century, is unique in Britain, with brass plates on the sides of some elegantly engraved with the names of their occupants. The heyday of Painswick was between the fourteenth and eighteenth centuries, when the town grew rich from the Cotswold wool trade and was a centre of cloth making, and houses were built from creamy-white stone quarried from Painswick Hill, with several of the more interesting houses in Bisley Street and the sloping Vicarage Street. The handsome Palladian mansion of Painswick House stands half a mile outside the village and contains a good collection of furniture and fine Chinese wallpaper. In St Mary's Street there is a set of stocks which were installed in the nineteenth century 'for the punishment of those who carry on carousels to the annoyance of neighbours.' Rather more effective as a deterrent than ASBOs, one is tempted to think.

You leave Painswick by heading north, along the B4073, bearing right off the road to pass the little church of Paradise and a golf course, keeping your old friend the A46 not too far away to your right. Your route skirts the summit of Painswick Hill, also known as Painswick Beacon, but it's certainly worth the short detour to visit the triangulation point with its splendid view; it's the site of another Iron Age hill fort and was populated by Royalist forces in the English Civil War. Beyond the hill and the golf course, woodland walking will dominate all the way to Birdlip, and indeed from the golf course you make your way north-eastwards through Pope's Wood, across the A46, then initially along a road and subsequently a path through beech woods. A break in the woodland comes at Cooper's Hill where there was once an Iron Age encampment, and you should certainly pause here to take in the views, which may extend to the Malvern Hills on a good day. At Cooper's Hill there is on each Spring Bank Holiday a cheese-rolling ceremony, where contestants plunge from the maypole at the top down the slope in pursuit of a mock cheese, and the winner receives a real 7lb Double Gloucester cheese as the prize.

Proceeding in a generally easterly direction, you pass two features of interest in close succession, namely the Haven Tea Garden and, a little off route, the ruins of Witcombe Roman Villa which dates from the first century AD and is owned by English Heritage. Continue on through Witcombe Wood, now swinging north-eastwards and emerging at a road about a quarter of a mile to the north-west of the village of Birdlip (62), whose unusual name is believed to mean 'steep place frequented by birds'. So many Cotswold villages and towns have intriguing names, any one of which might set the scene for either a historical or contemporary mystery. Indeed, so entranced may you be by the history and charm of the Cotswold Way or any other national trail that you might consider writing your own novel; it will then of course depend on both your tenacity to determine how quickly after your return your notebook or laptop is discarded and you find yourself resorting once more to the Easy section of the Sun Jumbo Sudoku Collection.

Birdlip to Cleeve Hill (15.5 miles) via Seven Springs and Dowdeswell

ENJOY: Crickley Hill, Devil's Chimney, Cleeve Common

From the Birdlip road you proceed along a woodland track to Birdlip Hill, continue north-eastwards along the scarp edge, then, having enjoyed the lovely views from here, go forward to the very busy A417 at the Air Balloon pub. Having crossed the road you veer westwards and sharply north-eastwards to reach the viewpoint and country park at Crickley Hill, a settlement dating back to Neolithic times, between 4000 and 3000 BC. Continue north-eastwards along the scarp edge to Shurdington Hill, here bearing right onto Greenway Lane, which takes you south-eastwards to the B4070; cross this road and continue along a minor road past Ullenwood Manor, then swing left north-eastwards along the edge of a golf course, going uphill. You lose a little height as you swing westwards, then bear right to mount the escarpment, going forward to Leckhampton Hill and the Devil's Chimney, a limestone rock which rises 50 ft from Leckhampton Hill. The slim rock was left after centuries of quarrying had gone on around it. The path now heads south-eastwards along the escarpment edge, providing superb views.

Swinging southwards, you cross the A435 at Seven Springs, originally believed, erroneously, to be the source of the Thames (the Thames Path begins from a place named Thames Head, several miles to the south of Seven Springs) then head north-eastwards, passing Wistley Grove and enjoying lovely views from Wistley Hill. You enter Lineover Wood, veering north-westwards and descending along the eastern side of the wood to the crossing of the A40 close to Dowdeswell Reservoir, just three miles or so east of Cheltenham; if you wish to break off to visit this bustling spa town, this is the obvious place to do so. The Way, however, heads just east of north and begins a six-mile journey through countryside devoid of towns and villages to the next big objective, Cleeve Hill. There is quite a stiff ascent from the A40 crossing but the gradient eases and the Way, using a mixture of paths and lanes through generally open country, rises to around 1000 ft, swinging in a more north-westerly direction to arrive at Cleeve Common and the summit triangulation point.

Cleeve Common

The Common is the highest ground visited by the Cotswold Way, at just under 1100 ft, and is designated a Site of Special Scientific Interest with its variety of butterflies and orchids; from the triangulation point and topograph there are magnificent views on a clear day.

After so many miles without amenities it's good to have the village of Cleeve Hill just below the viewpoint to your left, and you may wish to stay at the excellent Cleeve Hill youth hostel just a short way off route. My memories of Cleeve Hill (77.5) will forever be coloured by the recollection of kindly being given a lift back to this spot by the owner of the B & B where I had stayed, half an hour's walk away. It was only as he set off again that I realised I was without my essential guidebook containing all the route maps for the day.

Cleeve Hill to Stanton (14.5 miles) via Winchcombe and Stanway

ENJOY: Belas Knap, Winchcombe, Sudeley Castle, Hailes Abbey, Stanway, Stanton

The town of Winchcombe is your next significant objective, but while it's a deceptively short distance by road, the Way follows a much more circuitous route to get there; beyond the triangulation point it veers north-east then south-east, seemingly away from Winchcombe, heading to the left of a second triangulation point and a group of transmitter towers which may be useful landmarks in misty weather.

You now turn eastwards along a clear track, taking you to Wontley Farm, then swing north-eastwards, going forward to Belas Knap.

Belas Knap

Belas Knap is a Neolithic barrow, the building of the original shrine probably dating back to around 2500 BC, and it is said to be the best preserved ancient burial chamber in England, being used for burials for over seven centuries; it is 78 ft long, 60 ft wide and, at its highest point, 13 ft high, and an excavation in 1863 uncovered 26 burials as well as Roman coins and pottery.

Now you begin to lose height, heading north-eastwards to a lane, before turning briefly southwards to the top end of the delightfully named Humblebee Woods, then proceeding northwards past Wadfield where there was once a Roman villa and there is now a fine eighteenth-century farm. Straightforward field walking now follows, and you proceed confidently on into Winchcombe (84). During the Anglo Saxon period, Winchcombe was an important Mercian regional centre, and it later drew prosperity from the wool trade; the church of St Peter, dating back to the mid fifteenth century, boasts an impressive array of gargoyles on its exterior. The biggest tourist attraction in Winchcombe is Sudeley Castle, the last resting place of Katharine Parr, the sixth wife of Henry VIII. Although it looks splendidly ancient, the castle is in fact a reconstruction, having been demolished by Parliamentarian forces, and is said to be the model for Blandings Castle in the novels of P. G. Wodehouse. From Winchcombe the Way heads pleasantly north-eastwards across fields to Hailes, a hamlet that is best known for its abbey, now in ruins but at one time a wealthy Cistercian foundation; it was the destination of medieval pilgrims, having been presented in 1230 with what was believed to be a phial of the Holy Blood, though this was subsequently denounced as 'but honey clarified and coloured with saffron'.

Beyond the abbey ruins, the Way swings south-eastwards and climbs steeply round the south side of Hailes Wood, then veers north-east to the Iron Age hill fort at Beckbury Camp. Beyond the camp, enjoying excellent views, it goes forward to a track, in due course arriving at the B4077 at Stumps Cross where it turns north-westwards and now descends through the meadows to the hamlet of Wood Stanway and then the small but beautiful village of Stanway. The village boasts a Jacobean manor named Stanway House, guarded by a superb Jacobean gatehouse, and there is also a twelfth-century church, a huge tithe barn and a thirteenth-century watermill. Beyond the village you bear north-eastwards, initially through parkland and then fields, gaining height and soon arriving at the extremely attractive village of Stanton (92). You proceed up Stanton's long main street, on either side of which the houses, built in around 1600, are of golden stone with steeply pitched gables; the estate was owned by the architect Sir Philip Stott between 1906 and 1937 and it was as a result of his efforts that the appearance of the houses, as well as the medieval village cross, is much the same today as when they were built. Sir Philip's former home, Stanton Court, is a fine Jacobean house with superb grounds which are sometimes open to the public, and the original manor house, Warren Farm House, dates back to the sixteenth century. The church of St Michael and all Angels is Norman in origin; some medieval pews survive and deep grooves in their ends are said to have been made by the leashes of dogs brought inside by shepherds. Nowadays the village is one of the most unspoilt and stunningly attractive in the country, not just the Cotswolds, whether seen in the height of summer or the depths of winter, and indeed with snow on the cottage roofs and atop the surrounding hills, it looks like the perfect setting for archetypal English scenes in a major feature film. But don't expect to be joined by Hugh Grant or Renée Zellweger as you sit on the wooden bench outside the village shop licking your newly purchased Fab ice lolly.

Stanton to Chipping Campden (10 miles) via Broadway

ENJOY: Broadway, Broadway Tower, Dover's Hill, Chipping Campden

While on some long-distance paths the final miles can be a tiring anticlimax, this is certainly not the case with the last section of the Cotswold Way. Your route proceeds up Stanton's village street and south-eastwards up onto Shenberrow Hill; here you swing northwards along an escarpment track, with good views opening out to your left, but lose height as you follow the track eastwards to the western edge of Buckland Wood, then turn northwards and go forward to the pretty woodland of Broadway Coppice. Having descended through the woods, you emerge to see the village of Broadway directly ahead of you, and continue just north of east through the fields to arrive in the village. Broadway has been described as the 'show village of England' and boasts a long, broad main street lined with honey-coloured Cotswold stone cottages, with bay windows and the occasional thatch and half-timbering. In the centre of the village is the Lygon Arms Hotel, which dates back to the sixteenth century, and both Charles I and Oliver Cromwell stayed there at different times. Nowadays the village appears to be the sort of place for which the word 'honeypot' was invented, with shops catering for all tourist tastes and offering wares that are certainly not restricted to souvenirs of Broadway itself; indeed it will only be when the walker feels how much heavier his rucksack is at the start of the final part of the walk that he will realise the extent of his spending in the village, ranging from books of maddening lateral thinking puzzles conceived in Japan to rock-hard blocks of tooth-rotting toffee manufactured in Dundee.

Although your final objective, Chipping Campden, is just a few miles to the north-east, your route heads south-eastwards from Broadway, and you will see why as, after a steep climb, you reach another amazing viewpoint at Broadway Tower. The tower was built in 1800 by the Earl of Coventry as a folly with no purpose other than that it could be seen from his family seat at Worcester which was about 20 miles away. The top of the tower, at 1089 ft, just beats for height the highest ground in the Cotswolds on Cleeve Hill. Beyond the tower you do proceed north-eastwards, enjoying extensive views as you walk, before entering woodland and arriving at the A44 crossing at Fish Hill; beyond the A44, continuing north-eastwards, you cross a field and join the Mile Drive, a fine avenue providing lovely easy walking and good views to your final destination. From the Mile Drive it is a short walk on to the last great viewpoint of your journey, Dover's Hill, which provides an enticing prospect of the Vale of Evesham, and which was named after Robert Dover, who lived from 1582 to 1652. Described as a 'genial extrovert who loved pageantry', he was responsible for the founding of the Cotswold Olympics, and this hill was the venue for these games which were first held in 1612; sports employed over the years have included horse racing, coursing, jumping, wrestling, tug o' war, sword play and shin kicking!

From Dover's Hill the route veers sharply south-eastwards and drops down to Chipping Campden (102), the end of the Cotswold Way and a really lovely town with which to end your walk. Among its outstanding buildings are the open-sided Jacobean market hall, with timbered roof, dating back to 1627, the fourteenth-century Woolstaplers Hall, Grevel House which dates back to 1380, a mainly fifteenth-century church with a fourteenth-century chancel and a 120 ft-high tower, and the Hicks almshouses named after Sir Baptist Hicks who built the houses for the local poor. In addition, there is a rich array of what were merchant's houses, reflecting the fact that the town was once the centre of the Cotswold wool trade, and indeed a good dozen of Chipping Campden's wool merchants became Lord Mayor of London. The town was the setting for scenes in Pasolini's adult film version of *The Canterbury Tales* which was released in 1971.

Apart from a rather splendid badge available for successful conquerors of the Cotswold Way, there are no rewards for successful completion, just lots of happy memories. If it's a tangible reward for toil, sweat and back-breaking endeavour that you're after… well, perhaps you should have stuck to cheese-rolling down Cooper's Hill.

The South West Coast Path

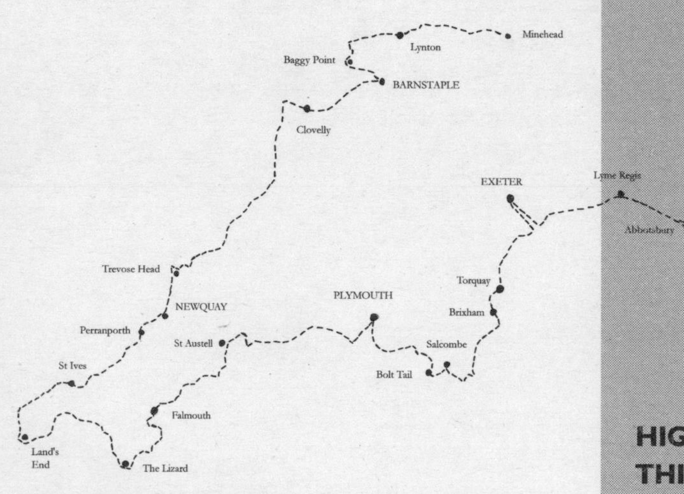

Designation: National trail.
Length: 628.5 miles.
Start: Minehead, Somerset.
Finish: South Haven Point, near Poole, Dorset.
Nature: A walk round the often rugged and spectacular coastline of the south-western counties of England, covering the entire coastlines of Devon and Cornwall, and sections of the coastline of Somerset and Dorset.
Difficulty rating: Strenuous, severe in places.
Average time of completion: 6–7 weeks in aggregate.

HIGHLIGHTS OF THIS WALK (There are hundreds on the Coast Path but to my mind these stand out as being of special interest):

- **Valley of Rocks**
- **Hartland Point**
- **High Cliff**
- **Tintagel**
- **Cape Cornwall**
- **Lizard**
- **Polperro**
- **Bolt Head**
- **Lyme Regis**
- **Durdle Door**

NB: All mileages assume the most direct routes are taken. Separate mileages are given for alternatives to seasonal ferries. No alternative routes, or mileages for these alternatives, are given in respect of ferries used by the Coast Path that run all year.

The statistics speak for themselves. This enormous coastal trek is a truly awesome logistical challenge for any walker, however fit or experienced. Yet foot-travellers whose ambition it is to complete all the big walks in Great Britain will at some stage have to rise to it.

The glorious coastal scenery of Somerset, Devon, Cornwall and Dorset, with high cliffs, quaint villages, cosy harbours, sandy coves and dramatic peninsulas, acquired popularity with holidaymakers and walkers long before any suggestion was raised of a continuous coast path. The idea of joining up the numerous existing rights of way along these coasts to create an unbroken route came from a wartime committee of the Ramblers' Association. It was given official blessing in the National Parks and Access to the Countryside Act of 1949, and thereafter each of the four county councils involved set about designating and waymarking the route. Progress was slow, and although most of the necessary work had been done by the end of the 1970s, there were still some sections that required negotiation at that time. Even at the time of writing, although a continuous route is available to walkers, not all the work has been done to provide a true coastal route throughout, and in one or two places it is necessary to detour to existing rights of way inland to maintain the continuity. The fact is, however, that no two walkers will follow exactly the same route for a number of reasons. There are some 'cul-de-sacs' to headlands that involve detours, and which may be omitted if time is pressing; for example, the Lulworth–Kimmeridge section of the Dorset coast is only open at certain times and an official inland alternative is prescribed. Some river and estuary crossings may be undertaken by ferry, and whilst many of the ferry trips are actually incorporated into the official route, even some of these do not operate out of season, and lengthy foot detours may therefore be necessary (suggested alternatives to seasonal ferries are shown in italics, but you may prefer to use taxis if short of time – I assure you it is not cheating!).

Unless you are incredibly fit and in the fortunate position of having sufficient time and resources available, it is unlikely that you will even contemplate trying to complete the South West Coast Path in one go. It is very easy to break it down into sections, and because communications with the rest of Great Britain are so good, you will have little difficulty in breaking off and starting afresh at a later time. The added advantage of a number of separate expeditions is that you can see the effects of each season on the coastal scenery. Summer is on the face of it the best time to be on the Coast Path, with seasonal ferries running, accommodation and refreshment easily available almost everywhere, and the best chance of settled sunny weather. However, springtime offers a dazzling array of colourful plant life, autumn can bring wonderfully crisp clear days with incredibly wide-ranging views, and those brave enough to walk sections of the route in winter can gaze with awe as the seas, driven by south-westerly gales, crash majestically against the rocks and cliff-faces.

Your walk needs to be planned with care, especially if you wish to walk the Lulworth–Kimmeridge coastal section and use the seasonal ferries, but having made the necessary enquiries and arrangements, you will find many of the hazards that are present on some of the other long-distance routes to be absent on the South West Coast Path. Most of the larger villages and towns on the route are well served by public transport, thus allowing considerable flexibility in planning your itinerary. Amenities are extremely plentiful, even out of season, although it is wise to enquire about accommodation in advance during the winter months. You will have little difficulty with route-finding, although you need to be careful to take the correct turning out of the towns and villages along the way. The simple advice, if you are walking from Minehead, is to keep the sea on your right! Furthermore, the ground underfoot is usually very pleasant to walk on, especially on the clifftops. Assuming you do decide to break up the South West Coast Path into sections, the hardest aspect will be the amount of up-and-down work. Do not think it is simply a case of ascending serenely on to the clifftop in the morning and gently descending in the evening. There are numerous breaks in the cliffs, with coves, combes, valleys, harbours and inlets, necessitating drops and climbs.

The whole route abounds with magnificent plant life and wildlife. The first part of the path, along the Somerset coast, traverses the fringes of Exmoor, famous for its ponies and also red deer which can often be seen in winter, especially in the oak woodland areas through which you will pass. The coastal heath round North Hill attracts stonechats and Dartford warblers, whilst further on you may see peregrines, ravens, shelducks, herons, egrets, redshanks and golden plovers. The Braunton Burrows in Devon host rare plants such as sand toadflax and water germander, while the sea around Lundy Island, clearly visible from the north Devon coast, has been designated a marine nature reserve and the island itself is host to some 40 species of bird. Many clifftops of Cornwall are decorated with tiny flowers such as spring and autumn squill, kidney vetch, thrift and bladder campion, while above you hover fulmars, kittiwakes, and lesser black-backed and herring gulls. Look out too for puffin, guillemots and razorbills on some of the small offshore islands. Off the Land's End peninsula, where gulls and auks breed along the cliffs, you may see grey seals and possibly even orcas and dolphins, whilst on the Lizard peninsula there is a remarkable variety of plant species rarely found elsewhere, including long-headed clover, pigmy rush and hairy greenweed. On many parts of the Dorset and south Devon coast, especially the Exe estuary, you may see winter flocks of avocet, shoveler, wigeon, teal, brent geese, grey plover and ringed plover, whilst the spectacular cliffs around Lulworth Cove in Dorset support a wonderful range of butterflies and orchids. Even very near the end of the route, on the cliffs round Durslton Head, you will see shags, guillemots, kittiwakes or fulmars. Birdwatchers will of course wish to train their binoculars in the hope of sighting rare and exotic feathered visitors, but others, having studied the map and seen there are six more vertical ascents to do before lunch, may well be forgiven for being more anxious to move onwards, even at the risk of not knowing their hoopoe from their shag.

Minehead to Lynton (21.7 miles) via Porlock

ENJOY: Selworthy Beacon, Culbone, Sisters' Fountain, Foreland Point

This is a long opening section, but it can be broken at Porlock. Minehead is a pleasant and popular seaside resort; Quay Town, the oldest part of Minehead, has a harbour dating back to 1616. You start your adventure by climbing steeply north-westwards out of the town on to North Hill, an area dotted with prehistoric mounds, using one of two alternative routes, the stiffer one proceeding via the ruins of Burgundy Chapel. Although there is a clifftop alternative, the official route from North Hill follows a path some way back from the cliff edge across an area of heathland, passing just to the north of the 1,013 ft Selworthy Beacon. A detour is possible to the left here to visit the Beacon and also the beautiful thatched village of Selworthy. You continue to Bossington Hill, passing Hurlstone Point and dropping down to the lovely Hurlstone Combe, proceeding through the combe to the pretty village of Bossington, which lies slightly inland. You then strike out towards Porlock Bay, and it is a straightforward walk beside the bay to reach the hamlet of Porlock Weir (9). As you proceed beside the bay, you pass just to the north of Porlock, with its small whitewashed houses and ample amenities. Beyond Porlock Weir you enter an extensive area of woodland, soon reaching the Norman Culbone Church, which is just 12 ft wide and is claimed to be the smallest medieval church in England.

A colony of lepers lived hereabouts in the Middle Ages and would follow services through a window. Beyond Culbone the walk is easy and quick, continuing through the woods and dropping to Yenworthy Combe, then going forward to Sisters' Fountain with its distinctive cairn and slate cross, a most refreshing spot in the heat of summer. There is the possibility of an alternative higher level route between Culbone and Yenworthy, set further back from the sea but providing splendid views to the Welsh coast.

You now leave Somerset and enter Devon. Lovely walking follows, the route proceeding through the beautiful woodland of the Glenthorne Estate, seen at its best in spring when the rhododendrons are in full bloom, and past a woodland lodge with its magnificent gate-pillars topped with wild boar heads. The walking becomes more open, with bushes and shrubs replacing the trees, and consequently much better sea views. You proceed past Wingate Combe, with its attractive waterfall, and go on down to Caddow Combe where there is a splendid view to the lighthouse on Foreland Point, the most northerly headland on the whole route; you should certainly detour to the lighthouse, from which there are glorious views across the Bristol Channel to south Wales. Beyond Caddow Combe you rise to Butter Hill, coming within sight of Countisbury church, then follow a path that runs parallel with the A39 down towards Lynmouth. Lynmouth has attractive thatched cottages as well as a picturesque harbour and promenade. In 1952 a freak storm flooded the village, resulting in the loss of 31 lives and the destruction of 100 homes. Having dropped to Lynmouth, you then make a zigzag ascent to reach Lynmouth's neighbour, the Victorian resort Lynton (21.7). The ascent involves three crossings of the water-powered Lynmouth Cliff Railway, which provides a rather easier link between the two places if you feel you have done enough climbing for one day and if your conscience permits.

As you continue your walk along the Coast Path, you will have your conscience tested not only by mechanical aids but by short cuts. Often you'll find there is a choice of path along the clifftops, with no suggestion as to which, if any, is the definitive one. You would be unwise to lose any sleep over having cut a sizeable corner rather too liberally, and could in any event respond to any suggestion of cheating by pointing to the fact that 150 or 200 yd missed in the context of 613 miles' walking is statistically insignificant.

Lynton to Ilfracombe (17.7 miles) via Combe Martin

ENJOY: Valley of Rocks, Heddon's Mouth, Great/Little Hangman, Combe Martin, Watermouth

Superb walking awaits you on the journey from Lynton to Combe Martin. You begin with an easy walk below Hollerday Hill to the famous Valley of Rocks, a remarkable dry valley surrounded by craggy outcrops, the most spectacular being Castle Rock, thought to be the result of glacial activity 10,000 years ago. Some road walking follows as you pass the Christian retreat centre at the mock-Gothic nineteenth-century Lee Abbey, and go forward to Woody Bay, through a predominantly wooded landscape. Beyond the bay, however, the woodland ends and you join an exposed cliff path which takes you to Highveer Point. Here you turn inland to round the gaping chasm of Heddon's Mouth, the cliffs falling away below you to a narrow channel of water before rising up equally precipitously beyond. You descend cautiously to cross the water just above Hunter's Inn, then climb steeply back up to the clifftop west of the Mouth.

Tremendous walking follows as you negotiate East Cleave and North Cleave, then contour the northern edge of Holdstone Down, descend to Sherrycombe and climb very steeply to Great Hangman. At 1,043 ft it is the highest point on the whole route, and there are fantastic views that include the Gower peninsula in south Wales as well as miles of Devon countryside. You then pass by Little Hangman, offering further great views, and drop down to Combe

Martin (34.1), which boasts one of the longest village streets in the country, extending as it does for some two miles along the A399. There are many typically Devon cottages with slate roofs and walls painted in a range of colours, and the church, which is at least 700 years old, is renowned for its 99 ft tower with battlements and tiers of gargoyles. The village's most unusual feature is the Pack o' Cards Inn which originally had four storeys, 13 doors and 52 windows, representing card suits, cards in a suit, and cards in a pack respectively. It should come as no surprise to learn that it was built by a gambler!

A predictably stiff climb out of Combe Martin is followed by a succession of small headlands and inlets; having passed the mock-Gothic Watermouth Castle and the attractive harbour at Watermouth, you go on round Widmouth Head and Rillage Point, interspersed by Samson's Bay. Beyond Rillage Point the route temporarily joins the A399, then bears right to make a zigzag climb to Beacon Point and Hillsborough, from which you can enjoy a fine view of Ilfracombe before descending to enter it. Built round its old harbour, Ilfracombe (39.4) is the largest seaside resort on the north Devon coast, with all the amenities you could wish for. I arrived here one freezing January afternoon, however, and I could not decide which was worst out of the long uphill detour to find my hotel, the newly-formed split right down my waterproof trousers, the central heating system in the hotel breaking down, or the absence of a decent crossword puzzle in my Sunday paper.

Ilfracombe to Saunton (15.9 miles) via Woolacombe

ENJOY: Torrs Walk, Morte Point, Baggy Point

The first part of the route from Ilfracombe westwards, known locally as the Torrs Walk, consists of a zigzag climb up to a lovely grassy area known as Torrs Park, from which straightforward up-and-down walking on well-defined paths takes you to the pretty village of Lee.

Here you briefly join a metalled road, dropping steeply to Lee Bay and then climbing back on to the cliffs for a superb four-mile march to Morte Point via Bull Point and its lighthouse, Damagehue Point, Rockham Bay and Whiting Cove. Until it levels out near the end, the coast path is constantly undulating, often plunging to sea level to meet grotesquely-shaped rocks that are constantly pounded by the surging surf, and the surroundings are further enriched by streams and waterfalls on the slopes. The ground levels out and a superb path, hugging the cliff edge with a grandstand view of the rock pavements and pillars below, brings you to Morte Point, with its spectacular jagged ridge of slate. It comes as no surprise to learn that the wild waters off this headland have seen numerous shipwrecks.

Beyond Morte Point the walking remains enjoyable but rather less spectacular, as you proceed to the sprawling holiday village of Woolacombe (47) with its jumble of hotels, boarding houses, shops and holiday homes. Beyond Woolacombe you continue beside the dunes of Woolacombe Bay and then, having passed the hamlet of Vention, you strike out westwards towards the prominent headland of Baggy Point. The walking is certainly bracing, and with westerlies blowing in off the sea it can seem like an endless trudge, but the reward, on reaching the Point, is a fantastic view which on a clear day can include Lundy Island and even the Milford Haven oil refineries of Pembrokeshire. Having rounded the Point, the last scenic highlight for some time, you have a straightforward descent to Croyde Bay. The walk onwards from Croyde to Westward Ho! is the most unexciting of the whole trail, and if you are pressed for time you should consider omitting it. It begins pleasantly enough, the route following alongside the B3231 Croyde–Braunton road with excellent views across Saunton Sands (55.3). This is popular holiday country but in January I found the amenities hereabouts sadly limited; my keenly anticipated hot lunch consisted not of the hoped-for plaice and chips in a cosy bar next to a roaring fire overlooking the surging seas, but a microwaved steak pie purchased from the Woolacombe village deli, and consumed at some speed on a bench before I lost all feeling in my fingers and toes.

Saunton to Bideford (22.3 miles) via Braunton and Barnstaple

ENJOY: Braunton Burrows, Barnstaple

The route does not cross the sands but having left the B3231 proceeds on to Braunton Burrows nature reserve. The Burrows are huge sand dunes clothed with tufts of grass, and are exceedingly difficult to walk on, but thankfully the route follows a wide track through the middle of the reserve, emerging at an area of mud and sand on the edge of the estuary of the river Taw. An official detour takes you through the Burrows along a boardwalk to view the meeting point of the Taw and Torridge estuaries. Once the estuaries have met, they form a single channel of water that flows into the bay, marked on the map as Barnstaple or Bideford Bay. Tantalisingly, you can look across this channel towards Appledore, no more than a mile away as the crow flies, but to get there on foot will require a good five hours' walking. The route turns left to follow the estuary inland, soon swinging left again alongside the river Caen, a tributary of the Taw, and, keeping Braunton Marsh to the left, follows the Caen to Velator on the edge of the sprawling community of Braunton. It is mechanical, uninteresting walking. At Velator you reach the course of the old Braunton–Barnstaple railway, turn right on to it and follow it. At first the walking is fast, if tedious, with the busy A361 close by to your left; about the most interesting thing is the sight on the map of a village just the other side of the A361 with the splendid name Heanton Punchardon. In due course, however, the Taw reappears to your right, and you follow alongside it as far as Barnstaple (68.1). Although this is comparatively dull walking, you are unlikely to be on your own. This section, along with much of the north Devon coastal section of the route, coincides with the 180-mile Tarka Trail named after the eponymous hero of Henry Williamson's much-loved novel. The riverside walk is also ideal for a gentle family stroll.

Barnstaple

Barnstaple is the largest town in the northern half of Devon, as well as one of the oldest towns in Great Britain, and until the Taw silted up, it once boasted an important harbour. Its heyday was in the eighteenth century, and it still has a largely Georgian centre. One of the most pleasant parts of the town is an eighteenth-century colonnade named Queen Anne's Walk, while St Anne's Chapel dates from the fourteenth century and once housed the grammar school that educated the poet John Gay, author of *The Beggar's Opera*. The town is an obvious place to stock up with provisions and also has a useful station with trains to Exeter.

The quickest way to cross the Taw (and now the national trail approved route), avoiding the centre of Barnstaple altogether, is via the new A361 bridge; if you wish to detour to the town, you can use the old crossing, the 16-arched Long Bridge which dates from the thirteenth century. Whichever way you cross the Taw, you go forward beyond the river onto another piece of old railway, this time the former Barnstaple–Bideford line. An alternative route, closer to the river, may be available but the railway walk is recommended. You are now walking along the south side of the Taw estuary, although you are often separated from it by grassland or marshes, and there are excellent views to Braunton Burrows and Baggy Point. A little way beyond Lower Yelland the route briefly forsakes the old railway to hug the riverbank by means of some rougher tracks and at one point a trudge through sand dunes, but at the village of Instow it regains the railway and passes a superbly restored signal box and platform. At Instow you reach the point where the Taw and Torridge estuaries meet, and can look directly across to Saunton Sands and Braunton Burrows. Now it is the Torridge that impedes progress; a seasonal ferry across the river to Appledore is available, but otherwise you must continue along the old railway, underneath the A39 and its impressive bridge crossing of the river, and on to the old Bideford station. Immediately beyond this, you cross the Torridge by means of the 677 ft long Bideford Bridge, with 24 arches that are all of varying lengths, and proceed into Bideford (77.6), the chief port of north Devon between the sixteenth and eighteenth century, with narrow streets that contain many seventeenth-century buildings. The town is no longer served by the railways but walkers may find refreshment in a restored railway carriage housed at the old station.

Bideford to Clovelly (18.9 miles) via Appledore and Westward Ho!

ENJOY: Appledore, Abbotsham Cliff, Green Cliff, Clovelly

Beyond the town you proceed beside the estuary along a rough sea wall – a breach in the wall necessitates an inland high-tide diversion – then proceed past the Appledore shipyard into Appledore village, which is as charming as its name suggests, with quaint narrow streets of trim cottages and Georgian houses. It has a long association with fishing, and the largest covered shipbuilding dock in Europe was opened here in 1970. At Appledore you arrive at the meeting point of Taw and Torridge for the third and last time, then follow the south side of the 'combined' estuaries to the mouth (there is one other brief high-tide diversion on this stretch). At long last you have reached the open sea again and, having gazed with satisfaction across to the huge white blob of Saunton Sands Hotel, you now swing left to proceed by Northam Burrows to Westward Ho! (85.4).

Beyond Westward Ho! the cliff walking resumes in earnest and the first climb brings a delightful view forward to Clovelly and Hartland Point and out to Lundy Island. (Although it's not part of the national trail, there is a walk available all the way round the island's coastline; if you've the time and means available it's certainly worth considering as the scenery and bird life are superb. Check the Internet or local tourist information offices for ferry details.). The lungs are certainly tested as you proceed on to Abbotsham Cliff and Green Cliff, then descend to the sea before a steep climb through a hazel and hawthorn thicket to Higher Rowden. A respite follows, as beyond Peppercombe you follow a delightful path through the oak and birch of Sloo Wood, with foxgloves adding constant splashes of colour. There is a steep descent to sea level at Buck's Mills followed by a very tough climb and then a pleasant but unspectacular walk along field edges, separated from the sea by thick woodland. At length you pick up the Hobby Drive, a clearly defined track that follows a somewhat serpentine course through the woods. It leads you to Clovelly (96.5), one of the showpiece villages of England, consisting of a tiny harbour at the foot of a single steeply-inclined cobbled street of stunningly attractive snow-white flower-decked cottages. It is a massively popular tourist haunt, so be warned. You may feel you've earned your refreshment here, but despite your hard work in getting here from Westward Ho!, it will get a lot tougher. A sobering thought for you before you set off from Clovelly: it has been calculated that on the entire walk you will cover 91,000 ft of ascent – three times the height of Mount Everest!

Clovelly to Hartland Quay (9.9 miles) via Hartland Point

ENJOY: Gallantry Bower, East and West Titchberry, Hartland Point, Upright Cliff, Damehole Point, Blegberry Waterfall

This is a short section but an unforgettable one and you should enjoy every inch of the ten miles. Initially the walking is easy as you keep a fairly level course through the woods but close to the sea, and glimpses through the rhododendrons reveal superb views, most notably at the quaintly-named Gallantry Bower viewpoint. Having passed the ornate early nineteenth-century Angels Wings viewing shelter you plunge to the sea at Mouth Mill, close to the impressive arched Blackchurch Rock. You rise again then drop to the modest Windbury waterfall past a riot of foxgloves and scabious, then pull clear of the woods and follow an open stretch along field boundaries close to the cliffs of Exmansworthy, Gawlish and East and West Titchberry. There are views back as far as Morte Point from here, and you should make the most of them, for soon you arrive at Hartland Point and swing in a much more southerly direction, losing the panorama of the coast you have enjoyed for so many miles. Tremendous walking ensues, however, as you drop to the waterfall below Upright Cliff and climb again, following a remarkable hanging valley known as Smoothlands, to Damehole Point. Here a glorious view opens up ahead, while all around you are fascinating rock formations with much to interest the geologist.

There is then an exposed and difficult scramble on to Blegberry Cliff, a descent to Blegberry Waterfall and a particularly severe climb to Dyer's Lookout. Gentler walking brings you to a road leading eastwards to the village of Stoke, while immediately seawards is Hartland Quay (106.4), a tightly packed, weather-beaten group of buildings including a museum that stand defiantly between sea and cliffs. Like many little settlements on the Cornwall or Devon coast, this is an exciting place to be in winter, as you stand watching the angry seas, whipped up by force nine gales, pound the harbours and surrounding cliffs.

Hartland Quay to Bude (15 miles) via Welcombe Mouth

ENJOY: St Catherine's Tor, Speke's Mill Mouth, Welcombe Mouth and the combes beyond, Morwenstow, Higher Sharpnose Point

Beyond the Stoke road you soon pass to the landward side of the huge sheer cliff known as St Catherine's Tor, then descend to the superb cascade of Speke's Mill Mouth before climbing on to Swansford Hill with dramatic views back to the Tor and Hartland Quay. Flat clifftop walking follows, the main hazard being the frighteningly close proximity of the path to the cliff edge round Milford Common. A track leads left to the hamlet and youth hostel of Elmscott, while the route goes forward to join a road that leads to Embury Beacon and the cliffs guarding the north side of Welcombe Mouth. So far so good.

Then the real work begins, as you negotiate a succession of massive combes: Welcombe Mouth, Marsland Mouth (where you enter Cornwall), Litter Mouth, Yeol Mouth, St Morwenna's Well, the Tidna, Stanbury Mouth, Duckpool, Warren Gutter and Sandy Mouth. Each involves a steep, often perilous drop down a narrow path, sometimes but not always stepped, then a footbridge crossing over a narrow stream, followed by a back-breaking climb to regain the lost height. Just before the Tidna you can detour to Morwenstow and its part-Norman church; its most famous parson was Robert Hawker, who first introduced the celebration of Harvest Festival here in 1843 and who would often repair to a cliff-edge driftwood hut close to the coast path to write poetry and enjoy a spot of opium.

Beyond the Tidna comes an outstanding promontory viewpoint at Higher Sharpnose Point, whilst at nearby Lower Sharpnose Point are the huge satellite tracking dish aerials of Cleave Camp which will remain visible for miles. Just above Duckpool, close to Steeple Point, is a fine view up the partially wooded Coombe Valley, but you will notice how much less wooded the combes are generally than in Somerset or north Devon. Beyond Sandy Mouth it is a much easier walk into Bude with just one innocuous descent to Northcott Mouth and climb on to Maer Cliff. Bude (121.4) is a popular surfing resort with a wealth of places advertising bed and breakfast, but the sign outside will tell you nothing about what lies within. Much will depend on whether the establishment is run for the benefit of the guests or the owners. In the former case, you can expect a welcome cup of tea and biscuits or cake, the run of the house, maybe even a lift to the nearest pub, a choice of breakfast time next morning and, when morning comes, bottomless supplies of every breakfast component known to civilisation. In the latter, access to any parts of the establishment outside one's bedroom will be carefully delineated, breakfast times and food provision (inevitably originating in the nearest cash-and-carry) will be closely prescribed, and curt notices will be found on walls with dire retribution promised for anyone daring to breach any of the house regulations, from wearing walking boots on the carpets to eating custard creams after 9.45 p.m.

Bude to Boscastle (16.5 miles) via Crackington Haven

ENJOY: Bridwill Point, Castle Point, Cambeak, High Cliff, Pentargon, Boscastle

Straightforward clifftop walking takes you on from Bude to Widemouth Sand, but coastal erosion round Great Wanson and Millook means that you must undertake two very considerable climbs by road, although there is some fine clifftop walking round Bridwill Point between these two ascents, with views back to those satellite dishes. Having left the road, you enjoy easier walking on the approach to Dizzard Point, with just one short drop into a beautiful wooded combe. However, beyond Dizzard Point the walking gets harder again, with a descent from Chipman Point being followed by a very stiff climb to Cleave. From here you strike out towards Castle Point and follow a piece of massive whalebacked and heather-topped headland, with tremendous views that stretch back as far as Hartland Point.

There is then a descent to the stream of Aller Shoot, a severe climb to the cliffs of Pencannow Point, and a descent to the pretty cove of Crackington Haven. This is roughly halfway from Bude to Boscastle and a good place to stop for rest and refreshment, as the seven remaining miles to Boscastle offer no facilities. They are seven unforgettable miles, starting with a climb to the majestic rugged headland of Cambeak and then a steady uphill trudge past rocks called the Strangles to the 732 ft High Cliff, the most elevated cliffs in Cornwall. There is a near vertical descent from here, followed by a climb up the side of the landslipped Rusey Cliff along a twisting narrow path, with the sea to your right and precipitous slopes of gorse, heather and bracken to your left. At length you regain the clifftop at Buckator and proceed easily on past Fire Beacon Point, Beeny Cliff and on to the Pentargon inlet with a quite splendid cascade.

Another climb brings you to Penally Hill where you have your first view of Boscastle, and it is then a steady descent down the cliffside to this beautiful village (137.9). Its harbour is the only shelter for miles along the north Cornwall coast, the narrow inlet snaking between high slate cliffs to a small stone jetty that was once used for exporting slate and grain. The village itself, with its narrow streets of slate cottages, lies half a mile from the harbour in the picturesque Valency Valley, and with its museum of witchcraft and multitude of craft and gift shops selling everything from leathers to curses, has given up without a struggle to the tourist trade. It suffered terrible flooding in August 2004 but has made a miraculous recovery. Thomas Hardy, who loved this area, was inspired hereabouts to write his novel *A Pair of Blue Eyes*.

Boscastle to Port Isaac (13 miles) via Tintagel

ENJOY: Ladies Window, Rocky Valley, Tintagel, Port Isaac

More tremendous walking awaits between Boscastle and Tintagel. You leave Boscastle and pass the headland of Willapark, its white coastguard building standing high above the southern entry to Boscastle harbour; curiously, further on in this section there is another headland called Willapark which gives fine views back to Hartland and the satellite dishes. Highlights as you proceed include the view out to Long Island, a spectacular tower of rock rising from the sea and a favourite gathering place for puffins, and the Ladies Window, a natural rock archway high above the sea. For me the best feature of this section is Rocky Valley, reached by a steep descent, it consists of a river guarded on either side by lush green banks, punctuated in spring with pockets of cow parsley, while immediately above stand rock stacks with almost surreal arrangements of jagged outcrops, ledges and faces. From there you go forward to Tintagel, obtaining excellent views to this historic site firstly from the second Willapark and then Barras Nose, this being the last piece of headland before you drop to Tintagel Haven.

Tintagel

To your right is the island promontory, reachable by bridge, known as Tintagel Head on which stand the ruins of Tintagel Castle that date back to the twelfth century. Excavations have revealed evidence of a Celtic monastery on the site, and legend has it that King Arthur was born and held court here or hereabouts. The village of Tintagel, formerly known as Trevena, is just off the route, and offers plenty of amenities; features of interest include the old post office building that dates from the fourteenth-century, and the Norman church of St Materiana which is much closer to the route.

Very easy clifftop walking now takes you past Dunderhole Point and Higher Penhallic Point to Trebarwith Strand where it is advisable to seek refreshment, as the five miles on to Port Isaac are tough. You begin with a colossal ascent, a big descent to the combe at Backways and strenuous climb up again, then after a brief respite you must negotiate three very steep-sided combes in succession, past Dannonchapel, Barrett's Zawn and Ranie Point. At Barrett's Zawn look out for an adit, or tunnel cut into the rock to allow easy access to the beach for the purpose of slate quarrying. At times the path is so steep and the ground so crumbly that hands as well as feet may be required! After Ranie Point things get easier, with one gentler combe, St Illickswell Gug, to negotiate before a brisk canter past Port Gaverne, once an important centre for the export of slate quarried nearby, into Port Isaac (150.9). This is a wonderful, typically Cornish seaside village, with narrow alleys of slate-built cottages quaintly arranged above a busy harbour.

Port Isaac to Trevone (17 miles) via Polzeath

ENJOY: Epphaven Cove, Lundy Beach, Lundy Hole, Pentire Point, St Enodoc, Padstow

The section from Port Isaac to Polzeath begins with an excellent and straightforward march round the headlands of Lobber Point, Varley Head and Kellan Head, from which you descend slightly inland to the small and totally unspoilt village of Port Quin, which lies at the end of a charming natural harbour. Towards the end of the nineteenth century its entire male population was lost when its only fishing vessel came to grief at sea. The western edge of the harbour is guarded by Doyden Point, close to which is a folly known as Doyden Castle. You pass the folly as you return to the cliffs and enjoy a great walk past Trevan Point and two delectable inlets, Epphaven Cove and Lundy Beach, the latter lying at the sea end of a wooded valley. Lundy Hole, just beyond, is a collapsed cave where you can look through a massive natural rock arch to the foaming sea far below. The Coast Path continues round Carnweather Point and round the neck of the twin headlands known as the Rumps where there are Iron Age fortifications and splendid views to the Mouls, a rocky island where seabirds regularly congregate. Next is Pentire Point, one of the best viewpoints on the north Cornwall coast; I am told that when conditions are right, even the Cleave Camp dishes may make an appearance! There follows a long and steady descent to Polzeath, a sprawling village with a popular beach and ample facilities.

Now you leave the coast for a while to follow a section of the Camel Estuary, beginning with an easy walk round Trebetherick

Point to Daymer Bay and passing the golf course at St Enodoc, although you should detour across the golf course to the church with its slightly angled thirteenth-century spire. The poet John Betjeman is buried in the churchyard.

A weary trudge over the dunes round Daymer Bay is followed by an easy passage round the edge of Brea Hill, topped by Bronze Age tumuli, and further dune walking takes you to Rock where it is necessary to use the ferry (year-round, save winter Sundays) to cross the estuary to reach Padstow (162.5). A seventh-century monastery was founded here by St Petroc and Walter Raleigh presided as Warden of Cornwall from the town's Court House. Its narrow streets of stone cottages and lovely harbour have a typically Cornish charm, somewhat shattered on May Day with the Obby Oss, a pagan celebration of the departure of winter. From Padstow you head back towards the coast, rounding St George's Cove and a large sandy expanse which includes the treacherous Doom Bar, where 300 craft, including three lifeboats, have perished. At the round tower of Stepper Point you reach the mouth of the Camel Estuary and enjoy a fine coastal walk to Trevone (167.9). You pass the oddly-shaped Merope islands, which are actually headlands that have become separated from the mainland, and after a steep descent and climb past the limestone cliffs at Porthmissen you come to the headland of Roundhole Point, from which you descend to the village of Trevone. As you negotiate this headland, watch out for a massive collapsed cave, taking the form of a huge hole in the ground.

Trevone to Newquay (18 miles) via Porthcothan

ENJOY: Park Head, Bedruthan Steps

From Trevone you negotiate a succession of bays including Newtrain, Harlyn and Mother Ivey's. The coast path stays close to the shore, only really rising significantly to round Trevose Head and its lighthouse, but soon dropping to Booby's Bay, the sands round Constantine Bay, and then Treyarnon Bay. These are all honeypots in the summer months and the walking itself is tame stuff. However, you then return to the cliffs and pass a number of long thin coves, enjoying the variety of colours; the yellow of wild buttercups, pink of the foxgloves, lush green of the clifftops, severe grey of the rocks, soft azure of the sea, and creamy white channels of foam with the tides. You descend to another little resort, Porthcothan, but ascend again to enjoy a tremendous cliff walk to Park Head, with the fascinating but highly dangerous Trescore islands nearby and views back to Trevose Head. Just beyond Park Head are the Bedruthan Steps, a sequence of large rock islands constantly pounded by the sea, and said to be used by the giant Bedruthan as stepping stones: of these, Queen Bess Rock was said to resemble the profile of the monarch until a rock fall in the 1980s, while Samaritan Island was named after a ship wrecked just off it in 1846. A well-signposted route gives you access to a grandstand view of the Steps, but venture out to them at your peril!

The walk on to Newquay is a walk of contrasts, with magnificent headlands topped with prehistoric forts and views inland to china clay spoil heaps being interspersed with descents to sea level and the tourist spots of Mawgan Porth, Watergate Bay and Whipsiderry. After rounding Trevelgue Head you proceed past Porth and a number of mini headlands, using a mixture of paths and roads to arrive in Newquay itself (185.9), a town with a proud fishing and mining history and now the biggest and most garish resort on the Cornish coast. I was fortunate to stay in a superb bed and breakfast where a fellow-guest extolled the virtue of organised walking. I remain ambivalent about this; whilst a guide will ensure you don't get lost and will draw your attention to features of interest, it must be irksome for the whole party to be forced to backtrack because some wretched soul thinks they may have left a bag of postcards behind at the last pub stop 45 minutes ago.

Newquay to Trevaunance Cove for St Agnes (15.3 miles) via Perranporth

ENJOY: Ligger Point, Perran Sands, St Piran's Oratory, St Agnes

Leaving the unsubtle joys of Newquay, you proceed round Towan Head, with excellent views across Newquay and its bay, and past Fistral Beach, renowned as the best surfing beach in the country. The route avoids the headland of Pentire Point East but skirts the western edges of the sprawling village of Pentire to arrive on the banks of the Gannel, a tidal river. There is a seasonal ferry at high tide, and a choice of summer or winter foot crossings, the latter requiring an extensive and unwelcome diversion upstream along the shores, and not usable for two hours or so round high tide. Once over the Gannel you proceed seawards alongside it, passing Crantock Beach and Rushy Green and passing through the dunes to return to the coast at Pentire Point West. You round this headland and then proceed past the cove and lagoon of Porth Joke, known locally as Polly Joke, going forward to Kelsey Head where you can look out to a National Trust-owned island called the Chick. There is a tough stretch of dune walking from here past Holywell Bay and on to the village of Holywell (189).

Beyond Holywell you climb on to the cliffs to round Penhale Point and pass an army camp, then continue to Ligger Point, from where there are good views ahead to the Perran Sands. You drop to these sands, which at low tide you can follow all the way to Perranporth, whilst at high tide you will be forced to endure a treadmill through the dunes. A brief detour inland across the dunes will take you to St Piran's Oratory, a sixth or seventh-century chapel and one of the country's oldest Christian buildings.

Beyond Perranporth (195), another popular holiday destination with a good range of amenities, you enter what was serious tin-mining country, with a number of old mining shafts nearby as you round Cligga Point, although in recent years tin-mining in

Cornwall has ceased completely. Beyond Cligga Point, the walking is straightforward on flat cliff tops, but there follows a steep descent to Trevellas Cove, then a big climb and further drop to Trevaunance Cove (201.2). From here it is an easy walk to St Agnes, once the centre of a flourishing tin-mining industry and today a pleasant village of sturdy slate and granite cottages, with old miners' cottages standing in a stepped terrace known as Stippy-Stappy. Trevaunance Coombe itself has had three harbours since 1632, all destroyed by the sea. The surroundings are certainly majestic.

Trevaunance Cove to Gwithian (15.9 miles) via Portreath

ENJOY: St Agnes Head, Wheal Coates, Western Hill, Crane Castle, Hell's Mouth, Godrevy Point

Progress beyond Trevaunance Cove is initially excellent, past St Agnes Head with excellent views to the Bawden Rocks, otherwise known as Man and his Man, where guillemots and razorbills often gather. The views from the heather-clad clifftops extend as far as Trevose Head. In due course you reach the nineteenth-century Wheal Coates engine house, a relic of the mining industry; engine houses drove the mining machinery and pumped water from the mine shafts. You drop steeply to the inlet at Chapel Porth, then climb up on to Mulgram Hill to get a good view of the mine.

There is then fast walking on a good level path, followed by a descent to the unremarkable village of Porthtowan, which is flanked by numerous old mineworkings, and indeed you will see more evidence of mining activity as you proceed towards Portreath. Much of this next section is quite easy, passing the perimeter fence of the Nancekuke defence area, but there are a couple of steep drops and climbs including a tricky descent to Sally's Bottom! You swing round the edge of Gooden Heane Cove, the path just inches from the sheer cliff edge, then descend to the village of Portreath (208), once a busy port and now a popular holiday village. From here you climb to the lovely cliffs of Western Hill, with good views back to Gooden Heane Point and forward to Navax Point and Godrevy Point.

The combes emerging at Porth-cadjack Cove and Bassett's Cove and their attendant drops and climbs slow progress a little, but once you get on to Reskajeage Downs the walking is good and quick. Highlights include the clifftop Crane Castle of Iron Age origin, and a great vertical chasm known as Hell's Mouth. As a road runs parallel with the coast path hereabouts, these are popular spots. Superb walking takes you out to Navax Point and then Godrevy Point, with grandstand views to Godrevy Island. The walk from Navax Point to Godrevy Point has two famous associations. It is the now unmanned nineteenth-century lighthouse on Godrevy Island that inspired Virginia Woolf's novel *To The Lighthouse*, and on a nearby reef, many of the personal effects of Charles I were lost in a severe shipwreck… on the very day of his execution. Not one of his better days.

Rounding Godrevy Point, you now begin the walk round St Ives Bay, enjoying fine views to St Ives, and the golden sands of Godrevy Cove. Make the most of these delights, as things will get tougher once you have passed the back of the beach to arrive at Gwithian (217.1).

Gwithian to Zennor (16.2 miles) via St Ives

ENJOY: St Ives, Clodgy Point, Mussel Point, The Carracks, Zennor Cliff, Zennor

For four miles beyond Gwithian you have to tramp through a large area of dunes, passing the holiday complex of Hayle Towans. The route is well waymarked and avoids the worst peaks and troughs but after the glories of Godrevy it is pretty grim stuff. At length you reach Hayle Estuary where there is a tantalising view across to Lelant and St Ives, but with no ferry available you must endure a tedious walk round the edge of the estuary. You begin with a trudge through a sorry industrial landscape to arrive at the nondescript village of Hayle (221.3), joining a road that takes you out of the village and across the river Hayle. Immediately beyond the crossing you fork right along a road which leads you into the village of Lelant, then as the main road bends left, you go straight ahead, north-eastwards, to the rough granite church of St Uny. Here you leave the road and cross the golf course, passing underneath the St Erth–St Ives branch line and across the dunes along the seaward side of the railway, with the pleasant prospect of St Ives Bay immediately to your right. You continue round the headland of Carrack Gladden, with the railway still to your immediate left, and arrive at Carbis Bay, where you climb away from the sea, crossing the railway and following roads towards Porthminster Beach. You cross to the seaward side of the railway once more and go forward into St Ives (226.7).

The official route follows the bay right round to St Ives Head, also known as St Ives Island, rounding the headland and going on to Porthmeor Beach, but it is perfectly possible to cut through the town to reach Porthmeor Beach rather more quickly. St Ives has a long history as a fishing port, has supported a flourishing pilchard fishery for many years, and is a magnet for visitors with its narrow cobbled streets of stone cottages, sandy beaches, picturesque harbour, beautiful bay and views seawards to Godrevy Island. It is very popular with artists too, and many galleries have opened in the town, including a Tate Gallery.

Leaving St Ives, you embark on a much wilder and more exciting stretch of coastline. The terrain can be boggy but the coastal scenery is majestic as you proceed past the headlands of Clodgy Point, Hor Point, Pen Enys Point, Carn Naun Point and Mussel Point; from Mussel Point there are good views to the Carracks, a group of islands where seals can be seen. You proceed on past the steep Tregerthen and Tremedda cliffs on to Zennor Cliff, a granite headland towering 200 ft above the sea. Just beyond this point you can detour to the granite village of Zennor (233.3) with its megalithic burial chamber known as Zennor Quoit, a museum with many exhibits relating to tin-mining, and the twelfth-century St Senara's Church. The church has a bench end which commemorates the mermaid who supposedly enticed the squire's son, and tenor in the village choir, out to sea and a watery death. How inconsiderate of her – did she not know of the nationwide shortage of amateur chorus tenors?

Zennor to Land's End (16.9 miles) via Pendeen Watch

ENJOY: Gurnard's Head, Porthmeor Cove, Bosigran Cliff, St Bridget's Church, Cape Cornwall, Aire Point, Sennen Cove, Land's End

From Zennor Cliff you continue past Pendour Cove, Porthglaze Cove and Treen Cove, with its old mine building, to the magnificent Gurnard's Head. The route cuts round the neck of the headland, but a detour to the headland and its promontory fort, Trereen Dinas, is strongly recommended. As you stride out to the next major headland at Pendeen Watch, the terrain continues to be juicy underfoot, but the scenery remains tremendous, with the coves of Porthmeor, Halldrine, Porthmoina and Portheras to your right, and the impressive Bosigran Cliff providing a splendid viewing platform just beyond Porthmeor Cove. Shortly before Portheras Cove you can detour slightly inland to visit the lonely church of St Bridget at Morvah with its fourteenth-century tower. From Portheras Cove you stride out to Pendeen Watch with its lighthouse that dates back to 1900. Between Pendeen Watch and Cape Cornwall, the next significant headland, there is a vast amount of evidence of tin-mining activity, with an abundance of disused mines, while just beyond Trewellard Zawn, at Levant mine, there is a restored beam engine, and close to Botallack there are two restored engine houses.

Shortly beyond the fort of Kenidjack you reach Cape Cornwall (243.9), the only piece of headland in England to be called a cape, and once believed to be England's most westerly point, although Land's End has since been given that distinction. You do actually move slightly east of south as you ascend to the next headland, Gribba Point, but after some splendid clifftop walking past Polpry Cove and Aire Point you follow the sands round the lovely Whitesand Bay and swing south-westwards again to reach Sennen Cove (249.1). The thirteenth-century church of St Sennen in the village of Sennen, a short detour inland from here, is the most westerly in England.

From here you climb on to Mayon Cliff and proceed, high above the sea, past Maen Castle promontory fort to Dr Syntax's Head, then having rounded the headland you can stand on the granite cliffs, gaze out to the Longships Lighthouse and find you have literally reached Land's End (250.2). There is no more land ahead of you and you must now turn eastwards to continue, this time along the *south*-facing coasts of south-west England. Land's End has become hideously commercialised, a big theme park having opened here in recent years, but it is still a magical place. Though you will have covered some 250 miles to get here from Minehead, many walkers hereabouts will have been tackling the rather longer trek from one end of the British Isles to the other; you may even see one such poor walker making his weary way onwards, exhaustion written all over his face, drawing upon his last reserves of willpower and inner strength… and wish him well for his remaining 875 miles to John o'Groats.

Land's End to Mousehole (12.6 miles) via Porthcurno and Mousehole

ENJOY: Gwennap Head, Nanjizal Cove, Minack, Penberth, St Loy, Mousehole

Having rounded Dr Johnson's Head and begun the long eastward trek towards Poole, your next major objective is Gwennap Head, where you will swing from south-east to north-east. The broad coast path maintains a fine clifftop course, past Nanjizal Cove, Pendower Cove, Folly Cove and the inlet of Porth Loe, and the headlands of

Carn Lês Boel, Carn Barra, Black Carn and Carn Guthensbrâs. Just before Gwennap Head is the holed headland of Tol-Pedn-Penwith, which is certainly worth a detour. Having rounded Gwennap Head you proceed past the small village of Porthgwarra and on to Porthcurno with its magnificent Minack Theatre, an open-air theatre that was begun in the 1930s and constructed in classical Greek style, with seating cut cleverly into the cliffs so that audiences can enjoy not only the play but the superb marine backdrop.

You continue round the inlet of Porth Curno, at the eastern end of which is a granite block known as a 'logan' rock, estimated to weigh about 65 tons, which 'logs' (rocks) at the slightest touch. In 1824 it was pushed over the cliff by a party of sailors; the incident caused such an outcry that Lieutenant Goldsmith, the ringleader, had to reposition the rock at his own expense! You proceed on past Cribba Head to the quite delightful hamlet of Penberth and its tiny cove, guarded by an impressive assembly of rocks and boulders, then on past the inlet of Porthguarnon, the charming wooded cove of St Loy, and the headlands of Merthen Point and Boscawen Point. You drop down to Lamorna Valley to round Lamorna Cove, then having passed the old granite quarries round Carn-du, you begin the long walk round Mounts Bay.

The next few miles see a return to civilisation as you follow a well-defined path past Kemyel Point and Penzer Point into Mousehole (pronounced Mowzel) (262.8), a pretty fishing village with houses of grey granite looking out on to a little harbour. On 23 December each year, fishermen gather to eat Stargazy Pie, in commemoration of one Tom Bawcock whose catch of fish supposedly once saved the village from starvation; it is made with whole fish whose heads poke out through the crust!

Mousehole to Porthleven via Penzance (16.8 miles)

ENJOY: Penzance, St Michael's Mount, Marazion, Trewavas Head, Wheal Prosper

It is a straightforward walk now, following a road into Newlyn, an important fishing village, and continuing into Penzance (266.4). The town boasts some excellent eighteenth-century houses, and gardens with sub-tropical plants. One of the most famous Penzance residents was Humphrey Davy, inventor of the miner's safety lamp, and a statue of him stands outside the imposing market house in Market Jew Street. An easy three-mile walk beside railway and road takes you from Penzance to Marazion, with great views to St Michael's Mount, to which access is possible from Marazion. Separated from the mainland by a tidal causeway, it is dominated by its superb castle, much of which dates back to the fifteenth century, and built on the site of a twelfth-century Benedictine monastery. Having left Marazion, a straggling but most attractive village with old cottages and winding streets, you begin heading resolutely south-eastwards to the Lizard. The walk on to Perranuthnoe is uninspiring, beginning with a road walk to Trevenner and then a section of beach walking, but beyond Perranuthnoe there is better walking with fine views towards the Lizard. Acton Castle, an eighteenth-century castellated mansion, is just a short way from the coast path to your left as you approach Cudden Point.

Having rounded the point, you soon reach Prussia Cove, named after a notorious smuggler who was known by his followers as the King of Prussia. The secluded Cornish coves were perfect spots to land contraband; Bessy's Cove hereabouts was once a landing place for smuggled brandy and named after the keeper of a nearby beerhouse. You then proceed past Kenneggy Cliff and its mine dumps, round Hoe Point and forward to the extensive Praa Sands and village of the same name. Good cliff walking on to and round Trewavas Head takes you past further engine houses, one of which,

Wheal Prosper, is owned by the National Trust. The coast between Megliggar Rocks, just beyond Trewavas Head, and Porthleven is liable to landslips, so follow signs carefully – and watch your feet – as you proceed past Tregear Point to Porthleven (279.6), once an important seaport, as indicated by the eighteenth-century Harbour House and nineteenth-century West Wharf. The 1890 Wesleyan chapel inspired the verse, 'They built the church upon my word as fine as any abbey; and then they thought to cheat the Lord and built the back part shabby!'

Porthleven to Lizard Point (13.4 miles) via Mullion Cove

ENJOY: Church Cove, Poldhu Cove, Mullion Cove, Kynance Cove, Lizard Point

Beyond Porthleven there is a tough stretch of beach walking round the edge of the Loe, Cornwall's biggest natural lake. Having passed Loe Bar, a thin piece of land separating the Loe from the sea, you join a more comfortable path, passing the memorial to the hundred victims of an 1807 shipping disaster, and continue past Gunwalloe Fishing Cove. You proceed past Halzephron Cliff to Church Cove, and the fifteenth-century church of St Gunwalloe which, though close to the sea, is sheltered from it by a bluff.

From there you continue to Poldhu Cove then climb steeply over Angrouse Cliff before descending to Polurrian Cove. Another climb takes you past a huge hotel, from which you descend to Mullion Cove (284) and its little harbour. This is one of the loveliest coves on the whole route, surrounded as it is by immense jagged cliffs and enjoying excellent views to Mullion Island. There is a steep climb up from the Cove and there follows an incredible six-mile walk to the Lizard via Predannack Head and Vellan Head, the coast path staying on the cliff edge almost all the way, with just one big drop and ascent round Kynance Cove. The cliff formations are remarkable, with numerous huge crevices and caves, and so many intriguing names: Ogo-dour Cove, Pengersick, Ogo Pons, Gew-graze, Pigeon Ogo. Gone are the trim fields and neat village communities, to be replaced by a gaping wilderness of heather and grass. Eventually you reach Lizard Point (293), turning eastwards, now walking on the southernmost stretch of land in Great Britain and passing the Most Southerly Cafe, the gimmickry of Land's End thankfully absent. Of more interest perhaps is the Lizard Lighthouse, built in 1751, and the Lion's Den, a huge hole in the cliffs caused by a collapsed sea cave. It's certainly quite satisfying to have reached this point on your walk: Mathew Lyons wrote in 2004 that Lizard Point 'has… that vertiginous sense of the world falling away to nothing.' Cheer up though, there's still some more walking ahead of you. Over three hundred miles of it.

Lizard Point to Porthoustock (14.4 miles) via Coverack

ENJOY: Devil's Frying Pan, Cadgwith, Beagles Point, Chynhalls Point

If the Most Southerly Cafe did not cater fully for your needs, further amenities are available in the nearby village of Lizard, and having made the detour inland you may also wish to inspect the pretty church of St Winwallo at nearby Landewednack. The Coast Path goes round Bass Point then starts heading north-eastwards, soon passing Hot Point. Lovely clifftop walking follows, with only minor undulations, taking you past the lifeboat chute at Kilcobben and on to the Devil's Frying Pan, a funnel-shaped depression leading to a remarkable rock arch between two cliffs. Just beyond is Cadgwith, almost your definitive Cornish fishing village with a busy harbour and whitewashed thatched cottages. Having descended to the village, you return to the clifftop for a time, then descend to Poltesco, site of a former serpentine works (serpentine being a type of local stone), and Kennack with its ugly caravan park just beyond. However, having passed the sands there and ascended to the cliffs, you enjoy an outstanding walk via

Carrick Lûz and the delectable Beagles Point to Black Head, with stunning views almost throughout and exceptionally beautiful spring flowers. There are a number of tough descents and ascents, Downas Valley being the most gruelling, and the slippery serpentine stone makes it hard to maintain footholds.

Beyond Black Head the walking becomes less strenuous but still interesting, with a good clifftop march followed by a visit to the fortification on Chynhalls Point and a walk round Dolor Point into the pretty village of Coverack (303.9). You leave Coverack along a lane followed by an ill-defined path which stays almost at sea level to round the aptly-named Lowland Point, beyond which you must negotiate Dean Quarries before coming to Godrevy Cove. You proceed along part of the beach, with views out to sea to the infamous Manacles rocks which have seen many shipwrecks, then go inland to the pleasant hamlet of Rosenithon before descending steeply to the village of Porthoustock (307.4).

Cornish cream teas

According to the South West Way Association, you will now be into the second half of your South West Coast Path pilgrimage, and may wish to celebrate with a traditional Cornish cream tea. Of course it may be that you've already sampled such fare over the preceding days and are therefore aware of what a lottery finding a really good tea is with so many different establishments catering for a huge tourist trade. One day, home-baked scones, home-clotted cream and home-made strawberry jam. The next, frozen scones, squirty cream and individual plastic containers of a red sugary glutinous additive-packed substance.

Porthoustock to Falmouth (18.7 miles) via Helford

ENJOY: Gillan Creek, Dennis Head, Helford, Glendurgan, Rosemullion Head, Pendennis Castle, Falmouth

A coast route is available from here, past the now unused quarries round Pencra Head and Porthkerris Point, although at high tide you will need to stick to a track beyond Pencra Head that leads to roads which you follow to Porthallow. Both routes provide fine views to Falmouth and are superior to the long-time official route which snakes tamely along inland roads and paths past the hamlet of Trenance. From Porthallow there is much better walking on a well-defined cliff-edge path to Nare Point, beyond which you go along the south bank of Gillan Creek round the twin villages of Gillan and Flushing. There are lovely views across the creek to the church at St Anthony-in-Meneage. Unless the creek can be waded (one hour either side of low tide) or a water taxi/ferry is available (please enquire locally) you must continue along the bank, a rather muddy and fiddly trudge, to the hamlet of Carne, and you are then able to follow roads round to the north side of the creek to continue.

From here, the route proceeds past the church and out to Dennis Head, from which there are fantastic views across Falmouth Bay to Falmouth, St Mawes and St Anthony Head lighthouse. Having rounded the headland, you now begin a glorious walk along the south bank of the Helford River, through mostly wooded and far less rugged surroundings, and with lovely views across the river. Soon you reach Helford (314) with its lovely whitewashed thatched cottages and the very popular Shipwright's Arms. From Helford you cross the river by seasonal ferry to Helford Passage.

[Alternative route, 8.4 miles: head westwards from Helford along a lane, then southwards on a metalled road through Kestle to reach a T-junction. Turn right and head westwards along roads to Mawgan. Turn right in the village to arrive at the B3293. Follow this north-eastwards through Gweek to Naphene Downs. Turn right to follow metalled roads eastwards via Nancenoy, Polwheveral and Porth Navas to Helford Passage.]

From Helford Passage you proceed seawards along the north shore of the river, passing the pretty village of Durgan and the stunning gardens of Glendurgan nearby, and the fifteenth-century church at Mawnan that stands in the lovely National Trust-owned

Mawnan Glebe. You then pass the river mouth and begin the walk round Falmouth Bay, rounding the attractive Rosemullion Head and enjoying fine forward views over the bay as you continue and descend to the popular Maenporth Beach. A brisk climb takes you on to Pennance Point, having rounded which you begin the long walk out to Pendennis Point. On the headland is Dennis Fort, a Tudor defensive blockhouse, and Henry VIII's Pendennis Castle. Road walking then brings you to Falmouth (326.1), a busy port and the terminal of the ferry to St Mawes which you must use to continue your journey. Save for winter Sundays, it is a year-round ferry service, but if for any reason it is not running or you do indeed find yourself here on a Sunday in winter, you have three options: a 34-mile road walk, a financially crippling taxi, or a day spent initially lingering over a lazy breakfast then pottering the narrow streets, enjoying fresh lobster at a cosy low-beamed restaurant… it's your decision.

Falmouth to Gorran Haven (21.6 miles) via Portscatho and Portloe

ENJOY: St Mawes, St Anthony-in-Roseland, St Anthony Head, Nare Head, Parc Caragloose Cove, Portloe, Caerhays, Hemmick Beach, Dodman Point

This is a long section, but if you have had a day off at Falmouth you may not object to the extra miles, and in any case you could break at Portloe. Having crossed Carrick Roads by ferry to the lovely St Mawes and its castle, also built by Henry VIII, you immediately need to use a seasonal ferry across the Percuil river to St Anthony on the Roseland peninsula. There is the possibility of a water taxi between Falmouth and Place; please enquire locally. *[Alternative route, 6 miles: follow the A3078 out of Mawes north-eastwards via St Just in Roseland, crossing the river at Trethem Mill then turning right along a minor road to Tregassa. Turn right here on to a minor road that proceeds just west of south via Gerrans and Bohortha to reach St Anthony-in-Roseland.]*

You soon pass the twelfth-century church of St Anthony-in-Roseland with its Norman south doorway, and connected to the nineteenth-century Place House, from which you stride out to St Anthony Head and its nineteenth-century lighthouse, and Zone Point with its fine views back across Falmouth Bay.

At this point you bid farewell to Falmouth Bay and enjoy an easy walk along flat cliff-top paths to the village of Portscatho, followed by a walk round the edge of Gerrans Bay to its eastern end at Nare Head. Initially the going from Portscatho is straightforward as you pass by the beaches of Porthcurnick and Porthbean, and then, beyond Creek Stephen Point, those of Pendower and Carne. Tougher walking follows as you then ascend to the cliffs, drop steeply to Paradoe Cove and then climb again to round Nare Head, with fine views from the headland. It is now a strenuous walk beside Veryan Bay to Portloe, the next village; having passed Rosen Cliff you have a near vertical descent, a mighty climb above Parc Caragloose Cove, and another big drop past Manare Point and Jacka Point to reach Portloe (339.3), a comparatively unspoilt and beautifully kept fishing village with a tiny harbour. Two miles west is Veryan with its thatched whitewashed circular cottages, said to be Devil-proof as there were no corners where Satan could lie in wait!

Enjoyable but tough clifftop walking past Caragloose Point takes you to the attractive twin villages of West and East Portholland, and a mile further on you reach Porthluney Cove. Close by is the majestic nineteenth-century Caerhays Castle, designed by John Nash who was also responsible for Brighton Pavilion and Buckingham Palace. You return to the clifftops, the slopes clad with bracken and outcrops of rock, then after dropping to the wonderfully unspoilt Hemmick Beach, you begin your assault on Dodman Point, which lies at the far eastern end of Veryan Bay and is one of south Cornwall's most prominent headlands. Although the ascent from Hemmick Beach is tough, the view from the memorial cross at the Point itself is tremendous, with a whole new coastal vista opening out to the east, including the broad sweep of St Austell Bay. There is then a long and difficult descent to Maenease Point, beyond which is the village of Gorran Haven (347.7) where you will no doubt hope for a meal after so much tough walking. The upside of Cornwall being so popular with holidaymakers is the easy availability of inexpensive cafes and takeaways, and your desire for sustenance after your day's walking will surely cause you to be more forgiving of the inevitable corniness of their names, whether My Plaice, For Goodness Hake, Cod's In His Heaven or Come Fry With Me.

Gorran Haven to Fowey (20 miles) via Charlestown

ENJOY: Chapel Point, Mevagissey, Charlestown, Polkerris, Gribben Head, Polridmouth Cove, St Catherine's Castle, Readymoney Cove, Fowey

This is another long day, but the middle part is quick and easy and there is the possibility of a break of journey at Charlestown which is roughly halfway. There's terrific cliff walking from Gorran Haven on to Turbot Point, down to Colona Beach and round the neck of the Chapel Point headland, where you begin walking round Mevagissey Bay. It is necessary to follow roads to pass into and through the undistinguished village of Portmellon and continue to Mevagissey, a picturesque fishing village with a lovely harbourside which can get very choked with visitors and cars in summer. Some up-and-down walking sees you round Penare Point and pass the ruins of Portgiskey, soon arriving at Pentewan with its huge caravan park, but from here you face a much more demanding section, with a number of steep climbs and descents. Early on there is a refreshing interlude at Hallane where a gushing stream meets the path in woodland before cascading into the bay, and shortly thereafter you round Black Head with its fine view over Mevagissey Bay.

You now begin the walk round St Austell Bay, enjoying rather easier walking as you pass the wooded cove of Ropehaven, but there follows one of the most savage switchbacks on the whole route. Gentler walking follows as you pass the popular beach of Porthpean and follow the clifftop round the edge of Duporth village, shortly reaching Charlestown (358). Its late eighteenth-century harbour, once extremely important for the export of local ore and china clay and containing two magnificent tall ships, is bordered by lovely old cottages, and was the setting for the BBC's popular *Poldark* series. The market town of St Austell lies just a mile further inland; the town has a long association with the china clay industry, hence the mountainous white spoil heaps, known as the Alps, which can be seen in the neighbourhood.

You continue round Landrion Point and alongside the extensive sands of Carlyon Bay with its massive eyesore of an entertainment centre. Then you have to negotiate, in quick succession, the Par china clay works, the residential sprawl of Par village, and a big caravan park at Par Beach. You return to the cliffs, meeting the Saints Way which crosses inland Cornwall, then drop to Polkerris. Its little assembly of cottages in a narrow valley make a picturesque sight, but the surroundings are sadly dominated by the china clay works and the village can get terribly crowded in summer.

From Polkerris you ascend steeply through woodland and now enjoy a fine cliff walk to Gribbin Head with its distinctive red and white striped daymark, which functions like a lighthouse but in the daytime, built in 1832. Rounding the headland and leaving St Austell Bay behind, you soon reach the delectable Polridmouth Cove, behind which is a serene lake, beautiful woodland and a road leading to Menabilly, a mansion that dates back to 1710 with gardens famous for sub-tropical plants. Menabilly was the home of the novelist Daphne du Maurier for many years and was the Manderley of her famous novel *Rebecca*. An easy field-edge walk is followed by a glorious promenade via the west bank of the river Fowey to the town of Fowey (367.7). The walk goes past the rocky Coombe Hawne, Henry VIII's St Catherine's Castle, and, with its lovely views across the water to Polruan, the pretty Readymoney Cove.

Fowey to Looe (11.7 miles) via Polperro

ENJOY: Lantic Bay, Pencarrow Head, Lansallos Cove, Raphael Cliff, Polperro

Once one of England's busiest ports, Fowey boasts an early fourteenth-century church, streets containing many sixteenth- and seventeenth-century houses, and a lovely harbour that is now a haven for pleasure craft. You cross the river by ferry to reach Polruan, which has a charming waterfront, quaint narrow streets, and a partially ruined square harbour-fort dating back to the sixteenth century. Having climbed out of Polruan you return to the cliffs, rounding Lantic Bay and its twin beaches of Great Lantic and Little Lantic, and stride out on to Pencarrow Head from which there are tremendous views that extend as far back as Dodman Point.

Beyond Pencarrow Head you proceed round Lantivet Bay, passing the gorgeous Lansallos Cove, a paradise of soft golden sands surrounded by formidable rock faces; look out for a rock cut lane used by farmers to facilitate the transport of seaweed from the beach. To your left you can see the tower of the fifteenth-century church of St Ildierna, easily reachable from the coast path and containing some fine sixteenth-century carved bench ends. There is now some tough up-and-down work but the way ahead is clear, the views superb and the cliff scenery majestic, most notably the natural arch on Raphael Cliff; at times the only sounds are those of the sea caressing the rocks and perhaps the warning tones of the bell buoy.

Beyond Raphael Cliff the going is easier, with an exhilarating promenade high above the sea and then a descent to Polperro, a gem of a village, with elegant Georgian houses, the famous House on Props (a house supported on wooden stilts and overhanging a brook), higgledy-piggledy narrow streets of cottages adorned with flowers, and a quite beautiful harbour. Although the coast path from Polperro on to Talland round Downend Point and by Talland Bay can be very crowded in summer, the crowds tend to thin out as you follow the cliffs to the promontory of Hendersick, looking ahead to St George's Island which will remain visible on and off for the next 60 miles. Beyond Hendersick you follow the cliff path round the edge of Portnadler Bay, joining a road near Hannafore Point and following it into West Looe, from which a road bridge takes you over the river Looe into East Looe (379.4). The towns offer contrasting forms of nourishment for the visitor; on my Sunday evening visit in August, West Looe offered a Methodist Church evening praise service with community hymn singing and the route to eternal salvation in the Lord, while East Looe offered hot pasties and clotted cream toffees.

Looe to Plymouth (20.6 miles) via Portwrinkle, Cawsand and Cremyll Ferry

ENJOY: Rame Head, Cawsand, Kingsand, Mount Edgecumbe, Plymouth

Undistinguished walking follows, as you pick your way round the housing developments and holiday complexes at Plaidy and Millendreath, but east of Millendreath the scenery improves with some pleasant woodland, good views back to St George's Island and the added attraction of Murrayton Monkey Sanctuary. You descend again to the twin villages of Seaton and Downderry, then after a stiff climb you continue to Portwrinkle (386.9). Beyond, there is a good climb up to the cliffs, alongside a golf course, but if firing is taking place on the Tregantle ranges you'll then be forced to the left to walk beside the B3247 road. Then, when you reach a fork, you bear right and follow the road round to the point where it arrives at Tregantle Cliff. If no firing is taking place, you may be able to stick to a coast route through the ranges. Both routes reunite at Tregantle Cliff and you now follow a signed path parallel with the road to Sharrow Point, from which you have to walk beside the road. You stay on the road through the straggling village of Freathy and for about a mile beyond it, before bearing right on to a path which snakes its way along the hillside amongst a vast profusion of holiday chalets. It is a relief to fight clear of them and proceed round Polhawn Cove and Queener Point to reach Rame Head. With its chapel ruin standing on cliffs 300 ft above the sea, this is the last major Cornish headland on the route and a significant landmark.

Rounding the headland, you proceed just north of east past Lillery's Cove, with only a short detour being required for you to reach the part-thirteenth-century church of St German, built all of rough slate. You go forward to Penlee Point, where you get your first view of Plymouth Sound, then head up the west side of the Sound and away from the open sea, walking through a predominantly wooded landscape to reach the attractive twin villages of Cawsand and Kingsand with their streets of quaint cottages looking out over Cawsand Bay, an inlet of the Sound. Beyond Kingsand you proceed on round Cawsand Bay to enter Mount Edgcumbe Country Park. The original sixteenth-century house of Mount Edgcumbe was burnt out during the Second World War, but the magnificent grounds survived intact and contain some interesting features including an eighteenth-century folly ruin and a splendid Orangery. You proceed through the grounds to Cremyll for the short journey across the Sound back into Devon and the huge port of Plymouth (400).

Plymouth

Although Plymouth was badly bombed during the Second World War, there is still much to see in the city. If you get to look at nothing else, try to visit the Hoe, a level headland and esplanade overlooking the Sound, with many monuments including a statue of Francis Drake who reputedly played bowls here while waiting for the onslaught of the Spanish Armada, and Smeaton's Tower, an eighteenth-century lighthouse. Elsewhere are ramparts of the seventeenth-century citadel, the Devonport dockyard and naval base, and the ancient Barbican area with its quaint narrow streets. This is easily the largest conurbation on the route, and you will have to turn your hand to all types of urban skills that you will have neglected while tramping through deepest Cornwall, such as walking along pavements rather than the middle of the road and remembering your PIN for the cashpoint.

Plymouth to Noss Mayo (13.8 miles) via Turnchapel

ENJOY: Jennycliff Bay, Wembury Point, Wembury Church, Warren Point

The ferry disembarkation point from Cremyll is Admiral's Hard, from which you walk via Royal William Yard to Firestone Bay and then on to Plymouth Hoe past West Hoe Pier. You continue along the waterfront walkway to the mouth of Sutton Harbour, passing the Mayflower Steps from which the Mayflower set sail in 1620, and the Barbican area with its fine old Tudor houses. You could choose to catch a ferry from the mouth of Sutton Harbour across to Mountbatten Point and the resumption of true coastal walking, but if you're a purist or the ferry isn't running, continue across the entrance of Sutton Harbour by the swing bridge and on to Laira Bridge via Breakwater Hill, with its huge South West Coast path signpost, and through the Cattedown district of the city. Once over the bridge, you proceed to Mountbatten Point past Radford Lake, Hooe Lake, the Clovelly Bay Marina and the Mountbatten Centre. It's certainly a long haul from Sutton Harbour and nobody could blame you for preferring the ferry! You then round the neck of Mountbatten Point, to reach the cliffs above Jennycliff Bay, an eastern inlet of the Sound, with tremendous views back to the city and across the Sound to Rame Head and Mount Edgcumbe.

The route continues down the east side of the Sound, with easy walking on low cliffs and no sense that you are so close to a great city. You pass Bovisand with its marine training school and holiday camp, go round Bovisand Bay to reach the rocky Andurn Point, and proceed past Renney Rocks on your right and the village of Heybrook Bay to your left. Beyond Heybrook Bay you pass round the site of the gunnery ranges of the now defunct *HMS Cambridge*. To your right, as you proceed past the ranges, is a great expanse of rock that tapers off at Wembury Point, and just out to sea beyond the Point is a prominent rock island called Great Mew Stone. Beyond the ranges it is easy walking alongside a rocky shoreline to Wembury church, beautifully situated on the hillside looking out to Blackstone Rocks on the shores of Wembury Bay. The route climbs high above the bay and you enjoy a splendid walk through the bracken with grandstand views to your next obstacle, the river Yealm. You drop down to Warren Point, situated on the riverbank, and a seasonal ferry crossing takes you across to the wooded east bank.

[Alternative route, 10 miles: return to Wembury church and follow minor roads northwards via Wembury village, Knighton and Hollacombe Hill, then turning eastwards via Spriddlestone to reach the A379. Follow this road eastwards through Brixton. A mile or so beyond Brixton turn right on to a road heading via Puslinch to the B3186. Turn right on to this road then first left via Bridgend and Noss Mayo to rejoin the route.]

The route turns right but by going left you soon reach the pretty village of Noss Mayo (413.8), situated alongside a tributary of the Yealm, looking across to Newton Ferrers on the other side. It is popular with the boating and fishing fraternity, its relaxed atmosphere epitomised by a notice I saw displayed in large letters in the village that read, 'Old fishermen never die – they only smell that way'.

Noss Mayo to Bigbury-on-Sea (13.2 miles) via River Erme

ENJOY: Mouthstone Point, Church of St Peter the Poor Fisherman, St Anchorite's Rock, Bugle Hole, Erme Estuary, Muxham Point, Ayrmer Cove

From the east bank of the river, the Coast Path proceeds along a track well above the Yealm, following it south-westwards to Mouthstone Point where the river flows into Wembury Bay, and then swinging south-eastwards again to continue beside the open sea. Having paused for a moment above Mouthstone Point to enjoy superb views back to Rame Head, you proceed on along a wide cliff path, which is in fact a nineteenth-century carriage drive cut by Lord Revelstoke, a local landowner. Enjoying fine views ahead across Bigbury Bay to Bolt Tail, the next major headland, you go on past Stoke Point and follow the edge of a strip of woodland to reach Stoke, where it is worth detouring down a steep hill to view the ruined fourteenth-century church of St Peter the Poor Fisherman.

Beyond Stoke the walking gets tougher, with a particularly steep descent and climb to St Anchorite's Rock, set impressively on a hilltop some way back from the cliff edge. From the Rock there is another big drop to the delightful inlet at Bugle Hole with a jumble of rocks set against steep gorse-clad cliffs, then follows a steady climb back on to the cliffs. The view up the Erme estuary is quite magnificent. You descend to Mothecombe Beach, then after a climb through woodland on Owen's Hill, you walk down to a slipway that provides the river crossing point to get over to Wonwell Beach. No ferry is available, and it is necessary for you to wade across the river, which you can do safely up to one hour either side of low water. Tide times are widely advertised enabling you to plan your arrival time carefully, but if you have time to spare you could detour to the pretty village of Mothecombe where refreshments may be available.

[Alternative route if the tides are unfavourable, 7 miles: proceed northwards along minor roads from Mothecombe via Holbeton to Ford, then follow a lane past Hole Farm to a footpath that heads north-eastwards, just west of Flete, to reach the A379. Turn right to follow the A379 over the Erme at Sequer's Bridge. Shortly beyond the bridge turn right on to a minor road heading southwards to Great Torr. Turn right at Great Torr on to a lane that heads south-westwards to Wonwell Court, from which a path runs to Wonwell Beach.]

Assuming you complete the crossing safely, you arrive on Wonwell Beach and stride confidently on past Muxham Point, giving you a lovely view back up the Erme, then embark on a very tough but exhilarating cliff walk to Challaborough. There is a good deal of up-and-down work but the rewards are unforgettable vistas of coves, rocks and often sheer cliff faces, including the shiny Dartmouth slate at Ayrmer Cove, as well as splendid views out across Bigbury Bay to Burgh Island. You drop to the popular holiday village of Challaborough, immediately beyond which is the little town of Bigbury-on-Sea (427). It is certainly worth detouring to Burgh Island, reachable across the sands from Bigbury-on-Sea at low tide and by sea tractor at high tide, and offering fine views from its hilltop.

Bigbury-on-Sea to Salcombe (13.5 miles) via Hope Cove

ENJOY: Inner Hope, Bolt Tail, Bolberry Down, Soar Mill Cove, Bolt Head, Sharp Tor, Overbecks, Salcombe

The Coast Path now leaves Bigbury Bay and begins wandering up the west side of the Avon estuary. A rather fiddly climb out of Bigbury-on-Sea beside the B3392 gives a fine view across the estuary, and you then follow the Avon inland, descending to the hamlet of Cockleridge. Just beyond Cockleridge you go down to the riverbank for a seasonal ferry crossing to Bantham on the opposite bank. At low tide and in calm conditions it is possible to wade across the river with extreme care, but this is not recommended.

[Alternative route, 7 miles: return to the B3392, following it north-eastwards to the inland village of Bigbury, turning right along a tidal road that follows the bank of the Avon to Aveton Gifford. Turn right on to the A379 here, cross the river then immediately turn right on to a lane heading for Stadbury Farm. A footpath then takes you south-westwards beside the Avon to Bantham.]

Having reached Bantham you may either go right out to Hams End, where you can gaze across a wide expanse of sand to the mouth of the Avon, or cut across the neck of this little headland. The Coast Path, now following Bigbury Bay again, then heads south-eastwards beside Thurlestone golf course, and round an inlet of the bay, with some large hotels dominating the scene, although things improve as you continue past Beacon Point and Woolman Point. Soon you get to the cosy sandy beach of Hope Cove, guarded by impressive outcrops of rock, while immediately adjacent are the twin villages of Outer Hope and Inner Hope. From Inner Hope, a particularly lovely village with a square of thatched whitewashed cottages and a backcloth of wooded hills, there is a brisk climb to Bolt Tail, which offers stunning views across Bigbury Bay and right back to Rame Head and beyond.

You now enjoy a magnificent cliff walk south-eastwards, passing another stunning viewpoint at Bolberry Down, and descending to Soar Mill Cove, an exquisite narrow inlet with a golden sandy beach, guarded by steep clifftops and rocky outcrops. After regaining the height lost, it is a marvellous walk on to Bolt Head along gorse and bracken-clad hillsides and down a grassy gully, and from Bolt Head, an important wartime lookout point with good views across to Prawle Point, there is quite an exciting rocky scramble round Starehole Bay to Sharp Tor. Called the Courtenay Way, it was cut in the nineteenth-century to provide ease of access for visitors to Bolt Tail. From Sharp Tor you continue to chart a precarious course along the side of steep-faced cliffs, now following the west side of the Kingsbridge estuary, passing the magnificent gardens of Overbecks then following roads into Salcombe (440.5). Originally a shipbuilding town with a castle built by Henry VIII, it is now a somewhat exclusive yachting and boating centre with little sympathy towards long-distance hikers. Indeed my February request of various bed and breakfasts for a one-night August stay as a Coast Path walker could scarcely have been met with more contempt if I had said I was a Colorado beetle seeking admission to a potato farmers' convention.

Salcombe to Stoke Fleming (19.8 miles) via Beesands and Torcross

ENJOY: Gammon Head, Maceley's Cove, Prawle Point, Start Point

An all-year ferry takes you from Salcombe to East Portlemouth, and there ensues a brief road walk to Mill Bay before an excellent cliff walk to Prawle Point, initially following the east bank of the estuary before proceeding more resolutely eastwards with the sea to your right. A narrow but unmistakable path weaves its way along the cliffs, with a dramatic drop to the sea on one side, and impressive rocky outcrops on the other; rocks along this section of coast include Pig's Nose, Ham Stone and Gammon Head! Beyond Gammon Head there is an almost sheer drop to Maceley's Cove, which like Soar Mill Cove is a lovely golden carpet standing between two towering columns of rock. You go on to Prawle Point, the southernmost headland in Devon, providing tremendous views back to Bolt Head and forward to Start Point, then beyond the headland you enjoy rather easier walking, much of it along field-edge paths close to the shore round Langerstone Point and beside Lannacombe Bay.

However, having passed Lannacombe Beach there is a much more strenuous walk to Start Point along a narrow ledge through the crags, before the lighthouse road allows an easier passage round the great schist outcrops of the headland to the Point itself. From here there are fine views across Start Bay which you will follow for some miles. You go back down the lighthouse road then descend steeply to sea level to reach Hallsands, consisting of a holiday complex and an old village that was ruined when, as a result of nearby shingle-dredging a century ago, it lost its natural sea defences and was exposed to the elements. It is certainly worth detouring to visit the ruined houses.

You continue past Tinsey Head and forward to the straggling village of Beesands, from which it is easy walking past the lake of Widdicombe Ley and Beesands Quarry to reach the busy and useful village of Torcross. There follows a walk along a shingle path beside Slapton Sands, used in 1943 for D-Day preparations by USA troops, but there is an inland alternative consisting of a path alongside the waters of Slapton Ley, a flourishing nature reserve. However, beyond Strete Gate you are forced away from the sea, there being no coast route available, using a number of lanes on the inland side of the A379 via Strete and Blackpool to Stoke Fleming (460.3). With your negotiation of Pig's Nose and Gammon Head still fresh in the memory, and the thought that you are in the area of Devon known as South Hams, you could be forgiven for refusing any more than a token rasher of bacon with your breakfast next morning.

Stoke Fleming to Paignton (20.3 miles) via Dartmouth

ENJOY: Dartmouth, Coleton Fishacre, Berry Head, Brixham

Just before Little Dartmouth you turn right off the road to return to the coast, and enjoy a good cliff walk past Combe Point and Compass Cove to the mouth of the river Dart at Blackstone Point, where there is a footbridge over a dramatic sea-washed gully. There is now a pleasant walk up the west side of the Dart, passing the ruins of the fifteenth-century Dartmouth Castle and its neighbouring church of St Petrox with lovely views over the estuary. Road walking then takes you into Dartmouth (463.3). Dartmouth, famous for its naval college, is a lovely town and boating resort, with many fine old buildings including a restored row of seventeenth-century houses on granite pillars known as the Butterwalk.

The Coast Path uses the year-round ferry to Kingswear to cross the Dart, then beyond Kingswear comes one of the toughest sections of all. The up-and-down walking begins almost at once as you proceed through a wooded landscape by the east side of the Dart, enjoying fine views across to the castle, to reach the Dart's real mouth at Inner Froward Point with its Second World War lookout buildings. Having enjoyed the view to Start Point you continue on past Outer Froward Point and Pudcombe Cove, walking immediately below the beautiful gardens and woodland of Coleton Fishacre but still high above the sea. From here to Sharkham Point via Scabbacombe Head and Crabrock Point the walking is often very severe, with particularly tough ascents from the intervening Scabbacombe Sands and Man Sands, and some awkward descents which can be very slippery in wet weather. Beyond Sharkham Point the walk out to Berry Head round St Mary's Bay is marginally easier but quite fiddly, and it is good to reach the headland with its country park, lighthouse and Napoleonic War fort.

Now you look out across Tor Bay, and its string of seaside resorts dominated by Torquay on the Bay's north side. You descend from Berry Head to sea level and soon arrive in Brixham (474), consisting of an early Victorian town centre and a fishing harbour where there are a number of early nineteenth-century houses. A stone on the quayside commemorates the landing of William of Orange here in 1688. You proceed past Churston Cove and Fishcombe Point and through woodland as far as Elberry Cove, then go round Churston Point to arrive at Broad Sands, but are then forced inland by the Torbay and Dartmouth railway, proceeding beside the line along the edge of Goodrington and as far as Goodrington Sands. You walk alongside the sands then climb briskly to Roundham Head before descending to the promenade of the very popular resort of Paignton (480.6).

After 20 miles you may feel you've done enough, so could be forgiven for making this your night stop, but having gained your second wind you may fancy a night out among the bright lights of Torquay, easily reachable by road from Paignton. This is Devon's largest resort, created largely in the nineteenth century, and with its stuccoed villas and sub-tropical trees and flowers, the nearest thing to a French Riviera resort in Britain. Many parts of the town retain a Victorian character but all the unsubtle trappings of a modern resort are there. On the Saturday night I was there in August, the town was packed with diners and clubbers, some dressed to kill in short skirts and high boots, others happy to amble the streets in vest tops, shorts and sandals. Wherever you stay around Torquay, you must just hope that the hotel you have chosen does not come complete with a waiter who responds to your inquiries with the single word '*Que?*' and a manager who goosesteps into the foyer and urges you not to mention the war.

Paignton to Teignmouth (12.8 miles) via Babbacombe

ENJOY: Hope's Nose, Babbacombe Bay, the Ness

You go forward from Paignton past Torquay Harbour. Fiddly but not unpleasant walking takes you via Daddyhole Cove and Meadfoot Beach away from the centre of the town, with good views across the bay to Berry Head, from which you go forward to the extraordinary piece of headland known as Hope's Nose at the very end of Tor Bay. Rounding the headland, you now begin the walk alongside Babbacombe Bay, some woodland walking taking you past Black Head to Anstey's Cove. A climb onto Walls Hill is followed by a descent to the beaches of Babbacombe and Oddicombe, beyond which you pass Petit Tor Point and follow a principally wooded course with limited sea views past Watcombe to Maidencombe. You are, however, at last emerging from the outskirts of Torquay.

The walk from Maidencombe to Shaldon is very tough, with a number of severe climbs and descents, and the hilltop views are often partially obstructed by trees, but the last rise brings a superb view to the river Teign and beyond, and a rapid descent from here brings you to the Ness, a tall tree-clad outcrop of sandstone at the mouth of the river. It is then a short walk to Shaldon from where a ferry journey takes you across the water to Teignmouth (493.4), one of Devon's oldest seaside resorts with many buildings dating back to the Georgian and early Victorian eras. Trivia buffs may care to note that the town was the birthplace, in 1791, of Charles

Babbage, regarded by some as the father of the computer; and, in 1000, of Elias Parish Alvars, known as the 'King of Harpists'.

Teignmouth to Exmouth (19 miles) via Dawlish

ENJOY: Powderham Park, Powderham Church, Topsham

From here to Holcombe you follow the sea wall, with the railway immediately adjoining it on the landward side. The railway, part of the London–Penzance line, is one of the most spectacular pieces of line in the country, with massive railway tunnels cut into the rocks. At high tide the sea wall is unusable and you must proceed inland along paths and then by the A379 to Holcombe. The main route leaves the sea wall just outside Holcombe and joins up with the other way in the village, and you then remain on the landward side of the railway, initially heading seawards to proceed parallel with it before retreating slightly inland on the approach to Dawlish. You join a minor metalled road and follow it to the A379, bearing right into a park and following the sandstone cliff edge before descending on a zigzag path and arriving by the boat cove near Dawlish town centre. Partly Regency in character, Dawlish was a favourite town of Jane Austen, and Dickens made it Nicholas Nickleby's birthplace.

An easy walk along the sea wall once more – or along the landward side of the railway at high tide – takes you to Dawlish Warren which boasts a large nature reserve but also a profusion of caravans and chalets. There you leave the sea wall and begin walking up the west bank of the Exe estuary, following a metalled road through the village and then on via Eastdon and Cockwood. Just beyond Cockwood you pick up the A379 which takes you on to Starcross, famous for its pumping house that formed part of Brunel's ill-fated Atmospheric Railway. At Starcross you can catch a seasonal ferry across the Exe to Exmouth where the true coastal walk resumes, but at other times it is necessary to continue up the side of the Exe to Topsham to cross the river there.

You leave the A379 to proceed along a minor road, with the railway to your immediate right and the lovely Powderham Park on your left, boasting a heronry and a castle that has been the home of the Earls of Devon since 1390. Having passed Powderham Church the road swings sharply left, but you go straight ahead on a track, cross the railway with extreme care and strike out on a path that continues alongside the estuary, and then beside the Exeter Canal which is separated from the estuary by an area known as West Mud. Soon you reach the ferry and use it to cross the estuary to Topsham.

[Alternative route if the ferry is unavailable, 4 miles: retrace your steps briefly and follow a minor road westwards to reach the A379 just east of Exminster, following it over the estuary to Countess Wear, turn right here and follow the road to Topsham.]

Topsham, for a long time an important port serving the nearby and easily accessible cathedral city of Exeter, is a pretty village with graceful Georgian houses and a genteel air; I remember stopping here for a cream tea and being asked to choose from a jam list!

In order to walk from Topsham to Exmouth, follow a minor road eastwards out of Topsham to Marsh Barton, joining a footpath and then a lane to bring you to the A376 at Ebford. Turn right on to the A376 and follow it through Exton, then beyond the Royal Marines' barracks, turn right down a minor road to Lympstone, a pretty village of thatched cottages and Regency villas and once a fishing port from which boats sailed as far as Greenland. At Lympstone you can then follow the East Devon Way, which hugs the railway on one side and the estuary sands on the other, soon bringing you into Exmouth (512.4). You have now negotiated your final river obstacle of the route.

Exmouth to Beer (19.4 miles) via Sidmouth

ENJOY: Ladram Bay, Peak Hill, Sidmouth, Weston Cliff, Branscombe, Hooken Cliffs

Exmouth, for a time the home of Lady Nelson, is the oldest resort in Devon, renowned for its red sandstone cliffs and bathing beaches, with buildings dating back to the eighteenth century. Follow the town's waterfront to get level with the very distinctive Maer Rocks out to sea; at the car park by Foxholes Hill, pick up a signed path heading for Budleigh Salterton ascending to the High Land of Orcombe, an area of grass above the beach. You proceed eastwards, ascend and then drop to Sandy Bay with its beautiful golden beach, and pass through an extensive holiday park before going forward to the triangulation point and viewpoint of West Down Beacon. You then descend to Budleigh Salterton, a pleasant resort with a number of eighteenth-century houses. Just beyond the town you detour briefly inland to cross the Otter estuary, beyond which it is easy walking along low clifftops past Brandy Head and Smallstones Point to Ladram Bay, a small inlet with striking sandstone stacks rising impressively behind.

There is then a climb to High Peak with its Iron Age hill fort, and soon after that you pass the tremendous viewpoint of Peak Hill, at just over 500 ft above the sea. There follows a very steep descent to Sidmouth (527), a town of fine Regency and Victorian buildings, and a tough ascent out of the town on to Salcombe Hill Cliff. This is followed by a big drop to Salcombe Mouth, another big climb to Dunscombe Cliffs, a plunge right down to the beach at Weston Mouth, and a massive ascent to Weston Cliff with tremendous views that extend back to Sidmouth and Budleigh Salterton and across large areas of Devon countryside. There is temporary respite with a level walk along Coxe's Cliff, and you briefly lose sight of the sea as you proceed through woodland just south of the lovely village of Branscombe. Easily reachable from the route, it contains thatched cottages, a thatched smithy that has been working since the fifteeenth century, and St Winifred's Church with a Norman tower and three-decker pulpit. You drop down to the sea again at the trippery Branscombe Mouth, then to reach Beer, the next village, you have a choice of routes. You may follow the top of Hooken Cliffs, offering superb views as far ahead as Portland Bill, or take the path through the undercliff area, formed as a result of a landslip in 1790, and now a fine centre of insect, butterfly and plant life. Both routes unite at Beer Head, the most westerly chalk headland in the country, from which it is a straightforward descent to the seaside village of Beer (531.8). A name like that could not fail to cheer a thirsty walker on a hot day.

Beer to West Bay (18 miles) via Seaton and Lyme Regis

ENJOY: Axmouth, Lyme Regis, Golden Cap, Bridport

From Beer you briefly return to the cliffs but soon drop down to the inlet of Seaton Hole and then, depending on the tide, follow the beach or a road on to the bustling resort of Seaton. You use the B3172 to cross the river Axe – a detour up this road brings you to the lovely thatched village of Axmouth with a church containing medieval wall paintings – then branch off along a track which skirts the inland side of a golf course, soon turning seawards on to Haven Cliff. You then proceed along a path through an undercliff created on Christmas Eve 1839 by a slip of an estimated eight million tons of rock. Virtually this entire walk is through dense woodland, and although you will not get lost, there are no landmarks to tell you where you are, and it can feel claustrophobic with very restricted sea views through the veritable jungle.

Emerging from the woods, you leave Devon and enter Dorset, and almost immediately arrive in Lyme Regis (540.4). Once an important port – Edward I used its harbour during his wars against the French and a number of ships departed the harbour to fight the Armada in 1588 – it is now a popular resort with strong literary associations.

Having enjoyed a stroll along the Cobb, a massive breakwater sheltering the harbour, and ambled along the pretty narrow streets of craft shops and cafes, you head for Charmouth, forced now well inland as a result of serious coastal erosion; the route is subject to change, so follow signposting and local guidance. You pass Charmouth and then proceed on to the cliffs again, further cliffslips having created a no-man's land of vegetation and rock between you and the sea, and ascend to Golden Cap, at 626 ft the highest cliff on the south coast. There is a steep descent to Seatown, a big climb to another excellent viewpoint at Thorncombe Beacon, a further drop to the sea at Eype's Mouth, then yet another ascent to West Cliff before a drop to West Bay (549.8). It is a two-mile walk from here to the attractive town of Bridport with its fine Georgian buildings and fifteenth-century almshouses; for centuries it has thrived on the rope-making industry, and the pavements used to be 'rope-walks' that were laid out for twisting and drying the cord and twine. West Bay itself comes as something of an anticlimax so soon after the timeless charm of Lyme Regis, with many of the less welcome concessions to the holiday industry; Meryl Streep's brooding stares and wistful gazes as the French Lieutenant's Woman, so effective when set against the Dorset coastline and the restless sea immediately beyond, would not carry quite the same gravitas if behind her stood nothing more stern and uncompromising than a mobile doughnut stand.

West Bay to Weymouth (22.5 miles; Portland loop route adds 13.1 miles) via Abbotsbury

ENJOY: Burton Bradstock, Chesil Beach, the Fleet, Abbotsbury, Weymouth

This is a very long section, but it is mostly easy walking and could be broken at the beautiful village of Abbotsbury. In any case it is effectively two sections in one, for you will certainly need an extra day for the loop route.

You climb steeply from West Bay on to East Cliff, then are forced inland, descending to cross the river Bride at Burton Freshwater, a short detour here bringing you to Burton Bradstock, a lovely village with 300-year-old thatched cottages and a fourteenth-century parish church. The route ascends on to Burton Cliff, then drops to Cogden Beach, where you begin a long walk by the shoreline. Progress is initially reasonably good, as you keep to the landward side of a strip of water named Burton Mere, but then you are forced on to the shingle of what is known as Chesil Beach, arriving soon at West Bexington. (Here an inland alternative to Osmington Mills begins, described later.) After some more shingle walking you join a surfaced lane that brings you to within half a mile or so of the western end of the Fleet. This is a lagoon separating the mainland from the long, thin, blue-clay reef of Chesil Beach whose massive shingle wall, in places 35 ft high and 150 yd wide, consists of pebbles thrown up by the stormy seas and increasing in size from west to east. It extends as far as Portland and although it could be followed, it is an extremely tough walk, especially in bad weather.

The official Coast Path veers to the landward side of the Fleet, contouring Chapel Hill topped by the fifteenth-century chapel of St Catherine, and skirting Abbotsbury (559) with its lovely thatched cottages, massive tithe barn built on the site of an eleventh-century abbey, and swannery which is seen at its best during the hatching season in late spring. There is a clearly-marked detour should you wish to visit the village. East of Abbotsbury you are forced well inland even of the Fleet, proceeding through heavily farmed land to pass over Merry Hill then swinging southwards past Wyke Wood to return to the Fleet at Rodden Hive. Progress is now very easy as you follow a clear level path beside the Fleet, incorporating numerous inlets and mini headlands, but always separated from the open sea by the great shingle wall of Chesil Beach. There may be a brief inland diversion at Tidmoor Point if there is firing on the Chickerell rifle range. You pass the Royal Engineers camp and, with views to the isle of Portland on your right and the suburbs of Weymouth now encroaching to your left, you proceed to Ferry Bridge, where you cross the causeway linking Weymouth and Portland.

It is at Ferry Bridge that you are able to pick up the Portland loop route, now part of the South West Coast Path. It merits a day's walk of its own, assuming you decide to do it; note that the centre and principal amenities of Weymouth are a couple of miles beyond Ferry Bridge so one option might be to continue into Weymouth then return to the loop route by bus next day. You start by crossing the causeway on to the island, immediately arriving at Fortuneswell. It is recommended that you tackle the walk in a clockwise direction, so that you swing north-east to Portland Castle, a fortress built by Henry VIII, before veering south-east. Initially the walking, past the houses of Fortuneswell and a Young Offender Institution, is unexciting, but shortly you arrive at Church Ope Cove where you join the coast. Nearby is the tiny thatched Portland Museum, which was the setting of the home of the heroine in Hardy's *The Well Beloved*. From the cove you proceed south-westwards towards Portland Bill along a rugged undercliff path, past some quarry workings, then along a road and low cliffs, admiring, on a clear day, the coastline to the east towards Lulworth Cove and St Aldhelm's Head. You proceed round the end of the headland, past the lighthouse and Pulpit Rock, then head just east of north along a splendid clifftop path, with tremendous views across Lyme Bay, to arrive at Fortuneswell again and go forward to return to the causeway and be reunited with the main route.

Back on the main route, you swing from south-east to north-east and follow a rather fiddly course along a mixture of roads, greens and narrow paths snaking between houses and the sea to enter Weymouth (585.4, mileages now include the Portland loop).

Weymouth

Weymouth is a pleasant seaside town with a large sandy beach, an attractive harbour, and many fine old buildings including Georgian and early Victorian houses and also Tudor cottages, and as you approach the harbour you will pass the impressive Nothe Fort, which was built as a defence against Napoleon. King George III took a great liking to Weymouth and it was here in 1789 that he became the first reigning monarch to bathe in the sea from a bathing machine, a device pioneered in the town in 1763. His immersion, to the sound of a band playing God Save The King, was apparently greeted 'with a mixture of awe and admiration'!

Weymouth to Lulworth Cove (11.9 miles) via Osmington Mills

ENJOY: White Nothe, Swyre Head, Hambury Tout, Durdle Door, Lulworth Cove

This is a short section but much tougher than the preceding one. Beyond Nothe Fort you turn sharp left down to the harbourside to cross the water by means of the Town Bridge, then follow the harbour seawards again and return to the seafront at the Esplanade. You leave the town, following Weymouth Bay beside the A353 coast road which you leave at Overcombe, following Furzy Cliff past Bowleaze Cove and then striking out to Redcliff Point. Pleasant and undemanding cliff walking takes you on to Osmington Mills (where the inland alternative from West Bexington – see below – rejoins the main route). Thirsty walkers will be delighted to note that the Coast Path here passes right through a pub garden! You continue along gentle cliffs to Ringstead Bay, passing close to the site of what is now the deserted village of Ringstead, the ruin of which, according to legend, was brought about by French pirates.

At Ringstead Bay the walking gets a lot tougher, with a big climb to the coastguard cottages of White Nothe, at 548 ft the highest point attained since Golden Cap. From here to Lulworth the scenery is truly magnificent, the Coast Path following the tops of sheer limestone cliffs high above the sea with some very steep climbs and descents, and tremendous viewpoints from the summits of Swyre Head and Hambury Tout. Between these two hilltops there is a depression from which you have a perfect view of Durdle Door, a natural arch of limestone and one of the most photographed coastal features in the country. A long descent from Hambury Tout brings you to Lulworth (597.3), a popular village of attractive cottages and shops built on the edge of Lulworth Cove, a quite remarkable natural inlet with two arms of Portland and Purbeck stone almost encircling the water. It is here that, if you have made the right arrangements, you now have the enticing prospect of a quite fantastic seven-mile coast walk to Kimmeridge. However, owing to Army activity, this walk is only usually available at weekends and holiday periods (details are posted on the website: simply doing a Google search under 'Lulworth Firing Ranges' will access them), and outside those times you will be forced to take a very tame inland walk instead. The most direct alternative, albeit still entailing an extra six miles or so, is to follow the B3070 via West Lulworth, Lulworth Camp and East Lulworth to West Holme, turning right on to a road that heads past East Holme to Stoborough, turning right again to follow a road southwards to Creech, and following metalled roads south-westwards and south-eastwards through Steeple to reach Kimmeridge. Worse, the B3070 is sometimes closed beyond East Lulworth, in which case the only way round is north-westwards along roads to Coombe Keynes and Wool, where you can pick up a road heading eastwards via East Stoke to West Holme. Or you could pick up a taxi. Whatever alternative you choose, you'll no doubt be cursing the vital day you wasted back in Penzance trying to find a shop that stocked your preferred brand of insect repellent.

INLAND ALTERNATIVE: West Bexington to Osmington Mills (17 miles, not used in the cumulative mileage reckoning) via Upwey

ENJOY: Limekiln Hill, Abbotsbury Castle, Hell Stone, Hardy Monument, Corton Down, Maiden Castle, Bincombe Down, Chalbury, West Hill

The inland alternative leaves the coast at West Bexington to follow a portion of the South Dorset Ridgeway, a prehistoric route with one of the biggest concentration of round barrows (burial mounds) in Britain. You proceed inland up West Bexington village street then steeply uphill to meet the B3157 on Limekiln Hill, turning right to follow the road. You pass an old limekiln that has been restored by the National Trust, then go forward to the Iron Age hill fort of Abbotsbury Castle. Leaving the B3157, the route continues eastwards across White Hill, immediately above Abbotsbury, then after crossing a metalled road, goes past a stone circle on to Portesham Hill. You cross another metalled road and soon reach the restored Neolithic (pre-Bronze Age) Hell Stone burial chamber, then enter an area of woodland and swing north-eastwards to arrive at the Hardy Monument. Built in 1844, this is named not after the novelist Thomas Hardy, but Admiral Thomas Hardy, Nelson's flag-captain at Trafalgar, and immortalised in Nelson's reputed last words, 'Kismet, Hardy' or as some are wont to say, 'Kiss me, Hardy!' The views from the monument are tremendous, extending right out to Weymouth and the sea beyond. It is then an easy walk south-eastwards on a good path over Bronkham Hill and Corton Down, passing a massive succession of Bronze Age (2200–650 BC) round barrows and with fine views to Maiden Castle to the left. First occupied 4,000 years ago, and fortified in the Iron Age, Maiden Castle is one of the largest earthwork fortifications in Europe, its perimeter extending more than two miles and its terraced ramparts rising to more than 80 ft.

From here you go forward to cross the B3159 just north of Upwey, where there's a useful railway station, then swing southwards on a lane parallel with the A354 Dorchester–Weymouth road, soon crossing this and proceeding eastwards over Bincombe Down. Swinging southwards, you drop steeply to the pretty village of Bincombe, then head south-eastwards to climb on to Green Hill, passing just north of the hill fort of Chalbury. From this point you veer north-eastwards, climbing steadily to West Hill which again is dotted with round barrows, then go south-eastwards again, dropping steeply down towards Osmington. You can now look back on West Hill and see a white horse cut into the hillside in recognition of the many visits to the area made by George III during his reign. The route joins a lane which soon reaches the pleasant thatched village of Osmington, crosses the A353 and takes a gentle climb and descent through fields, returning to the sea at Osmington Mills. Here the inland alternative ends. Certainly it will have made a change from coastal walking.

Lulworth to Winspit for Worth Matravers (16.1 miles) via Kimmeridge

ENJOY: Fossil Forest, Mupe Rocks, Bindon Hill, Arish Mell, Flower's Barrow, Worbarrow Tout, Tyneham, Tyneham Cap, Kimmeridge Ledges, Egmont Bight, St Aldhelm's Head, St Aldhelm's Chapel

Assuming the coastal route is open east of Lulworth Cove, you climb away from the cove, with tremendous views back down to it, and descend to the Fossil Forest which consists of lumps of rock which contained tree stumps from a forest that existed well over 100 million years ago. Here, fortunate walkers will pass through the gates into the restricted zone. The route through the area is guarded by yellow boundary posts and frequent warning signs, but despite this is totally unspoilt by development, and the absence of farming, owing to the military activity, has produced a wilderness landscape that is most unusual on the south coast of England. Beyond Fossil Forest and the grotesque formations of Mupe Rocks, there is a massive climb round Mupe Bay on to Bindon Hill with awesome sheer chalk cliffs.

You drop to the tiny cove of Arish Mell, steep chalk cliffs zealously guarding its entrance, then have another back-breaking climb to the Iron Age hill fort at Flower's Barrow and a huge drop to Worbarrow Tout, from which there are tremendous views back across Worbarrow Bay to Bindon Hill. There is then another big climb on to Gad Cliff, where you should detour to Tyneham. Having been evacuated in 1943 as part of the Allied invasion plans, the villagers never returned, and Tyneham is effectively a ghost village with ruined houses adjacent to a pretty green and pond, although the church is lovingly maintained and the school has been furnished to look just as it did before the evacuation. A high level walk takes you from Gad Cliff on to the tremendous viewpoint of Tyneham Cap, from which you begin descending towards Kimmeridge Bay. You go round the more modest headland of Broad Bench and pass the Kimmeridge oil well, leaving the restricted area and rounding Kimmeridge Bay, passing close to the tiny grey limestone village of Kimmeridge. From there you go past the ornate and recently repositioned Clavel Tower, built in 1820 as a folly and later used as a coastguard lookout, and some excellent walking follows on cliffs known as Kimmeridge Ledges, the Coast Path proceeding high above the sea and often perilously close to sheer drops.

You pass Rope Lake Head and the delightful waterfall and woodland at Egmont Bight, then climb steeply to the limestone peak of Houns-tout Cliff. Cliff slips have resulted in the diversion of the coast route away from the sea round Chapman's Pool and into the valley of Hill Bottom instead, but having risen from Hill Bottom you swing southwards to follow parallel with the coastline once more, negotiating a tough descent and climb at Emmett's Hill and going forward to St Aldhelm's or St Alban's Head, some 354 ft above the sea. Before you round the headland it is worth detouring to visit the square twelfth-century St Aldhelm's Chapel, and pausing to admire magnificent views which can extend as far as Portland. Now you proceed north-eastwards, initially on the limestone cliffs but then dropping to the combe at Winspit, from where it is an easy detour to the pretty village of Worth Matravers (613.4) with cottages of Purbeck stone and a church with some fine Norman features.

Worth Matravers to South Haven Point ferry terminal (15.1 miles) via Swanage

ENJOY: Tilly Whim Caves, Durlston Head, Durlston Castle, Swanage, Handfast Point, Old Harry, Studland

Beyond Winspit, you return to the cliffs, passing plenteous evidence of quarrying activity as you proceed on via Seacombe Cliff towards Durlston Head. At Dancing Ledges a swimming pool was cut into the limestone slabs by quarrymen almost a century ago, and further on you meet the Tilly Whim Caves, consisting of large black holes in the steep limestone cliff face. As you approach Durlston Head you enter Durlston Country Park, passing Anvil Point with its lighthouse, visitor centre and folly known as Durlston Castle, built around 1890 by one George Burt. You round Durlston Head, the cliffs hereabouts hosting a wide variety of seabirds, then descend to Peveril Point with its coastguard station and enter Swanage (621). It is a pleasant resort, the most striking architectural feature being the town hall, another gift of George Burt and worth visiting for its remarkable seventeenth-century façade, an example of the City of London style of the period which Pevsner curtly describes as 'overwhelmingly undisciplined!' Then again, Swanage is a holiday resort after all…

From Swanage you return to the cliffs, climbing on to Ballard Down with its five small bowl barrows – circular Bronze Age burial mounds – and enjoying a splendid walk along the tops of the virtually sheer chalk cliffs. Soon you reach the Foreland, also known as Handfast Point, where you look down on the dramatic assortment of crumbling chalk stacks of Old Harry rising from the water. If you feel sufficiently daring you can follow a perilous course along a narrow ridge towards the first of them, but it would be a pity to slip to your grief so close to the finishing line! Then you swing westwards and descend on a wide track, enjoying fine views to Bournemouth and beyond, soon arriving at the pretty village of Studland, with a lovely little Norman church and popular pub. The last two and a half mile stretch of the national trail consists of a walk either along the beach or through the dunes beside Studland Bay, keeping the Studland Nature Reserve to your left. Part of the sands bordering Studland Bay has been designated a nudist beach, and in summer you may feel somewhat overdressed in your T-shirt and shorts. You continue on the sands round Shell Bay to arrive at the ferry terminal at South Haven Point, where the official Coast Path ends (628.5).

The Sandbanks chain ferry will convey you from here across the mouth of Poole Harbour for a long walk or interminable bus ride into the centre of Bournemouth, where you will merge into the holiday crowds with no prizes for what you have done and nobody to even recognise what, if you have walked it all, is a truly stupendous achievement. If you have come to love the coastline and the constant presence of the sea, perhaps the best reward you could give yourself is a relaxing week's beach holiday where you can sit contentedly on your hotel veranda knowing that the nearest refreshment is no longer an excruciating thirty-minute tramp away over shingle or the nearest accommodation a body-battering 12 steep-sided combes away.

The Pembrokeshire Coast Path

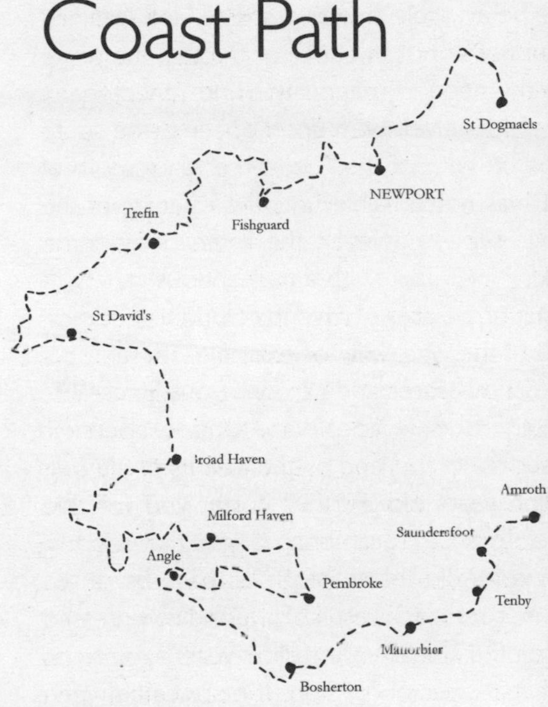

Designation: National trail.
Length: 176.5 miles.
Start: St Dogmaels, Ceredigion.
Finish: Amroth, near Saundersfoot, Pembrokeshire.
Nature: A walk along the often rugged and spectacular coastline of the Welsh county of Pembrokeshire.
Difficulty rating: Moderate to strenuous.
Average time of completion: 13–15 days.

HIGHLIGHTS OF THIS WALK:

- **Pen yr Afr**
- **Witches Cauldron**
- **Dinas Head**
- **Strumble Head**
- **St David's Head**
- **St David's**
- **Newgale Sands**
- **Pembroke**
- **Green Bridge of Wales**
- **Elegug Stacks**
- **Huntsman's Leap**
- **St Govan's Chapel**
- **Skrinkle Haven**
- **Tenby**

The Pembrokeshire coastline has always been regarded as an area of great historic and scenic interest. In 1952 it was designated as a National Park, and a suggestion was made that a continuous path along the coastline be available to walkers. The idea received enthusiastic support, but it was not until May 1970 that the route opened, largely due to the need for negotiation with landowners, who were not always cooperative. Even upon opening, the route was not continuous; the crossing of the Cleddau estuary south of Milford Haven on foot was not possible until the opening of the Cleddau Bridge in 1975. Now, however, the route offers some of the best coastal walking in Britain, with a tremendous variety of coastal scenery as a result of the area's rich and colourful geological past. The southern end of the walk will, for example, reveal rocks of old red sandstone, coal measures and carboniferous limestone; those were all sedimentary rocks, legacies of the Upper Palaeozoic era, deposited on the surface of the land by the actions of the sea, and are over 300 million years old. Further north, you will find examples of much older rock of Precambrian origin, that is up to and over 1,000 million years old. Much of this is made up of sea floor sediments, but some rock is as a result of lava and compressed ash of volcanoes that erupted at least 600 million years ago. It was 400 million years ago that a series of collisions took place between the mobile continental plates which raised the mountains of North Wales and twisted and folded the horizontal rock layers of north Pembrokeshire into the grotesque shapes of grits and shales that make the coastline so fascinating for today's visitor.

The first settlers arrived in the area in around 5000 BC, but it was the Iron Age dwellers, moving in 2,600 years ago, who were the first to leave their mark on the landscape. They did this with a succession of defensive promontory forts of which there remains much evidence today. In the years following the departure of the Romans – who had a negligible effect on Pembrokeshire life – Christianity flourished in this corner of Wales; St David is the most famous of a large number of devout monks and ascetics who lived and worked in the area. The cathedral of St David's, though not strictly on the route itself, is the principal architectural highlight of the region. The Norman invasion and subsequent colonisation of south Pembrokeshire by English-speaking settlers led to the so-called 'Landsker' or divide between the English-speaking peoples of that region and the largely Welsh-speaking peoples of the north. That can still be traced today; Welsh is heard more often in north than in south Pembrokeshire, and the place names tend to become more Anglicised as progress southwards is made.

The combination of majestic scenery and Iron Age and Christian relics is reason enough to visit the Pembrokeshire coastline, but there are many other attractions for the walker. Most notably, there is an abundance of wildlife and plant life. Heather, gorse and bracken are constant features, while spring yields generous quantities of snowdrops, daffodils, primroses and cowslips, and carpets of bluebells and foxgloves. Seagulls are in evidence at every step of the walk, but they are joined by many other seabirds including gannets, razorbills, guillemots, fulmars and choughs. Choughs, with their glossy blue-black plumages and red legs, are plentiful in Pembrokeshire despite going into decline elsewhere. Seals can also be seen, particularly in the autumn breeding season.

The walking, although demanding at times, poses no serious technical challenges; because the route keeps largely to the coastline, route finding is rarely a problem, with a clear well-defined coast path. Although the region is wonderfully unspoilt, there are many towns and villages on or near the route, so there will be no difficulties in finding food or accommodation, and public transport links are excellent. The most remarkable aspect of the walk is that, although at over 175 miles from end to end it is one of the longer national trails, the distance from start to finish as the crow flies is only 30 miles! It is therefore practicable to drive to the start, in the knowledge that there will be a comparatively easy and affordable journey back to the car from the finish, even though it does undeniably detract from one's sense of achievement on reaching the end to realise that the start can be returned to by motorised transport in less time than it takes to oven-cook a Bernard Matthews turkey roast.

St Dogmaels to Parrog for Newport (15.5 miles) via Poppit Sands and Ceibwr Bay

Enjoy: Pen yr Afr, Gernos, Pwllygranant, Pwll y Wrach, Morfa Head, Newport Sands

The route begins at the northern end of St Dogmaels on the banks of the river Teifi, a river noted for its salmon and sea trout, known locally as 'sewin'. Travellers by public transport who have been decanted at Cardigan will have an easy walk to St Dogmaels via the B4546. St Dogmaels is worth a few minutes' exploration; it boasts a number of elegant Victorian cottages, a ruined abbey that was founded in the twelfth century, and a nineteenth-century church containing an early Christian stone monument inscribed in both Latin and also Ogham, which was a script used by ancient British and Irish scholars. Thus was it possible to translate the previously baffling Ogham alphabet in 1848. The start of the route is clearly marked with bilingual signposts bearing the words 'Llwybr Arfordir/ Coast Path', and these signposts are provided liberally all the way to Amroth. The first two miles of the journey, heading north-westwards, are extremely easy, the route following the B4546 to Poppit Sands and then a narrow metalled lane uphill to the hamlet of Allt-y-goed. Here, the reassuring tarmac ends and you continue north-westwards, joining a path which offers excellent views to the mouth of the Teifi and Cardigan Bay across slopes clad thickly with bracken. Straight ahead is Cemaes Head, and here the route swings sharply south-westwards, a direction it will maintain for much of the way to St David's Head, which is over 50 miles away. The contrast between this magnificent clifftop scenery and the homely, gentle surroundings of the riverside communities of Cardigan and St Dogmaels is remarkable. Almost at once you reach Pen yr Afr (3); at nearly 600 ft above the sea this is the highest point of the national trail. The sheer cliff faces and the folds in the rocks, legacies of geological activity 400 million years ago, are remarkable.

The next highlights are the waterfalls at Gernos and the nearby cove of Pwllygranant, where there is some stiff up-and-down walking to do; beyond Pwllygranant is Ceibwr Bay, owned by the National Trust and noted for its fulmar colony. The rock folds were made 450 million years ago by Great Caledonian earth movements. No amenities exist here, and indeed there is nothing on offer until you reach Newport. Just beyond Ceibwr Bay is the scenic highlight of this stretch, namely Pwll y Wrach or the Witches Cauldron. It is in fact a collapsed cave, where the sea has gnawed away at soft rocks along a fault. The path descends steeply and crosses a natural bridge over a huge chasm between two faces of steep rock; once you have regained the height lost, the 'bridge' looks almost tightrope-like in narrowness.

There is some very tough climbing as the coast path rises to 500 ft again. Towards Morfa Head there are some frightening moments as the path snakes round a small inlet with a strip of grass less than a yard wide separating you from a straight drop of some 300 ft. Large areas of bracken on the upper slopes of the cliffs give way to monstrous shale faces that sweep to the water's edge. At Morfa Head, you get your first view of the superb sands of Newport Bay. The descent from Morfa Head is not easy; the path is very steep, and there are a number of awkward scrambles through outcrops of rock. It is necessary to drop right down to sea level and follow a path which runs beside Newport Sands (at low tide, if you wished to avoid Newport you could cut straight across the sands to the eastern end of Parrog, fording the Nevern estuary en route), and after crossing a stream, reaches a metalled road. The route turns right on to the road, immediately crossing the Nevern estuary and then straight away turning right to follow a path which continues towards Parrog (15.5), this time following the south edge of Newport Sands. At length it turns right on to a metalled lane that passes through Parrog.

By staying on the road you have used to cross the Nevern estuary, you will reach Newport, for centuries a thriving port, but now set back from the sea. It is a useful stopping-place, with a wide range of amenities; it boasts many attractive eighteenth and nineteenth-century cottages of various colours, Norman castle ruins, and a thirteenth-century church with many memorials to seamen in its churchyard, while the lane running down to the old harbour is overlooked by ancient limekilns. As you approach and enter Parrog and Newport you may be aware of a range of inland hills with a distinctly moorland feel. These hills, which dominate north Pembrokeshire, are called the Preselis.

Parrog to Goodwick (12.5 miles) via Fishguard

ENJOY: Aberrhigian, Aberfforest, Dinas Head, Hescwm

The coast path continues westwards through Parrog and there follows a splendid walk to Cwm-yr-Eglwys, with superb views back to Newport Bay and the Preselis. The two finest features on this section are the coves of Aberrhigian and Aberfforest, and although both coves entail steep descents and ascents, your efforts are amply rewarded. Shortly beyond Aberfforest the route meets a metalled road and drops to Cwm-yr-Eglwys. This is a small but bustling place, its most notable feature being the Sailor's Chapel of St Brynach, almost completely destroyed by a storm in 1859. At Cwm-yr-Eglwys you have a choice; you may follow a woodland valley walk to Pwllgwaelod, heading roughly westwards and avoiding Dinas Island (not actually an island; it ceased to be one 8,000 years ago, and is now a rugged peninsula), or you may continue on the coastline round Dinas Island via Dinas Head, using the coast path. If you are pushed for time, you may want to opt for the woodland route, which in summer is notable for its variety of butterflies. However the walk round Dinas Head is to be greatly preferred, given the right conditions. The views from Pen y Fan, the headland summit, are breathtaking; Pen yr Afr, now many miles back, is clearly visible, as is the whole of Fishguard Bay and the crests of the Preselis. There have been suggestions that the Wicklow mountains in southern Ireland can be seen from here, but even with a hundred per cent clarity and binoculars, I was unable to pinpoint them when I visited the headland. It's certainly very frustrating to reach a viewpoint topograph and find that the landmarks supposedly visible from it are not, the thick mist obviating any possibility of seeing the tower of St Peter's Church, one mile away, let alone Times Square, New York, a mere 3173 miles distant.

Slight anticlimax sets in as you descend from Pen y Fan to Pwllgwaelod, and begin the long walk round Fishguard Bay. There is more up-and-down work, following which the coast path negotiates the splendid little sheltered inlet at Hescwm, then climbs back up to follow the clifftops. Thereafter the going is more straightforward, the route keeping to field edges and passing a caravan park. Beyond this, however, there is more magnificent coastal scenery, culminating in the ruins of the late eighteenth-century Fishguard Fort on Castle Point. Three cannons still remain, as if warning off future invaders of these shores. At Castle Point the coast path turns sharply southwards to reach Lower Town, the old fishing port at the mouth of the Gwaun valley. Once a busy industrial port, it is now a haven for pleasure boats; the car park in the village is known to be given over for boats in the summer. You turn right on to the A487 and follow it briefly for a steep climb up into Fishguard (25.5), one of the largest settlements on the Pembrokeshire Coast Path with all the amenities you are likely to need. The route actually turns right off the main road shortly before the town centre and uses a footpath which snakes round the edge of the town to reach Saddle Point, high above the mini estuary created by the river Gwaun as it flows into Fishguard Bay. The views across the bay to Dinas Head are stunning, and there is the more immediate prospect of Castle Point, extending its face across the water like some giant sea creature. Beyond Saddle Point the coast path turns resolutely away from Castle Point, heading just south of west and dropping down to the A40. Turning right on to the A40, you proceed beside it as far as a roundabout, then take the second exit off it to cross the railway on a minor road and enter Goodwick (28). The town of Goodwick, which offers refreshment and accommodation, grew as a result of the advent of the railway (Fishguard railway station is in fact at Goodwick). A breakwater and lighthouse further round the bay mark the extent of what is known as Fishguard harbour, and it is the quay at Goodwick which serves as the Fishguard ferry terminal and boasts the smart new Stena Line buildings. I clearly recall enjoying a well-earned portion of chicken and chips on the quay on a Saturday night, with Goodwick's principal nightlife appearing to consist of the assembly, from 9 p.m., of cars and lorries beginning their patient wait for the 3.15 a.m. Rosslare ferry.

Goodwick to Trwyn Llwyd for Trefin (17.5 miles) via Pwll Deri and Abercastle

ENJOY: Cwm Felin, Strumble Head, Porth Maenmelyn, Pwll Deri, Carn Ogof, Mynydd Morfa, Abercastle, Pen Castell-coch

The route continues by leaving the minor road very soon after crossing the railway and bearing right (north-eastwards) onto a lane that heads uphill on to the cliffs again, via Harbour Village. Once the village has been left behind and the coast path is regained, you can look forward to many miles of totally unspoilt walking on a well-marked coast path, uninterrupted by towns or busy roads. The next objective of note is Strumble Head, one of the most prominent headlands on the map of West Wales. To reach Strumble Head from Harbour Village, however, it is necessary to head northwards to round Crincoed Point, and then north-westwards, turning away from Fishguard Bay at last. Most of the walking is straightforward without any severe descents or climbs. The first of two outstanding features of this section is the delectable wooded valley of Cwm Felin, where you momentarily forget you are on a coast path as you enjoy the brief sensation of sheltered woodland and rushing stream, a most refreshing experience on a hot day. Emerging from that, you come almost immediately to Carreg Goffa monument above Carregwastad Point, the landing place for the last military force to invade Britain, in February 1797. The plan was for 1,400 ex-convicts from France, under the leadership of Colonel Tate, an American, to land either near Bristol or in Cardigan Bay and raise a peasants' revolt which would divert attention from the main aim: an invasion of Ireland by 15,000 regular soldiers. The landing at Carregwastad was a mistake, and within two days the force capitulated nearby – not helped, one suspects, by the fact that many of the invaders had got themselves drunk on a cargo of wine from a ship that had been wrecked on the coast shortly before.

The walking is uneventful until you reach Strumble Head where you will swing south-west, and indeed for the next 30 miles or so south-west will be the predominant direction of travel. A coastguard station and a lighthouse, situated on the island of Ynys Meicel, serve to mark Strumble Head, although there are no amenities available. This significant headland, which offers views that stretch as far as the Lleyn Peninsula in north-west Wales, is a favoured spot for birdwatchers, and basking sharks and Risso's dolphins have been observed in the waters close by. The going thus far from Goodwick has been very easy, but it slows down considerably now as you embark on a stretch of coast where every headland is a volcanic intrusion, beginning with a succession of small hills of volcanic rock. The coast path ceases to be a reassuring strip of green or brown and loses all definition for a while as the route weaves its way through, or round, the outcrops of rock, negotiating streams, ponds, moorland and hillocks as it goes. Soon after rounding the astonishing cove of Porth Maenmelyn and passing the imposing promontory fort of Dinas Mawr, you have to make a steep climb to Pwll Deri, where you will find what is surely one of the most spectacularly-sited youth hostels in the country. Viewed from further south, it is hard to see what stops it falling into the sea. There is a respite for a few moments as the route turns right on to the hostel approach road, then turns right off it and sets off again along a ridge path. This leads to the wonderful viewpoint of Carn Ogof, providing spectacular vistas of the cliffs that you have recently negotiated.

Between Carn Ogof and Abercastle you will venture through some of the wildest coastal terrain in the British Isles, with hardly a house or even a road in view. If the wind is howling, the sense of isolation and ruggedness is accentuated even more. Soon comes the heather-clad mini headland of Penbwchdy, where the negotiation of craggy outcrops brings your activity more into the realms of scrambling than walking. Things get slightly easier beyond Penbwchdy, the coast path curling round the spectacular sandy cove at Pwllcrochan, guarded on all sides by formidable rocks. You then drop to the twin beaches of Aber Bach and Aber Mawr, passing a promontory fort at Carreg Golchfa just before Aber Bach; beyond Aber Mawr there is another climb and then faster walking along field edges with just one big fall and rise at Pwllstrodur. Though the walking is more straightforward, the scenery remains fascinating, with the summit of Mynydd Morfa, marked by a triangulation point, to the left, and the little headlands of Penmorfa (where there is a hill fort) and Trwyn Llwynog to your right. Shortly beyond Pwllstrodur you reach Abercastle, the first settlement since Goodwick. Although it has no amenities to speak of, it is a picturesque place, and its cosy harbour, guarded by the spectacular island of black rock known as Ynys y Castell, is a delight. Just beyond Abercastle, a detour inland takes you shortly to Carreg Sampson, a cromlech, or burial chamber, built by the Neoliths, who were amongst the first settlers in this area. From Abercastle to Trwyn Llwyd (45.5), providing easy access to Trefin with its variety of amenities, the walking is straightforward with no real up-and-down work, but there are numerous twists and turns as you make your way round a profusion of small inlets and headlands, of which Pen Castell-coch is the most fascinating. Coastal erosion has produced a particularly grotesque range of rock formations hereabouts, as well as small 'islands' of rock, and those who choose to end their day's march at nearby Trefin will enjoy a fine conclusion to their walk. So much of this section is indeed a paradise for geologists. In fact, some walkers may recall having visited the area on school field trips, where the interest consisted not so much in the rock formations as the flavour of the crisps chosen for the day's packed lunch, or the chances of getting off with Amanda in Form 5B.

Trwyn Llwyd to Whitesands Bay for St David's (11.2 miles) via Porthgain

ENJOY: St David's Head, Porthmelgan, St David's

Beyond Trwyn Llwyd, the coast path descends again to reach the fascinating village of Porthgain. Its harbour provides strong evidence of the area's industrial past, and the remains of the old brickworks, last used in 1931, can still be seen. The harbour is lined with banks of crushers, bins and shoots where stone quarried from nearby cliffs was broken, graded and deposited into the waiting ships. On climbing back on to the clifftops beyond the village, you will see numerous traces of the old quarries, the most notable of which is the old tramway cutting. There follows some splendid cliff scenery, with grandstand views to the fine beach of Traeth Llyfn, and then a descent to the little village of Abereiddi, where slate was once quarried. Its bay and sandy beach, popular with fossil hunters, are guarded by the rocks of Trwyncastell. After this succession of villages, civilisation is left behind as you embark on a stunning journey through completely unspoilt cliff scenery. You pass the sites of some ancient forts, then proceed through the beautiful valley of Pwll-caerog before making the strenuous ascent to the summit of Penberry.

Beyond Penberry the terrain takes on a distinctly moorland appearance, with granite boulders protruding from the great carpets of heather, and there is a succession of climbs through relentless thrusts of igneous rock. The walking has an incredibly remote feel, although you will not truly be on your own, as wild ponies can be seen gambolling contentedly among the tufts of heather. There is a marvellous profusion of wild flowers including sea pinks and oxeye daisies, and if you feel brave enough to venture to the cliff edge you may observe grey seals, which thrive in the unspoilt surroundings. There is a definite sense of building up to something, until at last you reach St David's Head, the largest igneous thrust of all. It is not quite the most westerly point in Wales – that will be reached in just a few miles – but it is a key place on the route. The reward for reaching, and rounding, the headland is a superb view to the nearby cove of Porthmelgan and Whitesands Bay beyond. Porthmelgan stands in the shadow of 595 ft Carn Llidi, an inland hill of mountainous appearance that towers over St David's and its surrounding countryside. Passing Coetan Arthur, another important Neolithic burial chamber, the descent to Porthmelgan is straightforward, as is the rise and drop to Whitesands Bay. This part of the walk is a popular tourist path and steps have had to be taken to curb the resulting erosion. Whitesands Bay (56.7), where I obtained refreshment from a useful cafe, has one of the best sandy beaches on the route, and offers a quick easy road link to St David's on the B4583. Its status as a major tourist attraction ensures there is no shortage of shops, tearooms, pubs and other amenities.

St David's

St David's, the smallest city in Great Britain, is not on the route, but it virtually demands a detour for a short visit at least, if not an overnight stay. The cathedral, which turns what would otherwise be regarded as a village into a city, dates from the end of the twelfth century, and was almost certainly built on the site of a monastery founded by St David in the sixth century. Situated in a leafy valley, the cathedral's most notable features include a decorated sixteenth-century roof and fourteenth-century carved choir screen. In the same valley as the cathedral stand the wonderfully romantic ruins of the fourteenth-century Bishop's Palace.

Whitesands Bay to Solva (12.3 miles) via Porth Clais

ENJOY: St Justinian's, Ramsey Island, Pen Dal-aderyn, Treginnis, Penpleidiau, Solva

The walk from Whitesands Bay to St Justinian's, just under two miles, is straightforward; the coast path follows a level course along the cliffs at a modest height above the sea, with the seductive sands of the bay immediately below and the might of Carn Llidi towering up behind. St Justinian's itself is more impressive for its fine setting than its buildings, which include a lifeboat station and a small roofless chapel. Immediately to your right across the water, as St Justinian's is reached, is Ramsey Island, the home of St Justinian himself, and supposedly the resting place of 20,000 saints. Legend has it that St Justinian, having had his head cut off by murderers on the island, walked across the Sound with his head in his arms! Accessible to visitors by ferry only at certain times of year, the island is a privately owned and farmed nature reserve, and is a nesting and breeding place for more than 30 species of bird including guillemots and razorbills. The strip of water separating the island from the mainland is Ramsey Sound, where fearsome rocks named the Bitches lie in wait to claim careless navigators, while an equally dangerous collection of reefs, known as Bishops and Clerks, lies a little further off the island. The Bitches, according to legend, were all that was left after St Justinian prayed for the destruction of the bridge linking Ramsey with the mainland because he was getting too many visitors.

Once past St Justinian's the walking, round the small bay of Porthstinian and beyond, gets considerably tougher. However, the cliff scenery is magnificent. At Pen Dal-aderyn an important moment is reached; this is the most westerly point on the Welsh mainland, and having rounded the headland, you will find yourself making significant progress eastwards for the first time on the walk. With Ramsey Island behind you and the prevailing wind on your back, you now have St Brides Bay for company, and will continue to do so for most of the next 30 miles. The coast path follows the bay in its entirety, from Pen Dal-aderyn at its north-westerly extreme to Wooltack Point at its south-west tip. The walking is magnificent almost throughout, beginning at once with the National Trust-owned cliffs of Treginnis and the splendidly named cave Ogof Mrs Morgan. There are exquisite views hereabouts to the rocky islands of Carreg yr Esgob and Carreg Fran, each of which guards the beautiful Porthlysgi Bay. The little hillocks of volcanic rock round Porth Henllys provide ideal platforms not only for views to the bay but also for views back to the hills at the southern end of Ramsey Island.

Less than a mile beyond Porthlysgi Bay is Porth Clais (63), a harbour that serves St David's, and though it has seen some industry, it now principally caters for the tourist trade. It is a superbly attractive harbour, with a thin stretch of water protected on each side by lines of tall cliffs. The route must turn inland and drop steeply to cross the water before rising again and returning to the cliffs overlooking the bay. About half a mile beyond Porth Clais is St Non's Chapel; though built comparatively recently, it was by St Non's Bay, on to which the chapel looks out, that St David, the patron saint of Wales, was supposedly born in the middle of the fifth century. Between St Non's Chapel and the next major settlement at Solva, there are no real difficulties, and you can make reasonably quick progress eastwards round the top end of St Brides Bay. Interest is provided by a succession of fine small headlands, namely Pen y Cyfrwy, Penpleidiau with an impressive fort, Carreg y Barcud and Ystafelloedd. Stone from cliffs at Caerfai Bay, sitting snugly between the first two of these headlands, was used in the building of St David's Cathedral.

Solva itself lies at the end of a narrow hooked harbour; it is actually a drowned river valley which submerged when the sea rose at the end of the last Ice Age. The approach to the village is wonderful, with fine views to the headland on the far side of the harbour. This headland, known as St Elvis Rock, does not point out to sea but curls inwards to provide the narrowest possible entrance to the harbour, which more than one observer has likened to Boscastle Harbour in Cornwall. Solva (69), a busy port in the early nineteenth century with a brisk trade in cloth, corn, timber and coal, is a cheerful jumble of houses around the harbour, with ample facilities for rest and refreshment, particularly in summer. It's also a nice easy name to pronounce! You're not far now from the stream said to mark the divide between the Welsh-speaking north of Pembrokeshire and the English-speaking south.

Solva to Little Haven (12.1 miles) via Newgale, Nolton Haven and Broad Haven

ENJOY: Newgale Sands, Druidston Haven

The route continues in dramatic style beyond Solva, with an ascent, a sharp drop and then a climb round the neck of the St Elvis headland. Very soon after this comes the promontory of Dinas Fawr, which although a cul-de-sac and not on the coast path itself, is well signposted and easily accessible. It is a detour well worth making; the walk to the tip of the promontory is along a huge whaleback ridge of rock, and the views throughout are magnificent. Returning to the main path, Newgale looks temptingly close on the map for those who have spurned refreshment opportunities in Solva, and there are good views to the village and its sands once Dinas Fawr has been left behind, but the march to reach it provides some of the toughest walking on the route. There are two big valleys to negotiate, each involving a knee-jarring drop and then a lung-testing climb almost immediately afterwards. The reward – apart from the traverse of a crystal-clear stream which may provide life-saving refreshment on a hot day – is an uninterrupted view of Newgale Sands, one of the finest stretches of sand on the coast of Great Britain. A brisk descent brings the coast path down to the A487 and right on to this road into Newgale (74). This little settlement, at the head of its 2-mile carpet of golden sand, not only marks the north-eastern extremity of St Brides Bay and an important 'corner' for you to have turned, but the nearby Brandy Brook Stream is said to mark the divide of north and south Pembrokeshire. Beyond Newgale, with the route now heading resolutely southwards, the cliffs temporarily cease. The A487 soon heads off inland, and you must choose between the sands, the shingle bank or a metalled minor road as you proceed towards Nolton Haven.

As the road veers slightly away from the coast, the route joins a footpath, running parallel to the sands, and then when the sands end the path swings round some old mine workings, and passes a huge towering mound of rock known as Rickets Head. It stays on the clifftop then swings inland to reach the pretty cove and village of Nolton Haven. The village once had a quay where coasters loaded anthracite from a nearby colliery, but only did so in the summer months as the ship insurers, Lloyds, refused to insure vessels for use during the wild winter months. The next in a veritable line of havens is Druidston Haven, with another fine sandy beach; some more tough up-and-down work is required here, the route heading slightly inland to join a metalled road which you follow round Druidston Villa. On leaving the road, however, and rejoining the coast path, the walking becomes straightforward, with an easy clifftop march towards the twin villages of Broad Haven and Little Haven. Though the sight of its buildings is hardly aesthetically pleasing, the great sweep of golden sand immediately in front of them is more so, and the prospect of a wide range of amenities in the village will encourage you to descend briskly southwards to reach its centre. Broad Haven, the larger of the two villages, became a fashionable resort in the nineteenth century and there is still a Victorian atmosphere about the place, especially on Trafalgar Terrace and Webbs Hill, where a neat chapel built in 1841 stands beside a stream. Little Haven (81.1) is a pretty place which, like Nolton Haven, also has a history of exporting coal. At the time of my visit Broad Haven boasted an excellent shop and post office where I recall parcelling up five days' worth of dirty clothes to send back home in an effort to lighten my rucksack. Whilst it certainly made life more comfortable for me as I continued on the walk, it is not a practice I would commend if you wish to return from your adventure to a partner who is still on speaking terms with you.

Little Haven to Marloes Sands for Marloes (12.5 miles) via Wooltack Point

ENJOY: Nab Head, Deer Park, views to Skomer and Skokholm, Gateholm Island

You turn another corner of St Brides Bay as you make the stiff climb out of Little Haven on to the clifftops. As far as Borough Head you are separated from the sea by a strip of woodland, then from Borough Head to the hamlet of St Brides, the route sticks to the coast path which stays on sheer clifftops at between 200 ft and 300 ft. Beyond Borough Head come the inlets of Brandy Bay and Dutch Gin; the highlight of this easy and straightforward section, however, is a waterfall down a virtually sheer cliff face fed by an innocuous stream that is crossed by means of a simple wooden plank. The route drops to the beach at St Brides (no amenities), then climbs back on to the cliffs to round Nab Head – a Stone Age site for the manufacture of flint tools – and proceeds almost due south, then south-westwards, round Musselwick Sands. Beyond these sands the coast path swings more decisively westwards for the final assault on Wooltack Point and the farewell to St Brides Bay. As you approach the headland, you pass the picturesque little inlet of Martin's Haven, guarded to its west by Haven Point. You may take a short cut across the neck of the headland, aiming due south from Martin's Haven, but few walkers will wish to spurn the opportunity to follow the headland – known as the Deer Park – right round. The Deer Park is the site of important Iron Age defensive embankments and there is not a deer to be seen. However, not only should the extra walking provide unbeatable views to the bay, and its magnificent coastline that has now been safely accomplished, but there are also views to Skomer Island immediately to the west. Further out to sea, a little to the south-east of Skomer, is the island of Skokholm. Both islands are amazingly rich havens of wildlife, including puffins, petrels and Manx shearwaters, and boat trips are available in season if you have the time and inclination to take a closer look. The rounding of the Deer Park is a crucial moment on the walk; not only does it complete the walk round St Brides Bay but it is roughly the halfway mark of the journey.

The good news for more timid souls is that the second half is gentler, less rugged and less remote than the first, although there is still some fantastic scenery to come. Now heading south-east towards St Ann's Head and continuing on the clifftops, you pass the ominously named Deadman's Bay and Albion Sands, beyond which stands Gateholm Island. The island is accessible at low tide and well worth visiting if you have time; there are some unusual cliff formations here known as the Three Chimneys, where horizontal beds of rock dating back 450 million years have been virtually upended into chimneys of eroded stone. Beyond Gateholm Island, there is then a quite magnificent walk above Marloes Sands (93.6), the golden carpet punctuated by outcrops of rock. With easy access to the amenities in the nearby village of Marloes, this is quite a popular spot for holidaymakers, and all the better for the absence of end-to-end candyfloss stalls, bucket-and-spade emporia, vulgar postcards, and scrawled blackboard signs proclaiming the availability of 'fish n chip's'.

Marloes Sands to Sandy Haven for Herbrandston (13.9 miles) via Dale

ENJOY: St Ann's Head, Mill Bay, Dale Point, Watch House Point, Little Castle Head, Lindsway Bay

The walking remains highly enjoyable and straightforward beyond Marloes Sands. Once round Hooper's Point, you pass a disused airfield to your left, now owned by the National Trust, and continue on past the sands of Westdale Bay. Nearby is the Cobblers Hole, a classic example of rock-folding in old red sandstone. The village of Dale is a short walk away across the neck of the peninsula, but if you wish to get a few more miles under your belt you will press on to St Ann's Head without difficulty, passing the mini headlands of Long Point and Little Castle Point, and two bays, namely Welshman's Bay and Frenchman's Bay. St Ann's Head, with its lighthouse that was built on the site of St Ann's Chapel, is another important stage on the route, marking the start of the walk alongside the channel known as Milford Haven, away from the coast. Just across Milford Haven from St Ann's Head you will see Rat Island on the south side of West Angle Bay, where the true coastal walking resumes, but to reach that point, tantalisingly close as the crow flies, requires at least two full days of hard tramping. The route continues north-eastwards now along the water's edge round Mill Bay, with its fine cliffs of old red sandstone; it was at Mill Bay that Henry Tudor (later

Henry VII) landed in August 1485 before capturing the English throne at Bosworth Field. You round two more bays, Watwick and Castlebeach, on the way into Dale, and encounter a particularly delightful wooded valley near Castlebeach Bay.

The tip of the headland beyond this bay is Dale Point, and on the headland is Dale Fort. Constructed in the eighteenth century as a defence against the French, it has been converted into a field study centre. You will pass other defensive forts around the mouth of Milford Haven as the walk progresses, and will thus appreciate the importance that was attached to the deep anchorage of the Haven and the naval installations to which it gave rise. The route joins the approach road to the fort and turns left on to it, dropping down to reach the picturesque village of Dale (101), its shingle beach providing fine views across Milford Haven. The village is an extremely popular sailing centre, with safe moorings available in Dale Roads off the shingle shore; it really only comes to life when the sailing season begins, although the village pub has catered for the needs of walkers all the year round. -

The walk round Milford Haven from Dale to Angle is the least exciting or rewarding section of the route, and some walkers may wish to miss it out altogether. If you have decided to stay with it, you will have your resolve tested almost immediately as you leave Dale, when you reach a tidal creek known as the Gann which can only be passed at low tide. If the creek is negotiable, it is then a straightforward walk round the edge of the sands and then south-eastwards to the pleasant but unspectacular Musselwick Point. Otherwise a tedious detour is needed to the nearest bridge crossing, following the B4327 Haverfordwest road northwards and over the creek, then as the road swings north-eastwards, soon branching off right on to a minor road heading for the hamlet of Mullock. You then turn right again and use footpaths to proceed southwards to rejoin the coast path just short of Musselwick Point. There is then an improvement as you reach Monks Haven with its wooded valley, lake, impressive castellated walls, and good views across to West Angle Bay.

Now, though you are not proceeding alongside the open sea, the cliff faces are still impressively rugged; the headlands of Watch House Point, Great Castle Head and Little Castle Head, complete with prehistoric promontory fort, are all delightful and give good views to the shoreline on the south side of the Haven and the charming Thorn Island lying just off West Angle Bay. The beach at Lindsway Bay, just before Great Castle Head, is also very attractive and unspoilt. However, you are now within sight of the oil refineries which, although fascinating in their way, do tend to detract from the beauty of the surroundings. Beyond Little Castle Head, you walk northwards to Sandy Haven (107.5), briefly joining a lane which takes you down to Sandyhaven Pill. Within shouting distance of the village of Herbrandston, this is another tidal creek that is bordered on both sides by pleasant stretches of sand, and again you must hope that the tide will be low enough for you to use the stepping stones and avoid another tiresome detour. The detour itself, if you are unfortunate enough to have to make it, consists of a walk up the road running parallel to and then across the creek; bearing right immediately after crossing over it, you follow the road down to the village of Herbrandston, at the south end of which you join a road that leads westwards back to the east bank of the Sandyhaven Pill to pick up the route. It certainly adds a few unwelcome miles to the walk, and may provoke amongst some hikers the obvious but no less painful quip that it is a bitter Pill to swallow.

Sandy Haven to Pembroke (16 miles) via Milford Haven, Neyland and Pembroke Dock

ENJOY: Neyland, Cleddau Bridge, Pembroke

Once across the Pill, whichever method is used to negotiate it, you soon proceed south-eastwards into oil country. In the late

1950s, when oil companies were looking for a suitable location to receive and refine crude oil from the Middle East, the broad, deep estuarine waters of Milford Haven proved an ideal choice, since the deep-water channel was able to admit oil tankers of over 250,000 tons. During the next decade and a half, a number of different companies adopted Milford Haven in this way, and many refineries were still operational towards the end of the twentieth century while considerable paraphernalia has been left by the companies that have gone. The result is a landscape which for the next few miles is dominated by massive chimneys, cylindrical storage tanks and jetties. The route, though staying close to the estuary and rounding South Hook Point to proceed eastwards, passes right beside the workings of the former Esso refinery, actually passing *underneath* an old jetty. Just beyond this jetty you leave the National Park, dropping down to the uninteresting Gelliswick Bay and briefly picking up a road which follows the bay round. As the road swings to the left, the route leaves it, turning right alongside a school playing field and then along roads heading north-eastwards through the village of Hakin, the route marked with acorn signs on the pavements. Eventually you drop down to the Victoria Bridge, at the head of the docks, and use the bridge crossing to enter the town of Milford Haven (112). The land on which the town stands was owned by Sir William Hamilton whose wife Emma became Lord Nelson's mistress. It was Hamilton's nephew Charles Greville who in 1800 planned and founded the port, and indeed the planned aspect is obvious from the neat gridiron of streets in the heart of the town. Following the collapse of the town's whaling and Admiralty shipbuilding trades, and the decline of its fishing industry, oil has become the town's saviour, although some refineries have closed down in the past two decades.

Having passed through the town, which offers the best range of amenities since St David's, the route leaves the centre by way of Hamilton Terrace, heading towards and then up the left side of Castle Pill. This is yet another tidal creek, on the shores of which various boatyards and an armaments depot have been built. Soon, you reach the B4325 and turn right on to it to cross Castle Pill by means of Black Bridge, from which you have a steep twisty climb, still on the B4325. The climb seems endless, but at last the crest is gained and the route turns right on to a footpath which heads south-east towards the estuary and round the edge of another vast refinery. The pipelines connecting the jetty and refinery are crossed by means of an extraordinary bridge where not only on either side, but above you, have been erected iron bars, mesh and barbed wire, so that you get the sensation of walking in a cage. In due course the path, passing above Wear Point, drops down to a metalled road which heads slightly north of east through the pleasant villages of Hazelbeach and Llandstadwell to rejoin the B4325 round the little town of Neyland (117). As you reach the town, you will rejoice at the sight, immediately ahead, of the Cleddau Bridge, which marks the furthest point of the journey up Milford Haven and the start of the long walk back to the lovely coastline that you have left behind.

Neyland is not a wildly interesting town; it is notable now only for its picturesque marina, although it was once a terminal for a packet service to Ireland and was actually known as Milford Haven before Greville's town adopted this name. Brunel was aware of the anchorage potential of Neyland for ocean-going ships, and established a special mooring here for the largest of his three steamships, the *Great Eastern*. The national trail leaves the town by passing into a strip of woodland at its north-east end, proceeding northwards through the wood above the marina to reach the A477. You turn right on to this road, which immediately crosses a creek, then half a mile or so later cross the estuary by means of the Cleddau Bridge, built in 1975. The bridge crossing is enjoyable, with good views not only to the estuary but to the waters of the Daugleddau which flow into the estuary, the settlements of

Pembroke Dock, Neyland and Milford Haven, and of course the ubiquitous chimneys and storage tanks of the refineries. However, anticlimax follows; after walking briefly further beside the A477, you bear right to walk in a south-westerly direction through a built-up area marked on maps as Llanion Park, arriving on the waterfront at Pembroke Dock (121).

You now follow a waterfront walkway from which there are good views to the Cleddau Bridge. Pembroke Dock, though certainly not the highlight of the walk, has a colourful past; after the Admiralty moved its operations here from Milford Haven town for economic reasons during the Napoleonic Wars, a new dockyard was built and remained operational until 1926. It was used during the Second World War as a base for boats protecting the Atlantic convoys, and as a result was bombed heavily by the Germans. You can still see the martello tower that was part of the dockyard's defensive system. Just before the tower the route turns a little west of south to pass alongside the Pembroke Dockyard, then strikes out south-westwards onto Barrack Hill and swings south-eastwards towards another major water crossing, this time a river, to enter the suburban settlement of Pennar. The river presents an impenetrable obstacle to straightforward progress westwards beside Milford Haven. As a result, it is necessary to head south-eastwards – *away* from the coast again – to the nearest available river crossing which is situated in the old town of Pembroke. After leaving the tarmac at the eastern end of Pennar, the route proceeds pleasantly but unremarkably south-eastwards through fields and woodland on the north side of the river, arriving at the A4139 and turning right on to it to cross the bridge and go forward into the old town (123.5). (Note that there is a brief tidal alternative at this point.) A glance at the map will indicate that since the roundabout on the south side of the Cleddau Bridge, you have done three sides of a big rectangle and could simply have stuck to the A4139 from the roundabout onwards, saving yourself considerable time and effort.

Pembroke to West Angle Bay for Angle (13.3 miles) via Monkton and Angle

ENJOY: Goldborough Pill, West Angle Bay

The old town of Pembroke is an undeniably attractive place, and is the highlight of the walk from the Cleddau Bridge back to the sea. Its main street contains many old houses, but its chief attraction is its castle with a spectacular riverside setting. With a keep almost 80 ft high and walls 20 ft thick, it was the birthplace of Henry Tudor in 1457, but parts of it date back nearly 300 years before that. You may either turn right immediately after crossing the bridge and walk round the castle walls to arrive at a road fork, or you may continue from the bridge to a T-junction, turning right to arrive soon at the same spot. The national trail takes the right fork, this being the B4320, and follows it through the suburban village of Monkton, heading just south of west. At a sharp bend in the road, at the southern foot of a marshy inlet, the route turns right on to a narrower road and shortly right again on to a footpath which proceeds through open country, describing a crude semicircle round the village of Hundleton and reaching a narrow road just west of the village. Walkers pushed for time can simply follow the road through the village and out the other side. Continuing roughly westwards towards Goldborough, you soon reach a very charming wooded valley, turning right on to a path that emerges from the woods and proceeds north-westwards past the tip of Goldborough Pill, rising gently with good views of Pembroke River. This is pleasant enough walking, as is the mild descent to another attractive wooded valley at Lambeeth, and the climb up the other side to Lambeeth Farm. The route continues along a path heading north-westwards, passing through an area of woodland and then alongside an approach road to Pembroke power station which now monopolises the scene to the east.

The route leaves the approach road, turning right on to a footpath then left onto a lane which leads to the tiny hamlet of Pwllcrochan.

Though its pretty church boasts a proud spire, pointing in determined fashion towards heaven, it is dwarfed completely by the towering chimneys immediately behind. The route turns right onto another metalled road which leads down towards the south bank of Milford Haven, with the oil refinery immediately to your left. The road peters out but the way forward is obvious as the route now re-enters the National Park and proceeds beside the Haven. It drops down to Bulwell Bay, with the town of Milford Haven visible straight across the water, then cuts round the neck of two mini headlands, Popton Point and Sawdern Point. Fort Popton was built on Popton Point in the last century to defend the Haven and was subsequently incorporated into an oil terminal. Once past Sawdern Point, you reach Angle Bay. For much of the walk round the bay, famous for its cockles, there is no path and you will have to pick your way through rocks, seaweed and often soggy sand to make progress. Moreover, the scene to your left for the early part of the walk on the foreshore is dominated by the refinery installations.

Things do pick up; the refinery is left behind, and soon after joining a lane you arrive at the village of Angle (135), a useful stopping-place and the last spot for many miles with a reasonable level of amenities. Continuing on round the bay, still following a lane, you pass the Old Point House Inn which contains a fire that supposedly has not gone out in 300 years, then you round Angle Point, and continue past a lifeboat station away from Angle Bay. Excitement now wells up, as the long trek round the Haven is nearly over and the open sea is just a short way away. Heading slightly north of west, the route continues along the modest clifftops past Chapel Bay, then at West Pill swings south-westwards to West Angle Bay (136.8). Thorn Island, on which stands an island fort that was built in 1854 and was later converted into a hotel, can be seen just a short way into the Haven, and across the Haven you will see out towards St Ann's Head. The inland section is over and true coastal walking resumes.

West Angle Bay to Freshwater East (19 miles – direct route) via Castlemartin

ENJOY: Sheep Island, Guttle Hole, Green Bridge of Wales, Elegug Stacks, Huntsman's Leap, St Govan's Chapel, Bosherston (off route), Stackpole Head, Barafundle

The five miles on to Freshwater West provide walking that is truly breathtaking; Rat Island, Sheep Island with its traces of an Iron Age settlement, Guttle Hole and the bays of East and West Pickard all bring scenes of rugged splendour, the benign green-coated upper slopes giving way to sheer sandstone faces that in turn plunge to the boiling frothing waters. Freshwater West is one of Pembrokeshire's finest beaches, the covering of the grey shingle on the foreshore resembling a huge shadow across the golden sands. On the southern edge of Freshwater West is a preserved seaweed collector's hut where edible seaweed was gathered to be made into laverbread, still a popular delicacy in parts of South Wales; the seaweed is boiled and reduced to a black mush, then dipped in oatmeal and fried. Behind the foreshore of Freshwater West stands a long line of grass-topped dunes, known as the Broomhill Burrows. These are diminutive in comparison with the monstrous sandstone piles nearby, but tower nobly above the beach like a miniature mountain range. You may, if you wish, follow the sands, but at high tide it will be necessary to resort to the Burrows, eventually turning right on to the B4319 and going forward by road to Castlemartin (145.5), temporarily leaving the sea behind. The reason is that the coastline from here to Elegug Stacks is owned by the Army and accessible only on special guided tours. Indeed, the whole of the coastline between here and Bosherston, and the areas immediately inland from it, is used for Army activity and it is vital to check with local tourist information offices or on the Internet to ensure that the spectacular coastal route eastwards from Elegug Stacks is open and available on the day you are walking this section. The alternative is a miserable road walk along the B4319 beyond Castlemartin via Merrion, Sampson and Bosherston.

The main route stays on the road east of Castlemartin then joins a metalled road heading south-westwards to the sea just west of Elegug Stacks. On reaching the sea, the route turns left along the top of limestone cliffs for what is one of the finest parts on the whole national trail. The section commences in spectacular fashion with two fine natural features just out to sea: firstly the Green Bridge of Wales, a wide and dramatic rock arch that rises majestically from the surging waters, and secondly Elegug Stacks, which are two huge limestone teeth shooting upwards out of the sea, and perfect nesting places for seabirds such as guillemots, kittiwakes and razorbills. The scenery is no less splendid as you continue south-eastwards via Flimston Bay, Bullslaughter Bay, Mewsford Point and the Castle, passing a number of Iron Age forts. There are caves, arches, grotesquely-shaped gaps in the rock known as blowholes because of the spray blown up through the gaps by the swell of the sea, and a succession of terrifyingly tall and steep limestone faces, with the narrowest channels of seawater darting through the gaps at the bottom. Care does need to be taken near to the blowholes, which may be quite alarming to vertigo sufferers in the party. The steepness of the rock faces is attributable to huge earth movements known as the Armorican Orogeny that took place a small matter of 250 million years ago, and which upended the limestone bedding planes on the sea floor. It is the faulting in the rock, and accompanying marine erosion, that has led to the amazing cliffscapes on this section. The most famous fault of all on this section is Huntsman's Leap, a narrow slit in the rock 200 yd long and over 100 ft deep but in places only a few feet wide. It got its name from a huntsman who is said to have successfully cleared it on his horse, only to die of fright when he realised what he had done!

As if this natural beauty were not enough, shortly beyond Huntsman's Leap comes one of the most famous landmarks of the whole route, namely St Govan's Chapel. Dating back to the thirteenth century – although the original chapel is thought to date back to the sixth century – this tiny stone structure neatly fills a cleft in the cliff that is so small it seems inconceivable that anyone could build on it. Indeed, the only way to enter it is by leaving the coast path and taking a steep flight of steps that drop directly into its austere interior. By exiting from the west of the chapel it is possible to descend to the beach. At the point where the flight of steps leaves the coast path to reach the chapel, a road comes down from Bosherston; this may be useful to walkers who have had to travel to Bosherston from Castlemartin by the inland route because of firing activity, although this road is also closed at certain times. From the chapel it is a short walk along the coast path to St Govan's Head, offering superb views to Stackpole Head a short way to the north-east. Having got round the headland, you proceed north-eastwards past the little creek of New Quay to the lovely sands of Broad Haven – not to be confused with its namesake on St Brides Bay. This Broad Haven is definitely more interesting, not only for its sublime surroundings but also its lagoon, set back from the beach with a carpet of heather along one edge and banks of limestone at its inland end. Separating Broad Haven from Bosherston are a series of lily pools, created by the Earl of Cawdor in the eighteenth century for his Stackpole Estate. Surrounded by woodland, the pools provide a pleasant contrast to the awesome ruggedness of the nearby cliffs, with the lilies at their best in June. Paths on either side of the pools allow a short circular walk via Bosherston, and it is one of the pool-side paths that the eastbound walker will use to get to Broad Haven if Army activity has kept him away from the coast all the way from Castlemartin.

Bosherston is a pretty place with whitewashed cottages and a thirteenth-century church, and you may be fortunate enough to obtain refreshments in season. Proceeding from Broad Haven, and rounding the modest Saddle Point, the next objective is Stackpole

Head, another fascinating study in limestone, and on rounding this headland, you have a lovely view of the golden sands of Barafundle Bay. Proceeding round the bay, the coast path continues to Stackpole Quay, believed to be the smallest quay in Wales, and once used as a base for the export of limestone. In fact it is at this point that limestone gives way for the time being to old red sandstone, and as the coast path continues via Greenala Point – site of an Iron Age camp – and Trewent Point, the cliffscapes provide a pleasing contrast of lush green and rich brown. Rounding Trewent Point, the route drops down to Freshwater East (155.8), a bay with a village of the same name on the hillside above it. It certainly lacks the charisma of Freshwater West although accommodation should be found here if needed. I endured one of my least agreeable nights on the national trail at Freshwater East; my host at the bed and breakfast had forgotten he had promised to provide me with an evening meal, and although he did deign to cook for me, there being no pub for miles, the food was simple and expensive. There was no bath, the shower spewed out only ice-cold water, and I slept so badly that I was reduced to sitting up in bed between 2.40 a.m. and 4.30 a.m. solemnly reading from cover to cover the entire stock of the previous year's brochures so that by the time I dropped off again I knew by heart the opening hours and admission fee for every steam railway, glass works and adventure fun park within a radius of 40 miles.

Freshwater East to Tenby (13.2 miles) via Manorbier

ENJOY: Swanlake Bay, Manorbier, Skrinkle Haven, Church Doors, Giltar Point, views to Caldey Island, Tenby

From Freshwater East to Giltar Point the walking is truly magnificent. Proceeding round the bay, you pass another Iron Age camp and continue on to West Moor Cliff, on which is a triangulation point at a height of just under 300 ft. Between the cliffs of West Moor and

East Moor is the lovely Swanlake Bay, and beyond East Moor is Manorbier Bay giving easy access to the nearby village of Manorbier.

Manorbier

The village is best known for being the birthplace, in about 1145, of Giraldus Cambrensis, or Gerald the Welshman, the author of a vivid account of life in medieval Wales. He was born in Manorbier Castle, a splendid Norman fortification which stands at the south-west edge of the village. Nearby is a fine twelfth-century church that boasts an impressive tower and a brass memorial to the SS *Satrap*, lost off the nearby coast in 1915.

East of Manorbier the cliff scenery is quite outstanding, a firm path following the cliff edge past a succession of narrow chasms in the sandstone. There is a slight inland detour to avoid the old military installations on Old Castle Head but there follows a quite delectable stretch of coastline past Skrinkle Head and Lydstep Point. Skrinkle Haven consists of three tiny coves, the largest of which is blessed with a beautiful sandy beach and huge limestone cliffs with twin caves cut into the cliff face on the east side. The most easterly of the three coves contains Church Doors, a remarkably tall and thin natural arch of limestone. Lydstep Point, a few minutes beyond, is bypassed by the official route, but a detour is almost mandatory to view the incredible cliff formations – further legacies of the Armorican Orogeny – with huge vertical thrusts of carboniferous limestone interspersed with caves and arches, all constantly vulnerable to the raging seas. There are good views to Caldey Island, where a religious community founded in the sixth century is today maintained by Cistercian monks who sell perfumes and toiletries they make from wild flowers found on the island. Boat trips run to the island in season.

The way drops to the beach at Lydstep Haven with its intrusive holiday park, and there is a stiff climb back on to the cliffs. However the walking soon improves as the route proceeds to Giltar Point past the viewpoint of Proud Giltar, near to which is the splendidly-named hamlet of Bubbleton and Valleyfield Top. (Access to Giltar Point may, again, be restricted by Army activity, in which case you will be diverted by Penally to South Beach, north of Giltar Point.) After rounding Giltar Point, from which there are fine views, there is another drop and a lovely walk along the firm sands of South Beach to arrive at Tenby (169).

Tenby

This is a justifiably popular resort, with a beautiful harbour, excellent sandy beaches, a commendable restraint on tacky concessions to the tourist trade, and fine views over the sea – more specifically, Carmarthen Bay – to Caldey Island, Giltar Point and the lovely coastline towards Saundersfoot. Arguably the town's most impressive feature is its now ruined castle, built in the twelfth century on a rocky headland, but there is so much else to see, including fine fourteenth-century town walls, quaint narrow streets, rows of Georgian and Regency houses, the part-thirteenth-century church of St Mary (possibly Wales' largest parish church) the fifteenth-century Tudor Merchant's House, and, across the beach, St Catherine's Island, dominated by a nineteenth-century fortress.

Tenby to Amroth (7.5 miles) via Saundersfoot

ENJOY: Monkstone Beach, Monkstone Point

Whether you choose to stay within sight of the sea, effectively avoiding the centre of Tenby, or prefer to cut through the town centre, you will exit from it beside North Beach, following Waterwynch Lane just east of north, and enjoying a grandstand view back to the town. The lane peters out just before the tiny hamlet of Waterwynch and there is some tough walking along the coast path towards Saundersfoot, including a particularly steep climb out of the thickly wooded Lodge Valley. The fact that this coastline faces eastwards, and is thus sheltered from the prevailing winds, has made it easier for woodland to thrive here. Once you have regained the clifftops, there are fine views to Monkstone Beach – another glorious stretch of sand – and the nearby wooded headland of Monkstone Point, which you arrive at shortly. There is an optional but highly recommended detour to the Point itself, from where Amroth, the end of the walk, is visible.

There is then a very straightforward walk, most of it through woodland, down to Saundersfoot along the coast path, although the sands can be followed all the way from Monkstone Point to Saundersfoot, and indeed on to Amroth just three miles beyond Saundersfoot, if the tide is right. Another type of rock, known as coal measures, can be found hereabouts, and a tight fold in that rock has produced a remarkable cave just south of Saundersfoot Harbour. Saundersfoot (173) was in fact established in the nineteenth century as a port for exporting good anthracite coal mined from nearby pits, but mining stopped after the outbreak of the Second World War. It has now become a popular yachting centre and holiday resort, although with none of the charisma or charm of Tenby; my impression of it was of a rather garish place, dominated by tourist amenities of the most unsubtle kind. The last little section of route begins in an unusual fashion, as Coppet Hall Point is negotiated not by means of a traditional coast path but through a number of tunnels built for narrow-gauge railway lines that conveyed coal-bearing trains to Saundersfoot. You remain on the old railway lines, but this time above ground and by the sea, to Wiseman's Bridge. The coal measures can be unstable and you should be aware of the possibility of diversions caused by rock falls.

At Wiseman's Bridge the route turns right on to a metalled road and follows it uphill out of the village, then turns right again on to a path that descends to Amroth (176.5), another village with mining connections. The sands here were used for a full rehearsal for the D-Day landings, witnessed by Churchill, Montgomery and Eisenhower. If you arrive at low tide, it is worth venturing on to the sands where you may be able to observe tree stumps and roots that are the remains of an ancient forest noted by Giraldus Cambrensis in 1183. On arriving at Amroth, it is an easy road walk past the castle, a comparatively modern structure, to the plaque on a block of stone in the shingle, marking the official ending of the walk, both in English and in Welsh. It is most satisfying to see on the plaque, above the recognition of the opening of the route by Wynford Vaughan Thomas in 1970, the words 'Poppit Sands 180 Miles' (though if the most direct route, avoiding detours, has been taken, it will have worked out a few miles less!). Having experienced the feelings of satisfaction, you must then work out how to get home. It is a long and anticlimactical walk to Kilgetty, the nearest railway station; moreover, trains back to civilisation from there are slow and infrequent, and if you are relying on public transport you will have to grin and bear the frustration of a journey of possibly several hours, however anxious you are to tell your nearest and dearest all about your epic encounter with Proud Giltar or your fleeting dalliance with Mrs Morgan.

Offa's Dyke Path

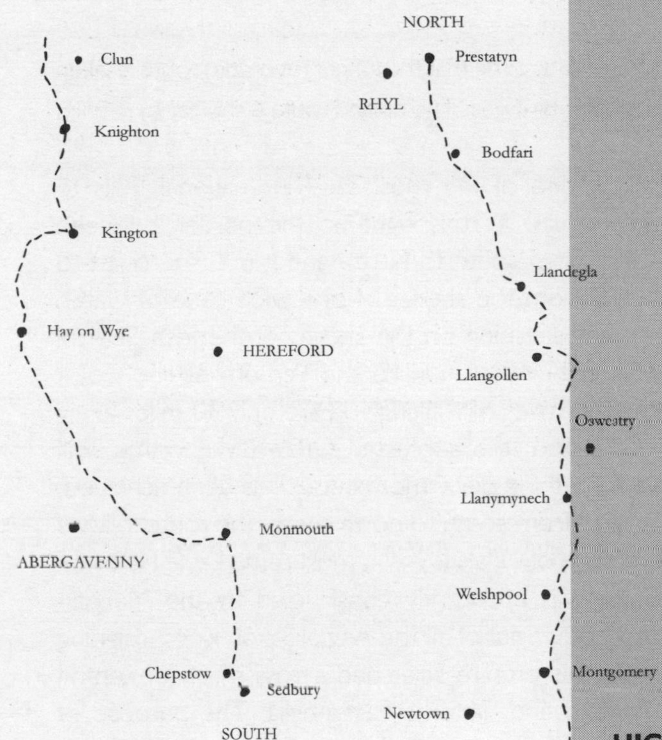

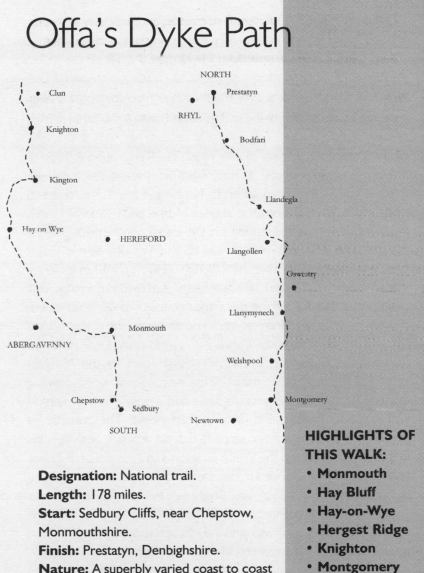

Designation: National trail.
Length: 178 miles.
Start: Sedbury Cliffs, near Chepstow, Monmouthshire.
Finish: Prestatyn, Denbighshire.
Nature: A superbly varied coast to coast walk following the English/Welsh border based on the eighth-century Offa's Dyke earthwork.

HIGHLIGHTS OF THIS WALK:

- **Monmouth**
- **Hay Bluff**
- **Hay-on-Wye**
- **Hergest Ridge**
- **Knighton**
- **Montgomery**
- **Chirk Castle**
- **Moel Fammau/ Jubilee Tower**

Difficulty rating: Moderate to strenuous, but many easy sections. Some strenuous sections could become severe in bad weather.
Average time of completion: 11–12 days.

NB: The distances given assume that the longer (riverside) route is taken between Brockweir and Bigsweir. The upland route is shorter by 1 mile.

Offa's Dyke Path is one of the most satisfying national trails to attempt and accomplish. It runs right up the border between England and Wales, from south to north, and it is a true coast to coast route, starting from the shores of one wide band of water, the river Severn, and finishing on the shores of the Irish Sea on the coastline of North Wales. Unlike the Pembrokeshire Coast Path, where after 180 miles of walking you are only 30 miles away from where you started, the successful Offa's Dyke walker will really sense that something quite momentous has been achieved. Moreover, on its way from south to north shore, the route follows virtually all that remains of Offa's Dyke, a most remarkable historical feature. The Dyke was apparently constructed by the Mercian king Offa, the most powerful of all the Anglo-Saxon kings, reigning from AD 757–796; his empire stretched across much of central and southern England and, latterly, East Anglia. The purpose of the Dyke was to mark an agreed, definite frontier between his kingdom of Mercia and the Welsh kingdoms to the west of it. There had been numerous border disputes and fluctuations for several hundred years, but peace was finally achieved in 780 and it was in 784 that work began on the Dyke. Although many historians believe that its purpose was primarily to serve as a frontier marker, it also enabled trade between Mercia and Wales to be controlled, and may have prevented or hindered cattle raids. Moreover, it has been suggested by Frank Noble, who played a prominent part in establishing the national trail, that the form and siting of the Dyke points to its main purpose being a defensive one.

Whatever its purpose, the Dyke was – and still is today – an awesomely impressive construction. Though each owner of the land through which the Dyke was to run had responsibility for the work on their section, the dimensions were similar throughout; the earth bank of the Dyke was on the whole 6 ft high and 60 ft wide, and it was always ditched. It covered a distance of 149 miles. Remarkably, 1,200 years later, 81 miles of the Dyke were still standing, and it was suggested that these remains could become the basis of a long-distance path.

The result is a journey which provides a fascinating exploration of our past, and wonderfully contrasting and unspoilt scenery from beginning to end. On no other national trail is there such diversity. Many sections could be accomplished by the most ill-equipped novice, but as many again will impose the greatest technical demands on even the hardiest traveller. One aspect common to every stretch of the route, besides the bilingual signposting ('Llwybr Clawdd Offa – Offa's Dyke Path'), is the ubiquitous stile – there are hundreds – but this should not detract from your enjoyment of the variety of surroundings. There are moors and mountains, forests and pastures, switchback hills, gentle riverside strolls, canal paths and aqueducts. There are also many chocolate-box villages and towns, and in fact you are never very far from places of habitation or amenities which are plentiful throughout.

Sedbury Cliffs to Monmouth (18.5 miles) via Chepstow and Redbrook

ENJOY: Chepstow, Wintour's Leap, Devil's Pulpit, Tintern Abbey, River Wye, Kymin, Monmouth

The start of the walk is at Sedbury Cliffs, on the English side of the border. If you have arrived at Chepstow by public transport, the easiest and pleasantest way to get to the start is actually to cross the river from the town centre, join the national trail and simply follow it backwards to the beginning! It is worth pausing upon reaching the start, marked by an inscribed stone, so you may enjoy the fine views down and across the Severn estuary; this is the widest stretch of water you will see until you reach Prestatyn nearly 180 miles away. Nearby is the magnificent Severn Bridge, opened in 1966, with its enormous centre span of 3,240 ft, the older of the two Severn crossings.

Then you turn your back on the Severn and head back towards Chepstow, proceeding slightly north of west alongside a fragment of the Dyke. It is good to see it making an appearance at once, as if reminding you of the over-riding theme and purpose of the journey. You cross the B4228 Beachley–Sedbury road, and the route continues in broadly the same direction, descending through a field to reach a housing estate. At length you reach the banks of the river Wye and swing right to follow a path high above the river and reach another area of housing, turning left briefly on to the B4228 and left again on to a path which meets the A48 (2).

There is easy access from here across the Wye to Chepstow, a town full of interest with steep medieval streets, a sixteenth-century gatehouse, and an impressive castle begun by the Normans in 1067 and finished during the thirteenth century to defend a strategic bend in the Wye. Beyond the A48, the route follows a mixture of paths and lanes running alongside the B4228, heading north-eastwards away from Chepstow. The highlight of this section is Wintour's Leap, a superb viewpoint on steep limestone cliffs high above the Wye. The route continues by the B4228, briefly proceeding to the east of it, before returning and at last leaving it for good at Dennel Hill, turning left to pass through the magnificent woodland on the eastern side of the Wye. The woodland opens out to give exquisite views to the Wye and in particular the remains of Tintern Abbey. The best viewpoint is at Devil's Pulpit, a small limestone outcrop from which it is said the Devil tried to corrupt the monks at Tintern. It is possible hereabouts to pick up a path leading down to the ruins of the abbey, which was founded in 1131 by Cistercians. It was a victim of the dissolution in 1536, although the abbey church with its rose window is almost intact.

Having passed the Pulpit and swung eastwards, you leave the woods, swing sharply to the west and go downhill to reach Brockweir. You may either choose to follow alongside the Wye to Bigsweir Bridge (11.5), or take a shorter but tougher route across St Briavels Common, with the Dyke clearly visible in places. This route starts with a brief walk along a metalled road heading north-eastwards, then follows a long woodland climb on a stony track, the reward being a sensational view back to the Severn Bridge and beyond. Flatter walking ensues, then a massive descent through woodland and an easy valley walk to Bigsweir. The Wye valley is a naturalist's paradise; the waters attract kingfishers, dippers and herons, while in the woodland areas – themselves a happy mixture of lime, oak, ash and beech – the observer may spot buzzards, woodpeckers, sparrowhawks and tawny owls. The Wye round Bigsweir is particularly noted for its glasswort, and the woodland walker in spring should look out for wood anemone, wood sorrel, dog's mercury and violets. Incidentally, this is the only section on the national trail of any length where a choice of route exists. Having done and greatly enjoyed both, I think I would commend the longer but flatter valley route to the comparatively inexperienced walker who is getting acclimatised to the demands of a long-distance walk.

At Bigsweir Bridge the route turns right on to the A466 but then bears almost immediately right again onto a metalled road and shortly left onto a path, climbing steeply through woodland and then following the right fringe of the woods past Coxbury Farm. It is tough going but soon comes the reward in the form of a lovely walk through Highbury Wood, high above the Wye on the stony ridge of the Dyke. Progress northwards is easy and fast, and it is a shame to drop down to Lower Redbrook (15) and bid farewell to the Dyke, which will not be seen again for well over 50 miles. The route turns right to follow the A466 briefly, then soon turns right again, joining the B4231 Newland road (entering Wales at this point) and climbing steeply. Shortly the route bears left on to a farm track and proceeds north-westwards, still climbing initially through open fields and then through woodland to reach the Kymin. At 800 ft, this is a wonderful viewpoint; immediately below is Monmouth, but well beyond the town in the distance you will observe the very distinctive hill known as Skirrid Fawr, which will often be seen for the next 20 miles or so. Close by the viewpoint is the Naval Temple, built in 1800 to commemorate a number of late eighteenth-century admirals. There is then a steep descent to Monmouth, initially along a path that, heading north-west, drops into further woodland, keeping the metalled access road to the left. The route swings round to join the road briefly before bearing left again along a path that leads to the A4136, which you then follow to the left to cross the Wye and arrive in the town (18.5).

Monmouth

Monmouth contains many Tudor and Georgian buildings, including several fine inns, and is a lovely place to spend some time. Among the many buildings of note are the Georgian Shire Hall, built in 1724, a museum devoted to Nelson, the ruins of an eleventh-century castle, the preserved seventeenth-century Great Castle House which became the headquarters of the Royal Monmouthshire Engineer Militia in 1875, and a two-storeyed gatehouse that was built in 1260 as one of four medieval gates into the town. The gatehouse is built on Monmow Bridge, the only Norman fortified bridge that survives in Great Britain; the river Monmow, over which the bridge passes, flows into the Wye just south of the town. The town also boasts statues of Henry V, who was born in the castle, and Charles Rolls, of Rolls Royce fame.

Monmouth to Pandy (16.8 miles) via Llantilio Crossenny

ENJOY: St Michael of the Fiery Meteor, White Castle, views to Skirrid/ Sugar Loaf

By contrast with what has gone before and what awaits later, the next section of the walk, from Monmouth to Pandy, is a gentle journey through peaceful rolling countryside. Whilst it is very pleasant, it could not be described as spectacular, although the 1,596 ft summit of Skirrid Fawr, becoming increasingly prominent as the walk continues, is a constant feature of the landscape.

Having proceeded south-westwards down the main street of Monmouth, the route turns right on to the B4233 Abergavenny road, and shortly left on to the metalled Watery Lane. As the road bends sharply left – shortly before terminating at Bailey Pitt Farm – you turn right on to a path that soon enters King's Wood, climbs quite steeply, and heads just south of west, picking up a track that descends gently to a metalled road just east of Hendre Farm. You turn right on to the road, then just beyond the farm buildings turn left to follow a path through fields heading north-westwards, keeping the river Trothy – another tributary of the Wye – on your left. Close by is the site of the now obliterated thirteenth-century Cistercian Grace Dieu abbey. On reaching a road you turn left on to it and immediately cross the Trothy, then soon turn right on to a path which continues through rolling pastures, with the Trothy now to your right. The path swings from north-westwards to just south of westwards, and stays very close to the water to reach a hamlet which rejoices in the splendid name of Llanvihangel-Ystern-Llewern. The little church is dedicated to St Michael of the Fiery Meteor, which conjures up images of fire-and-brimstone rhetoric traditionally beloved of Welsh non-conformist chapel preachers, although its setting could hardly be more peaceful or idyllic.

You cross a metalled road here and go south-westwards on a path through fields, in due course reaching another road, turning left on to it and following it steeply downhill. Then you bear right and head north-westwards, passing directly in front of an imposing house called The Grange and crossing an area of orchard before reaching another road, turning right on to it and following it to Llantilio Crossenny (27.5). This is near enough the halfway mark between Monmouth and Pandy, and offers a perfect incentive, in the form of the Hostry Inn with its reputation for excellent beer, to rest weary limbs and perhaps make friends with other Dyke walkers.

From Llantilio Crossenny, the route strikes out marginally north of westwards through open country to the little settlement of Treadam, then turns right to follow a track northwards to White Castle, the highlight of the section. It was one of three border castles built as a defensive triangle to guard the border land against Welsh raids, and although the round-towered stronghold of White Castle is now a ruin, it is nonetheless a most impressive one. The route then heads north-westwards again through very pleasant open farmland to reach the B4521 at the intriguingly-named hamlet of Caggle Street, turning right on to the road. Just past the little village chapel you turn left and continue north-westwards, initially along a path and then a metalled lane, through Old Court, then beyond this hamlet you turn right up a path leading to the hilltop village of Llangattock Lingoed. The Hunters Moon Inn, which was built in the seventeenth century, has changed little since, and there is also a pretty church which dates back to the thirteenth century. The route leaves the village on a path heading north-westwards through open country and, soon after leaving the village, there is a delightful narrow wooded valley or dingle to negotiate.

Having lost some height from Llangattock Lingoed, a steep climb is required to bring you within sight of Pandy. Continuing north-westwards, you reach a metalled road immediately north-east of the hamlet of Great Park and join a footpath just the other side, leading you to a lane which shortly reaches another metalled road. There follows a descent north-westwards along a path, keeping the little village of Wern-Gifford on your left, to the village of Pandy (35.3) on the busy A465 Abergavenny–Hereford road in the valley of the river Honddu. If you have spent the day hiking here from Monmouth, this descent represents a fine climax to the day's march; it is an easy and not excessively steep downward incline through fields, with the giant Skirrid Fawr towering to the left and the Black Mountains directly ahead. Pandy offers a good range of amenities, as does the neighbouring village of Llanvihangel Crucorney, which boasts an Elizabethan manor house and fine gardens. It is at Pandy that you will wish to pay particular attention to the weather forecast for the next day, for immediately ahead lies the assault on the Black Mountains, a much tougher proposition than anything encountered so far. I had the good fortune to arrive at Pandy during a spell of settled summer weather, so was able to spend a relaxing night here without worrying about what next day would bring; my contented evening stroll was enlivened by a football match that was in progress on the village playing field. With the peak of Skirrid Fawr gazing benignly down on the Honddu valley and across to the Black Mountains, the setting was bewitching indeed and an obvious distraction to away players who, mesmerised by its beauty, could be forgiven for losing concentration in defence and gifting the home side a few soft goals.

Pandy to Hay-on-Wye (17.5 miles) via Hatterrall Hill

ENJOY: Hatterall Ridge, Llanthony, Hay Bluff, Hay-on-Wye

An early start and a good breakfast are essential for walkers aiming to reach Hay on Wye from Pandy in one day, for there is no refreshment or proper shelter of any kind until you get to within a mile of Hay. The start is deceptively innocuous. You take a path heading westwards away from the A465 at the south end of Pandy, crossing the river Honddu and the Abergavenny–Hereford railway almost immediately, and reaching a narrow metalled road. You follow this westwards through the hamlet of Treveddw then cut off a sharp corner in the road, rejoining it further on and following it to a crossroads, turning right. Having climbed quite steeply, you promptly descend again, before branching off left on to a path just before the hamlet of Tre-wyn. By this time you may feel a little like a taxi-ing aircraft waiting for its take-off slot. However, having joined this path, you begin the ascent to Hatterrall Hill, and the crest of a magnificent mountain ridge, which you will follow all the way to Hay Bluff and beyond. It is a stiff climb, and also a long one. Do not be deceived by a triangulation point at just over 1,500 ft; it is only on Hatterrall Hill at 1,740 ft that the crest is properly gained and the gradient eases, but in fact you will continue to gain height gradually. In fine clear weather, this ridge walk, lasting some ten miles, is one of the most thrilling walks you will ever accomplish. With only sheep and Welsh moorland ponies for company, you pass through totally unspoilt heather moorland, dotted with bilberry and crowberry; to your left you gaze across the formidable Black Mountains range, and to your right across a massive area of beautiful border countryside.

Between your ridge and the higher peaks of the Black Mountains lies the enchanting Vale of Ewyas. It is possible to drop down to this valley not far beyond Hatterrall Hill – although it will be a tough climb back up again – to visit the village of Llanthony with its twelfth-century Augustinian priory, while further up the valley at Capel-y-ffin, easily reached by road, there are the remains of the more recent Benedictine abbey of St Anthony. You could stay on the metalled road from there all the way to Hay if you did not fancy trying to find your way back up to the ridge again. If the weather is bad, you may in fact have second thoughts about tackling the ridge at all; the ground is liable to turn into an instant quagmire, and the terrain is so exposed and so prone to low cloud and mist that without proper equipment you could be in some danger. If you decide against it, it is simple enough to follow the A465 south-westwards to Llanvihangel Crucorney where you will pick up the road that runs to Hay via Llanthony and Capel-y-ffin. Walking the ridge in fine settled weather, I met another walker who carried nothing but a stick, flask and guidebook and informed me his equipment was being carried by car. It is something of a risk to entrust one's bags to the local taxi service when walking a national trail. And not just the risk of your finding, ten minutes after the taxi's trundled off down the road with your worldly goods, that it's taken your day's packed lunch as well. While one hopes that there are not too many drivers who would stoop to helping themselves to the contents of the bags, one can never be entirely easy in one's mind that the driver will locate the exact accommodation at which he has been asked to leave the luggage. Few things will be more disconcerting for the exhausted walker than to arrive at Oaklands Cottage in Church Road where he has booked for the night only to find, six telephone calls later, that his bags have been deposited at Oaklands House in Church Lane which he passed some seventy-five minutes ago.

You continue along the top of the ridge, gradually gaining height, following not only the eastern edge of the Brecon Beacons National Park, but also the border between England and Wales. A triangulation point is situated at the spot where the ridge reaches 2,000 ft, but you continue to climb to 2,306 ft, the highest point on the whole of the national trail. To the right, as you proceed, is a parallel ridge and the 2,100 ft summit of Black Hill, while to the left is the 2,260 ft summit of the Twmpa, separated from your ridge by the Gospel Pass which is followed by the metalled road between Capel-y-ffin and Hay. It is a justifiably popular motor route but the ridge walk is a thousand times better. Having passed the ridge summit, and descended sharply by about 100 ft, you then have a choice. You may either veer slightly left along a path which soon arrives at the triangulation point of Hay Bluff (48.5) and continues to a road which you then follow to the right. Or you can do what in fact the official route does which is to pass round Hay Bluff, leaving it to your left and following a path that arrives a little further down the road. The former course is to be recommended, since Hay Bluff is a wonderful viewpoint and a place to linger on a clear day. After following the ridge for so many miles, you suddenly see it falling away in front of you and are treated to a breathtaking panorama across the lovely

Radnor countryside, with fine views to Black Hill and the Twmpa. Sadly, beyond Hay Bluff you must begin your descent. The early part of it is spectacular; you drop 600 ft in half a mile, although the steepness is mitigated for walkers by a carefully constructed path which, for erosion prevention, should be followed rather than cut round. In due course you reach the road, where you will see a prehistoric stone circle over the road as you reach it, and possibly, as I did, a rather less than prehistoric ice cream van.

You turn right on to the road, the path of the alternative route meeting the road a little further along. As the road bends slightly right, you leave it by bearing left on to a field path heading slightly west of north, and this general direction is maintained all the rest of the way to Hay. The path skirts the western edge of Tack Wood, briefly joining a track at Cadwgan Farm before heading out into open fields again, with Hay-on-Wye now directly ahead of you. You drop down steeply to arrive at a metalled road, bearing left on to it, then turn right to enjoy a very pleasant pastoral walk into the town (52.8), with the beautiful waters of Cusop Dingle to your right. Once a border fortress – the town is built right on the border, and boasts Norman castle ruins and thirteenth-century town walls – it is now one of the loveliest old towns in Britain, combining bygone charm with an impressive range of amenities and an abundance of fine shops and restaurants. It is known as a book town, for in 1961 one Richard Booth opened a huge second-hand bookshop here, many other bookshops have opened since, and a major book festival is held here every year. Bibliophiles can find books on every conceivable topic, from rolling stock on the Fenchurch Street–Southend line down the ages to inter-war Northern non-league football, and you can be sure that if there is insufficient room in your rucksack, traders will post your chosen book home for you. Even those without a literary bent may succumb to the array of reading matter on offer, and keen walkers wishing to round up the party next morning for the next stage of the hike should not be surprised to find at least one of their number sitting in a dusty corner of the children's bookshop flicking nostalgically through the pages of *Billy Bunter's Postal Order* or the 1972 *Beano* annual.

Hay on Wye to Kington (14.7 miles) via Newchurch and Gladestry

ENJOY: Bettws Dingle, Disgwylfa Hill, Hergest Ridge

It is with some reluctance that you will leave Hay, although if time is available it is worth detouring one mile up the B4351 to the pretty village of Clyro, where the famous diarist Francis Kilvert was curate from 1865 to 1872. Having left the town, the route follows the left bank of the Wye, heading just east of north, then heads slightly away from the river and proceeds north to cross the A438. From here you get a fine view back to Hay and the Wye valley. You turn right to walk beside this busy road but soon turn left and head north-westwards on a path that goes along the edge of Bettws Dingle, a deep wooded valley with a waterfall. It is a lovely shady spot on a hot day, although there is an eerie feel about the lines of closely packed conifers. A substantial climb through the woods, still heading north-westwards, brings you to a minor road where you turn right. The route follows the road to a T-junction, and turns right here, following the road until, shortly before Catworthy Court, the road bends to the right. You turn left here on to a path which meets another road at Cae-Higgin and then turn left again to follow this road briefly. Just before Cwm-yr-eithin the route turns right on to a farm lane that heads northwards. You gain further height here, but the reward, as you look back, is a superb view back to the Black Mountains, Hay Bluff and the Twmpa.

You cross another metalled road and head north-westwards towards Newchurch, soon passing the 1,167 ft summit of Little Mountain to your left, which although modest compared with Hay Bluff, is still well over 800 ft higher than the Wye valley that you forsook a few miles back. It is easy to detour to the summit, on which stands the site of a Roman camp. Beyond Little Mountain you drop very steeply towards the buildings of Gilfach-yr-heol. Just before them you bear right on to a lane and follow it to reach the pretty village of Newchurch in the valley of the river Arrow. When you reach the B4594 you turn right on to it and pass through the village. You then turn right again, this time on to a path heading north-eastwards and, climbing steeply again, continue on to Disgwylfa Hill, reaching 1,250 ft. This is wonderful walking on springy grass with glorious views across miles of totally unspoilt countryside. You begin to descend and drop down to a crossroads of paths where you turn left, soon reaching Hill Farm and, beyond that, a metalled road. Still maintaining a height of over 1,000 ft, you turn right on to the road. At Hill Farm, at the time of my visit, there was a welcome water tap provided for walkers, and some amusing doggerel extolling the benefits of this free refreshment!

Having turned right on to the road beyond Hill Farm, you shortly turn left along a path that heads northwards to a metalled road a little way east of Hengoed, then having crossed the road you proceed on a path heading north-eastwards past Stonehouse Barn and a disused quarry. You drop very steeply to reach a metalled road, and turn left on to this road, following it to the village of Gladestry (63). You then turn right on to the B4594 to pass through the village, in which the Royal Oak pub offers the first on-path refreshments since Hay. Even though the town of Kington is only a few miles away, it is worth stopping at Gladestry, as in order to reach Kington you must tackle Hergest Ridge which means another substantial climb, this time up to almost 1,400 ft. Beyond the village, you turn right on to the Huntington road and shortly left on to an excellent path which, heading north-eastwards, ascends on to the bracken-clad ridge. Although perhaps lacking the grandeur of the ridge between Hatterrall Hill and Hay Bluff, this is marvellous open walking. The ridge, where once a racecourse stood, is blessed with a lovely grass surface, making progress very easy, and there are tremendous views in all directions, stretching up to 30 miles on a clear day.

Having proceeded north-eastwards to gain the top of the ridge, you then swing eastwards to make the descent. With some reluctance (unless the weather is bad) you drop down off the ridge to meet an area of forest to your left, and at the edge of the forest you join a metalled road which you follow eastwards to arrive in Kington (67.5), on the English side of the border. To your right, as you follow this road, are Hergest Croft Gardens, which have a fine variety of trees and shrubs and in summer provide a rainbow display of azaleas and rhododendrons. Kington is a small market town on the banks of the river Arrow, which you last saw at Newchurch. There has been a settlement here since Norman times but virtually nothing here remains from that era. The town does boast a large thirteenth-century church and late Victorian clock tower, but arguably the most charming corner is a row of well-kept whitewashed stone cottages looking out on to Back Brook, a tributary of the river Arrow. You will see these cottages on your way out of the town. Though the town certainly lacks the interest of Monmouth or the charisma of Hay, it is a hospitable place, with plenty of shops and ample facilities for eating, drinking and sleeping. My bed and breakfast host not only offered me delicious warm home-made bread but also, as I arrived on a scorching August afternoon, a dip in his paddling pool that he had filled for his three small children. Bliss!

Kington to Knighton (13.5 miles) via Dolley Green

ENJOY: Bradnor Hill, Burfa, Evenjobb Hill, Hawthorn Hill

To exit from Kington it is necessary, having passed Back Brook, to cross the busy A44 that bypasses the town to the north, and head north-westwards to Bradnor Green, initially on a lane and then a path which climbs very steeply. Having passed Bradnor Green you cross what is the highest golf course in England at well over 1,000 ft, and though care is needed as you cross the fairways, the views are once more astonishing. The route, still heading north-westwards, stays well to the east of the nearby 1,282 ft summit of Bradnor Hill, then swings north-eastwards to climb on to Rushock Hill. This is quite demanding but exhilarating walking. It is on Rushock Hill that you are reunited with the Dyke, and for much of the next 70 miles you will be walking either along or beside it. You turn left to follow the Dyke, briefly heading westwards and passing a trio of eighteenth-century yews named the Three Shepherds. Soon you reach the 1,230 ft summit, providing views that stretch back to the Black Mountains, before beginning a big descent, passing to the left of the Knill Garraway Wood. You then turn right, heading northwards, keeping to your left the summit of Herrock Hill, which is just a few feet lower than Rushock Hill.

Now you descend rapidly, swinging westwards again just beyond Herrock Cottage and following a lane through a small patch of woodland to reach the B4362 at Lower Harpton, where you return to Wales. You turn right and follow this road for a few hundred yards as far as the ancient Ditchyeld Bridge which crosses the Hindwell Brook, although motor travellers use a more modern bridge beside it. A signpost here points the way to such delightfully-named places as Evenjobb and Presteigne. The national trail turns left on to the road signposted for Evenjobb, but soon leaves it, turning right on to a path that skirts the western edge of a large area of woodland. Having lost the Dyke shortly before Lower Harpton, you are now reunited with it, and begin one of the finest sections of Dyke-side walking on the route. As you swing to the left to head decisively north-westwards on to Evenjobb Hill, you pass a settlement known as Burfa, while in the woods to your right is an Iron Age fort known as Burfa Bank. At Burfa the route passes a magnificently restored timber-framed house. It has the splendid name Old Burfa, which sounds as though it ought to be a large camper van or other cumbersome vehicle driven by Sid James in one of the Carry On films.

Beyond Burfa it is quite delightful walking on to Evenjobb Hill. You cross a metalled road just east of the village of Evenjobb then proceed through Granner Wood, heading north-eastwards. You swing north-westwards, emerging from Granner Wood and climbing in open country towards another area of woodland called the Hilltop Plantation, just to the east of the farm at Pen Offa. You pass a summit of 1,218 ft within the plantation, then, still heading north-westwards, drop down into open country to meet a metalled road. Crossing it, you turn north-eastwards and head in a virtually straight line quite steeply downhill towards the Lugg valley. The Dyke is clearly visible for much of the journey from Burfa to the Lugg valley, and makes a splendid spectacle, while views to the west are quite magnificent. As you continue northwards towards Knighton and beyond, you may find the route following the top of the bank, but often the bank is so thickly laden with trees and other vegetation that progress along the top of it is not feasible and the path proceeds beside it instead. At the bottom of the hill you reach another metalled road which you cross, heading north-eastwards over pleasant meadows to cross the river Lugg and climb gently to arrive at the B4356 at Dolley Green (75.5).

From there you proceed initially north-westwards along a lane before turning north-eastwards and ascending steadily on to Furrow Hill, picking up a track briefly before turning sharp right and shortly left to follow the Dyke over Hawthorn Hill. At 1,300 ft this is the highest ground since Hergest Ridge, with excellent views all around; Presteigne can clearly be seen to the south-east, and on a clear day it is possible to see back as far as the Black Mountains. Still maintaining a height of well over 1,000 ft, the route turns slightly west of north to cross the B4355 Norton road and shortly afterwards turns right on to it. Soon you reach a junction with the

B4357, and you turn left on to this road, reaching the hamlet of Rhos-y-meirch and bearing right on to a narrow minor road then immediately right on to a path which proceeds slightly east of north, following the Dyke to Knighton. You pass just to the west of the prettily-named hamlet of Jenkin Allis, and the 1,066 ft summit of Ffrydd, then drop very steeply, passing the edge of a golf course and then through a small section of Great Ffrydd Wood. At the bottom of the hill the B4355 is crossed, and it is then a short walk to the main street of Knighton (81).

Knighton

Known in Welsh as Tref-y-Clawdd or the Town on the Dyke, because stretches of the Dyke can be seen around the town, Knighton boasts a number of seventeenth-century houses round a marketplace, a prominent Victorian clock tower, a little railway station on the Swansea–Shrewsbury line, and plenty of shops and accommodation. It is often trumpeted as the halfway mark on the national trail, but it is still some eight miles short of halfway. Of particular interest to the walker in the town is Offa's Dyke Park, containing the stone that commemorates the opening of the national trail here in 1971, and the Offa's Dyke Information Centre.

Knighton to B4386 for Montgomery (18 miles) via Newcastle, Churchtown

ENJOY: Panpunton Hill, Cwm-sanaham Hill, Llanfair Hill, Graig Hill, Churchtown, Edenhope Hill, Montgomery

This section is the toughest of the whole route, but it is also very rewarding. Several splendid stretches of the Dyke are still in evidence and the border countryside is absolutely delightful, with tremendously varied plant life and wildlife. Walkers should keep an eye out not only for foxes and rabbits but also weasels and polecats, while the spring brings plentiful amounts of primroses and early-purple orchids. At Knighton you cross back into Shropshire, and much of this section will be on the English side of the border. The start is deceptively easy, as the route drops to the river Teme which skirts the northern fringes of the town, then turns left to follow the south bank of the Teme north-westwards on a path, and crosses the railway and river. Almost immediately beyond the river you go over a metalled road, then climb very steeply on to Panpunton Hill. Initially you head north-eastwards, then on Panpunton Hill turn north-westwards – this will be your direction of travel as far as Llanfair Hill – and embark on a splendid high level promenade, following the Dyke as you go. You continue on to Cwm-sanaham Hill, with views across the Teme valley to the site of Knucklas Castle, an Iron Age fort. There follows a precipitous descent to a metalled road at Selley Hall, then after crossing the road you regain the lost height quickly and proceed past Garbett Hall, where a water tap should be available, on to Llanfair Hill, now rising to 1,400 ft. You are able to walk along the bank of the Dyke here, and there is a real feeling of being on top of the world, with fantastic views across miles of lovely countryside.

You reach a metalled road, turning right on to it and now heading slightly east of north. The road arrives at a crossroads where you turn right again, then almost immediately left to leave the tarmac and embark on another big descent to Lower Spoad, this time walking parallel to the Dyke. There is brief respite for the walker as the national trail, having crossed the B4368, proceeds across the meadows adjoining the river Clun, and over the river itself, beside which is the beautiful half-timbered farmhouse of Bryndrinog. Then you rise and shortly reach another metalled road, just east of the village of Newcastle, which contains a useful pub, at the halfway point of the national trail (89). Then, after going straight over the Newcastle road and refreshing yourself from another route-side tap, you head north-eastwards on to Graig Hill. This is an ascent of almost inhuman severity. The Dyke, bedecked with larches, climbs with you.

There follows a rather easier descent, the route coming down to cross three lanes in close succession just west of Mardu near the hamlet of Upper Mount where there is also an attractive pond. Swinging north-westwards, you proceed up a little valley through a small patch of woodland, then turn north-eastwards and climb steeply up to another metalled road at Hergan. Crossing the road brings no respite; you continue to climb as you head northwards to Middle Knuck, temporarily sharing your route with that of the Shropshire Way which has come up from Clun. Beyond Middle Knuck the climbing temporarily ceases, and after crossing a metalled road you descend steeply through woodland, heading slightly east of north, towards the delectable hamlet of Churchtown (92). As you approach the hamlet, the woods suddenly clear to give you the prospect of an open downward incline, dotted with trees and given added summer colour by patches of rosebay. Snugly nestling in the valley with a hill rising steeply behind is the church of St John, and you drop down to meet it. It is a lovely place to stop and take stock before embarking on the next climb, although despite its suffix 'town' the hamlet boasts no amenities whatsoever.

Having crossed straight over the metalled road by the church, you head just west of north and tackle perhaps the most gruelling ascent of all as you climb on to Edenhope Hill, which some say offers the best view on the entire walk. In winter the path gets very muddy, and in the summer it is crumbly and stony; when the latter conditions prevail, as they did when I walked it, you should be careful where to put your feet for fear of inadvertently creating a miniature landslide as I managed to do. Reaching a metalled road, you cross it and descend quite steeply to the river Unk, then ascend again through Nut Wood, heading north-westwards. This is the last big climb for a good few miles. You emerge from Nut Wood into fine open countryside, passing another pond, and for a while you pass along the ditch of the Dyke. Having crossed the lane that carries the Kerry Ridgeway, back now in Wales, you descend, slightly east of north, enjoying really lovely views to the Vale of Montgomery, with Corndon Hill dominating the scene to the north-east. You reach a metalled road, turn left on to it and pass through Cwm, then continue north-westwards, follow the road to a sharp right hand bend and continue straight on along a path that continues in the same direction through Mellington Wood, with Mellington Hall to your right.

In due course you reach a driveway, turn left on to it, and almost immediately come to the B4385 Montgomery–Bishop's Castle road. Continuing in the same direction, you turn left on to this road and having crossed the Caebitra river, returning to England, you arrive at a crossroads with the A489 Newtown–Church Stoke road. There is a most welcome pub here, named the Blue Bell Inn (96). The hard graft is temporarily over, and immediately ahead of you is some easy, level walking through fields and woodland. Having crossed the A489, you straight away turn right on to a path which immediately passes Brompton Hall then follows an almost straight line north-westwards for the final three miles to the Montgomery road. The path faithfully follows not only the course of the Dyke, clearly visible through this section, but also the English/Welsh border. As you near the B4386, the next road crossing, you get a lovely view to Montgomery, and indeed having arrived at the road (99), you have only a one-mile detour to the left to reach it. Montgomery is a beautiful little town, with a church dating from the sixteenth century, a Georgian square, some attractive half-timbered houses, and the hilltop ruins of a thirteenth-century castle, although an earlier castle was built here by Roger de Montgomery in 1072. There are majestic views across the Vale of Montgomery from beside the ruins of the later construction. After my long, hot walk from Knighton I felt I deserved a cream tea and unfortunately found myself presented with a huge plate of barely digestible teacakes and scones, the crumbly texture of which invited comparison with the soil on the climb up from Churchtown.

B4386 to Four Crosses (17.4 miles) via Forden, Buttington and Pool Quay

ENJOY: Beacon Ring, Montgomery Canal, River Severn

The next section of the route begins as easily as the previous one finished, since, having crossed the B4386, it continues along the flat in a north-westerly direction. You ford the river Camlad, returning to Wales, and then cross over a metalled road before swinging slightly east of north to walk alongside the B4388 just east of the village of Forden. You cross the A490 Welshpool road, and strike out north-eastwards on a path that proceeds through Kingswood and arrives at a narrow lane. Joining this and continuing north-eastwards, you embark on an upland area known as the Long Mountain, and although this sounds formidable, the going is not especially difficult. You climb very steeply then turn left into a forest, following the route carefully, as it is essential not to lose your way amongst the numerous tracks in the trees. Forest walking is not to everyone's taste, but there are breaks in the trees giving fine views north-westwards to Welshpool. There is also a lake called Offa's Pool which sounds historic and romantic, but it is simply part of the waterworks system of the Leighton Estate through which you are now travelling.

If all goes well you arrive at a narrow metalled road at Pant-y-bwch, join a path the other side and head eastwards then north-eastwards to reach Beacon Ring, rising to well over 1,300 ft, with a triangulation point and an Iron Age hill fort at the summit. This is another tremendous viewpoint, with splendid views to the Severn valley and the Shropshire hills, and you should make the most of it, for there will be no better view for the next 15 miles at least. Continuing north-eastwards, the route skirts the eastern fringes of the Cwmdingle plantation, then turns north-westwards and drops down to the Severn valley at Buttington. The descent is not especially steep, but it is messy with numerous stiles and fields to be negotiated, and a couple of very brief stretches of lane walking. At length you reach the B4388 Montgomery road at Buttington (108.5) and are temporarily reunited with the Dyke, of which beyond Buttington you will see little for some 12 miles. However, I was consoled by the presence, at Buttington, of the Offa's Dyke Business Park. Sadly there was insufficient time to explore the Offa's Dyke Carpet Warehouse, Offa's Dyke Bankrupt Electrical Wonderland or even a discount store named Offa's Offers.

Having turned right on to the B4388, you soon turn off to the left to cross the Shrewsbury–Aberystwyth railway line and reach the A458 Shrewsbury–Dolgellau trunk road. Turning left on to it, you immediately cross the river Severn, which you last saw at the start of your walk. The route then turns right on to a path, but by continuing along the A458 you will reach Welshpool (see Glyndwr's Way chapter) in just under a mile. You head north-eastwards across meadows to the ghastly A483, a trunk road that links the north and south Wales coasts, which you follow briefly to the right before turning left to walk beside the Shropshire Union Canal. Built in the late eighteenth century during a canal boom, it fell into disuse with the advent of the railways to the area, but has now been restored for the benefit of walkers, wildlife enthusiasts and barge travellers. In many ways it is a shame not to be able to follow the lovely towpath all the way to Four Crosses (where the national trail does pick it up again) but presumably in deference to the course of the Dyke, the route leaves it at Pool Quay.

Crossing the A483 and still heading north-east, you instead embark on a walk along an embankment on the west side of the Severn, which is part of the Severn flood defence system. It is pleasant but hardly breathtaking stuff; the highlights, for want of a better expression, are the three Criggion radio masts and the sight of the Breiddens across the river, a range of heavily quarried hills rising to 1,200 ft. Near Trederwen the route leaves the riverside, turning hard left then right to proceed briefly through intensely farmed countryside, temporarily rejoining the Dyke. You cross the B4393 and shortly afterwards arrive at Four Crosses (116.4) where, having crossed another B road (an arm of the B4393) you are forced to renew your acquaintance with the A483, following it through the village. Four Crosses is one of the defunct stations immortalised in the song 'The Slow Train' written by Michael Flanders and Donald Swann.

Four Crosses to B4500 for Chirk (16.4 miles) via Llanymynech and Trefonen

ENJOY: Llanymynech Hill, Moelydd Uchaf, Selattyn Hill

When the route was opened the A483 was followed for the next mile and a half to Llanymynech, but now the path turns left just beyond Four Crosses on to a metalled road, and then right to pick up the towpath beside the canal again. You follow this north-eastwards on its east bank, until the B4398 comes in to meet it, and it is a straightforward road walk to Llanymynech (119). The towpath section is lovely; there are sturdy brick bridges, lovingly restored locks and mile posts, pleasant views and no traffic noise, but the undoubted highlight is the aqueduct over the river Vyrnwy. At the crossroads in the village, which sits right on the English/Welsh border, you turn left on to the A483, then as the road bends right you turn left up a lane, and immediately right on to a path that climbs on to Llanymynech Hill. You head initially north-westwards then swing north-eastwards, briefly rejoining the Dyke as you round the edge of a golf course. Route-finding is a little fiddly, so follow the waymarks carefully. There are excellent views from the hillside, notwithstanding the fact that the elevation is nothing like as lofty as some of those encountered south of Montgomery. Llanymynech Hill has been mined for both copper and limestone; the hillsides show ample evidence of this, and as you swing north-westwards and drop very steeply, you cross the old Tanat valley mineral railway line. Having crossed the A495 you shortly turn left on to a lane that passes through Porth-y-waen, proceeding a little north of west, then at Cefn-y-blodwel you turn right on a path which leads towards Nantmawr (despite the Welsh sounding name, you are back in Shropshire). You soon turn right on to a metalled road to enter the village – a straggling collection of houses tightly packed into a little valley – then shortly bear left up a path that heads north-westwards through fields and woodland to the summit of Moelydd. Despite its comparatively modest height of 935 ft, there are tremendous views to the Berwyn Mountains to the west and the Shropshire hills to the east.

Swinging north-eastwards, you descend again, using a lane to pass by Ty-canol, then when this lane reaches a metalled road, you cross straight over and proceed along a path to Trefonen, crossing a charming brook in the shade of some trees at a field edge. You join a road that proceeds along the south edge of Trefonen, but soon turn left and head just west of north along a path that skirts the east side of the village, soon rejoining the Dyke. Continuing in the same direction, you rise then, having crossed the Croesau Bach–Oswestry road, drop very steeply by road to the Morda valley. This is a lovely spot, and there is the added bonus of a pub, formerly a mill, at this point. After what has been fiddly walking all the way from Forden, it is good, once you have climbed out of the valley, to enjoy a lovely stretch of path through Candy Wood and then across common land beside a disused racecourse to the B4580 road (128), heading initially just west of north, then just east of north. The views, through the gaps in the trees, are again delightful, and there is plenty of Dyke to see. By detouring right on to the B4580, in two miles you will reach Oswestry, a picturesque market town, which although largely rebuilt in the nineteenth century, has a number of seventeenth-century houses including Llwyd Mansion. There is also a part-Norman church, an early fifteenth-century grammar school (since converted into cottages) and castle ruins within a public park.

Though the Dyke continues over Baker's Hill, the national trail north of the B4580 prefers to follow a road that proceeds round the east side of it. At Carreg-y-big, however, the route turns left off the road and there follows a really fine section of path walking, initially northwards and then just east of north, following both the Dyke and the English/Welsh border for roughly four miles. Only at Orseddwen is the route briefly diverted from the Dyke on to a nearby track, but it soon rejoins it and proceeds along the western edge of Selattyn Hill before descending to cross the B4579 at Craignant. The route then climbs out of the valley, but before descending to the next major valley, that of the Ceiriog, there is a dramatic section at Nanteris involving a very steep wooded descent and climb almost immediately afterwards. This section has been less than affectionately described by walkers as the 'dirty dingle' although there is now a fine wooden stairway so progress is not quite so awkward now as it was. The descent to the Ceiriog is slow but rewarding, the route following the bank of the Dyke (the last piece of Dyke-side walking you'll be doing on the route), and there are fine views ahead to the sandstone walls of Chirk Castle. On arrival in the valley, you cross two roads in quick succession, the second being the B4500 Chirk–Glyn Ceiriog road (132.8). Although the official route heads north-westwards away from the B4500 and is described below, there is the possibility here of leaving the route and heading just north of east to visit Chirk Castle, then either returning to the B4500 or continuing to join the main route just north-east of Crogan Wladys. It is certainly worth seeing the castle (but do check opening times in advance) with its massive rectangular structure, unusually wide battlements, round towers at each corner and a fifth tower over the gateway. Inside the castle there is some fine sixteenth-century decorative work and some Stuart portraits which include Charles I and Charles II.

B4500 to Llandegla (15.5 miles) via Froncysyllte

ENJOY: Pont Cysyllte, Castell Dinas Bran, Valle Crucis Abbey, Egylwyseg Mountain

From the B4500 you climb steeply out of the valley and head north-westwards to Crogan Wladys. You then swing north-eastwards along alternate sections of footpath and metalled roads to drop to the A5 and the Vale of Llangollen. You are now back in Wales and will stay there for the rest of the journey. You cross the A5 and follow a path to the A483, turning left on to it to cross the Llangollen branch of the Shropshire Union Canal, then turn immediately left again to follow the canal towpath on its north side. There is easy access across the canal to the amenities of Froncysyllte (137) if they are required. This is delightful walking, culminating in the magnificent Pont Cysyllte aqueduct. Designed and built by Thomas Telford and William Jessop between 1795 and 1805, it carries the canal across the river Dee, at a height of 120 ft above it. The official route crosses the canal by the swing bridge and drops to the B5434, using this road to cross the Dee then turning right at the T-junction beyond it. As an alternative you can continue on the canal towpath over the aqueduct, although you need a good head for heights! Immediately beyond the canal there is a pub, very popular with canal users as well as walkers. Indeed the thirsty walker, who arrives at the pub after a tiring hike from Oswestry, may be somewhat peeved to be kept waiting at the bar behind the narrowboat traveller, shod in nothing heavier than deck shoes or flip-flops, and whose most strenuous outdoor activity that morning has consisted of hopping briefly ashore for the Sunday papers and fresh supplies of sunblock.

Just beyond the aqueduct, the towpath walk ends and the route bears left to pass through the little village of Trevor, soon reaching the A539. After briefly following that road to the left, the route turns right to head north-westwards into the Trevor Hall Woods, climbing steeply, and you should follow the signposts carefully amongst the packed conifers. Near the north-west tip of the woods, you reach a narrow metalled road and follow it to the left, north-westwards. Though seasoned walkers dislike tramping on tarmac, this particular march, along a rugged hillside, is a joy; to the left are fine views to the Vale of Llangollen, with the town of that name clearly visible further up the valley, and you can see the Berwyn Mountains rising up impressively behind. To the right, Trevor Rocks enhance the ruggedness of the scene, and soon to your left is the magnificent sight of Castell Dinas Bran, perched on a steep hillside and bypassed by the route. Once an Iron Age hill fort, a castle was built here in the thirteenth century for the princes of the Welsh kingdom of Powis, and although it is now a ruin, many of the walls and towers survive. It is certainly worth climbing it if you have the energy.

You continue along the road, looking down on Valle Crucis, a Cistercian abbey founded in 1189, and then at Rock Farm you turn right off the road on to a path to enjoy a tremendous walk along the western slopes of the limestone Eglwyseg Mountain, which at its highest rises over 1,640 ft. The path follows a ledge cut into steeply-packed scree with the craggy upper slopes of Eglwyseg forming an impressive sight to the right, while to your left is an area of forest called the Foel Plantation, and ahead are views to the summit of Cyrn-y-Brain, around 1,850 ft high. Swinging slightly north of east, you arrive in a secluded area of woodland and meet a road by an attractive stream; this lovely little oasis in such wild country is known as World's End (144.5). You go northwards up the road through the woods, heading steeply uphill, and emerge on to open moorland, continuing slightly east of north, then as the road begins to bend more to the right, you turn left to follow a path across the heather moor. This is some of the highest ground covered on the path since leaving the Black Mountains behind, with an elevation of well over 1,500 ft. Heading north-westwards, your path enters an area of thick woodland and descends. After wet weather this path can be extremely muddy, and even in a time of drought, when I walked it, it was very spongy, although boardwalks cover the worst sections. There is quite an eerie stillness about the woods, and even in bright sunshine the conifers produce dark shadows across the path. At length you emerge at the hamlet of Hafod Bilston (which may be marked on some maps now as Nant-yr-Hafod) and having crossed a metalled road you proceed, still north-westwards, along a path through fields to reach the A525 Wrexham–Ruthin road. You cross it and follow a lane north-westwards, almost immediately crossing the A5104 Bala–Chester road, and continuing into Llandegla (148.3), the prelude to a sustained section of remote high-level walking, and an obvious place for an overnight stop.

Llandegla to Bodfari (17.7 miles) via Clwydian Range

ENJOY: Foel Fenlli, Moel Fammau, Moel Arthur, Penycloddiau

Barely 30 miles separate you from journey's end, but you are now confronted by the formidable Clwydians, a range of heather-clad and, in parts, forested hills of Silurian sandstone overlooking the Vale of Clwyd, some topped by Iron Age hill forts. Unlike the walk over the Black Mountains, where there was one big climb only, the traverse of the Clwydians involves numerous ascents and descents, making it an altogether tougher proposition. Leaving Llandegla, you proceed north-westwards on the floor of the valley of the river Alyn, through pleasant farmland. You turn westwards to cross the B5431 then soon afterwards begin to climb, following a path initially north-westwards then south-westwards to a metalled road at the splendidly-named settlement of Tyddyn-tlodion, and turn right to follow that road just west of north. Soon you reach a five-pronged junction of lanes and paths. Your route is more or less straight ahead, again just west of north, keeping an area of woodland to your right. Now you begin your tramp over the Clwydians in earnest, passing over the hills of Moel y Plâs and Moel Llanfair, swinging briefly north-eastwards, then heading north-westwards again to negotiate Moel

Gyw. As might be expected, there are two substantial uphill trudges but you are rewarded with splendid views. As you pass over Moel y Plâs, you can admire Llyn Gweryd lake in its delightful setting to the south-east, with woodland guarding its southern and western shores, while on your left you will look down to the Vale of Clwyd, a broad expanse of rolling countryside, which will remain in view throughout your traverse of the Clwydian range. On this southern section of the range there are especially good views to the town of Ruthin which boasts a ruined castle and fourteenth-century church. Beyond Moel Gyw there is a drop to the A494 (154.5) with road links to Mold and Ruthin; the roadside pub marked on some OS maps was a motel at the time of writing.

The national trail turns right on to the A494 then shortly left on to a path heading north-eastwards through fields as it contours the next hill, Moel Eithinen. Then, as if tiring of these lower slopes, it bears left at a crossroads of paths and climbs steeply north-westwards to skirt the southern edge of Foel Fenlli, which boasts an Iron Age hill fort on its summit. The avoidance of the summit itself is for erosion prevention rather than to give walkers an easier time! Beyond Foel Fenlli the route swings north-eastwards, descending steeply to reach a narrow metalled road at Bwlch Penbarra. It is marvellous walking; the northern Clwydians form a splendid spectacle ahead, the Vale of Clwyd stretches out below, and at your feet lie acres of heather which form a blaze of colour in late summer. Having crossed the road, you proceed initially north-westwards, then north-eastwards, climbing all the time, towards the climax of the walk along the Clwydians, namely Moel Fammau, or Mother Mountain, and the mother of all the Clwydians at 1,818 ft. The climb is on a good wide path and the views are still excellent. At the summit of Moel Fammau (158.5) is the Jubilee Tower, built in 1810 to mark the golden jubilee of George III, and though it was never finished and fell into disrepair, some restoration work has been done. The views are incredible; not only should you enjoy the neighbouring Clwydians and your new friend the Vale of Clwyd, but the Wirral is clearly visible from here, and on good days it may be possible to make out Snowdonia and even Liverpool Cathedral.

You drop down very steeply off Moel Fammau as you head north-westwards on to Moel Dywyll, then swing slightly east of north to skirt the summit of Moel Llys-y-coed. There is another dramatic plunge to a metalled road, heading north-westwards, and indeed that will be your direction of travel all the way to Bodfari, where most walkers who have started that morning from Llandegla will wish to call it a day. Crossing the metalled road you climb again, keeping the summit of Moel Arthur and its hill fort to your left, then drop down again to another metalled road and after crossing it you embark on your last significant climb this side of Bodfari to the summit and hill fort of Penycloddiau. A large coniferous forest has been cultivated on these slopes, and the route passes along the eastern fringes of it on the way up. The views back down the Clwydians are majestic – it is especially satisfying to identify the Jubilee Tower, which is now a mere speck in the distance – and you can also look down on the historic town of Denbigh in the Vale of Clwyd. You are spared the ascent of Moel y Parc, the last really spectacular hill in the range, which lies straight ahead, but instead the route chooses to bear left, just north of west, round the base of the hill. There follows a long and anticlimactical descent on a path which swings in a more northerly direction to reach a metalled road near the Grove Hall. You turn left on to the road and follow it briefly, then as the road bends south-westwards, you continue westwards on a path which crosses the river Wheeler and reaches the A541 at Bodfari (166). You are now barely 100 ft above sea level. Refreshments are available here, although it would be wrong to set one's expectations too high; having pounded all the way from Llandegla during the day I made a beeline for a house advertising teas and found that far from offering cosy armchairs and a pot of freshly brewed lapsang souchong with generous slabs of Victoria sponge, all that was an offer was a vending machine at the back of a shop!

Bodfari to Prestatyn (12 miles) via Rhuallt

ENJOY: Mynydd y Cwm, Marian Ffrith, Prestatyn Cliffs

The route turns right on to the A541, following it briefly, then bears left up a lane, crosses a metalled road and continues north-westwards on a path, climbing steeply. You turn right to head north-eastwards round the eastern edge of another hill fort at Coed Moel-y-Gaer, then bear left, just west of north, to meet a metalled road. Crossing it, you join another road that heads uphill, just east of north. Having passed St Michael's of the Fiery Meteor many miles back and almost felt the fire-and-brimstone message, it may appear somewhat ironic that the map should announce that at this stage you are proceeding through Sodom. Whatever temptations of the flesh arose in the area that gave rise to the name Sodom, there seems little to beguile you over the next few miles, in terms of scenery or amenities. Leaving the road at a kink in its otherwise unerring north-easterly direction, you bear left on to a footpath and proceed north-westwards, skirting the summit of Cefn Du. North-westwards is now your direction of travel all the way to the A55. Beyond Cefn Du you pick up a metalled road, which you follow to a road junction, where you turn left then immediately right onto another road. At the next junction you bear left on to a path which contours the southern slopes of Moel Maenefa then drops dramatically to reach a metalled road. You turn left down the road, then just before St Beuno's College bear right to contour the hillside, soon bearing left at Maen Efa to drop down to the A55. This is the main trunk road across North Wales, carrying traffic from the Midlands to the holiday paradises of Llandudno and Colwyn Bay, and the busy port of Holyhead; the national trail bears right to proceed briefly alongside it before thankfully using a footbridge to cross it. From the footbridge it is a short walk into the village of Rhuallt

(170.5), the only habitation of any consequence between Bodfari and journey's end, and offering refreshment at the Smithy Arms. You exit from the village along a metalled road heading north-westwards as far as Brynllithrig Hall, then turn right and proceed north-eastwards, climbing again to reach a metalled road at Bodlonfa. This climb, on to the slopes of Mynydd-y-Cwm, is arduous indeed, but you can be reassured that there is nothing worse to come.

Turning left on to the road, you follow it through an area of woodland. Where this ends, you turn right on to a path that heads initially just east of north, then north-westwards across two metalled roads and past some old mine workings, and over the hill known as Marian Ffrith, the last Clwydian on the route. The northernmost Clwydian, Moel Hiraddug, lies off the path to the north-west. Having descended to Tyddyn-y-cyll you change direction, heading north-eastwards, still going downhill. You cross a road, then at Bryn Cnewyllyn bear eastwards to Marian Mill Farm, swinging north-westwards past a waterworks through a patch of woodland at Hentryn Hall.

Beyond Henfryn Hall you reach a metalled road, following it briefly to your right before turning left on to a path that soon reaches the A5151 at Ty Newydd. Crossing it, you head north-westwards along field paths, interspersed with a small road section, to Bryniau, situated just to the east of the viewpoint of Graig Fawr. Now journey's end is within sight. After so many miles of nondescript trudging, you ascend the slopes of Coed yr Esgob and are treated to a splendid march along the top of cliffs around 700 ft high, looking down on the town of Prestatyn and the Irish Sea. This area is a nature reserve and a lovely climax to the walk, with views which on a good day stretch as far as Snowdonia and Anglesey.

At length you drop down off the hilltop and into the town of Prestatyn. You then follow a succession of roads north-westwards which head unerringly into and out of the town centre, and down to the sea, the road to the seafront rejoicing in the unusual name of Bastion Road. Prestatyn was the northern end of Offa's Dyke, though all traces of the earthwork have now disappeared from the area. The town, a popular holiday resort with four miles of fine beaches, is a very pleasant place to end your walk from Sedbury, but before you start to relax you must walk to the stone at the end of Bastion Road and close to the seashore, marking the official end of the route (178). Immediately adjacent is a splendid Offa's Dyke Centre where you may be invited to sign a book to certify your completion of the walk and purchase appropriate souvenirs. Despite the somewhat anticlimactical final miles, it is with a heavy heart that most travellers from Sedbury will head back to the town's railway station to commence the homeward journey, having enjoyed a walk that is so full of history, great scenery and wonderful variety. At least, however, you will have your memories to sustain you, to say nothing of the parcel from that little bookshop in Hay that is awaiting you at home, containing priceless copies of a dust-jacketed *Trouble at St Judes* and a first-edition *Fly Fishing* by J. R. Hartley.

Glyndwr's Way

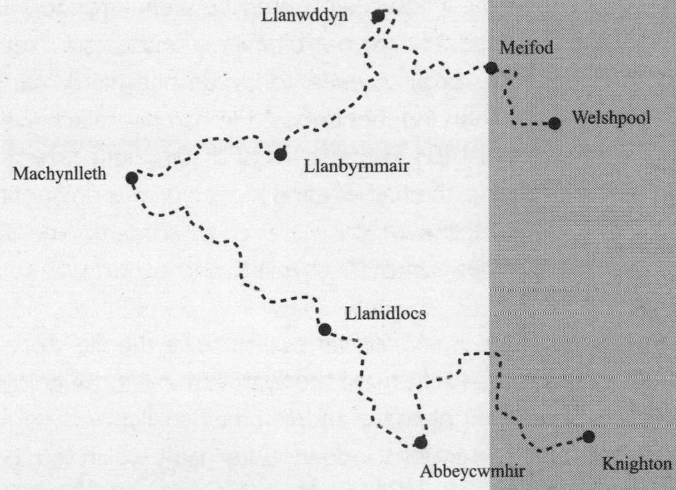

Designation: National trail.
Length: 134 miles.
Start: Knighton, Powys.
Finish: Welshpool, Powys.
Nature: An often rugged tramp through the heart of the remote mid-Wales countryside in the steps of Owain Glyndwr.
Difficulty rating: strenuous.
Average time of completion: 8–9 days.

HIGHLIGHTS OF THIS WALK:

- **Beacon Hill**
- **Ysgwd-ffordd**
- **Abbeycwmhir**
- **Clywedog**
- **Dylife**
- **Foel Fadian**
- **Machynlleth**
- **Abercegir**
- **Lake Vyrnwy**
- **Welshpool**

Glyndwr's Way is one of the newer national trails, opened in 2002, and one of just two national trails that run exclusively through Wales. Unlike many of the other national trails, it does not follow a particular geographical or historical feature but simply sets out to provide a walk through the remote and unspoilt countryside of mid Wales, with its superb scenery and great variety of wildlife. It gets its name from the uncompromising and heroic Welsh warrior Owain Glyndwr, who lived between around 1360 and 1415 and mounted a fierce but ultimately unsuccessful revolt against the oppressive English; even today despite his defeat he remains an icon of Welsh independence. He had himself crowned king of a free Wales in 1404 in the town of Machynlleth, which he established as his capital, the halfway and indeed pivotal point of the National Trail route. Moreover, it is believed by some that he died at Darowen, a few miles east of Machynlleth and a short way south of the route.

However, the route does not set out to trace the life story or the deeds of this remarkable man; the walk is there to be enjoyed for what it is, namely a pleasant and at times challenging journey through some very fine country indeed, using paths which with only a few exceptions are well defined and well waymarked. That said, there is a good deal of fiddly walking where navigation could pose problems, especially in bad weather, and there is a huge amount of up-and-down work, with some exceedingly steep climbs in places. The area covered by the route is remote, and although two towns, Llanidloes and Machynlleth, are visited en route, there are some lengthy stretches with no amenities to speak of. Posing a particular logistical challenge is the 28-mile walk from Llanidloes to Machynlleth, which does not pass through a single settlement of any description, the only chance of refreshment being at a moorland pub some way off the route.

Like the Pembrokeshire Coast Path, the end of the route is curiously close to the start, and it may come as a surprise and possibly even faint disappointment to the walker, having completed the 134 miles from Knighton to Welshpool, to find that he is only a short road journey away from where he started. Less kindly folk may suggest that he would have achieved his objective much more quickly, and boasted a rather cleaner pair of boots, by doing the whole thing by road in the first place.

Knighton to Felindre (15.75 miles) via Llangunllo

ENJOY: Llangunllo, Beacon Hill

You begin in Knighton, where for the first and only time you may meet walkers doing Offa's Dyke Path which also passes through the town. The town was the site of a major victory for Owain Glyndwr against the English in 1402; there are many old buildings, some dating back to the seventeenth century, but its most prominent feature is the huge clock tower right in the centre of the town, built in 1872. You exit from the town to the south-west, then swing north-west to climb steeply and enjoy a most attractive woodland walk. Emerging from the woods, you swing sharply south, following a road downhill to Little Cwm-gilla then turning west to climb steeply uphill – your first of many tough ascents during the walk – on a clear track, passing the splendidly-named Ebrandy House. There is a descent and a sharp left turn which could easily be missed, the path now heading south-westwards and affording excellent views ahead. Your walk along a well-defined track is sadly cut short and you swing further south-west to drop down to the valley floor at Cefn-suran, and after a gentle climb, you descend steeply to the Lugg valley and the village of Llangunllo (6.5). There's a curious pub here, which at the time of writing doubled up as a community shop. Turning right (north) off the main street you head northwards along the road, leaving it to climb steeply to pass underneath the railway, the very beautiful Heart of Wales line linking Shrewsbury and Swansea, completed in 1868.

Now you leave civilisation behind and head out into the moors, using firstly field paths then a clear track to climb north-westwards towards Beacon Hill, the climax of this section. You bear right (northwards) at a junction of tracks near Upper Ferley, and now proceed just east of north on a track that just keeps on climbing, eventually levelling out in an area of woodland adjoining Pool Hill and Beacon Hill. You turn sharply left (north-west) and with Pool Hill to your left and Beacon Hill to your right, cross an ancient earthwork named Short Ditch and embark on a splendid march through the heather moors. There is a fair amount of up and down walking, but the gradients are generally modest and progress is rapid along an excellent track. A mile or so from Pool Hill you round Stanky Hill which lies to your left, and here you leave the main track and turn right, north-eastwards, along the eastern edge of what is rather grandly called Black Mountain. You need to follow the waymarks carefully as your path becomes much less obvious; this is still quite remote moorland terrain, even though you have lost a little height, and there are few waymarks to guide you. At length, however, you pick up a more obvious track which maintains a north-easterly course and goes uphill to cross a minor road at Cefn Pawl.

Over the road you swing north-westwards to continue across moorland, still maintaining your height, then plunge steeply down into the Teme valley, swinging eastwards then north-westwards to hit the valley bottom on the edge of the village of Felindre (15.75) on the B4355. This is an obvious place to break after your first day on Glyndwr's Way, as the village offers food and accommodation.

Felindre to Abbeycwmhir (15.75 miles) via Llanbadarn Fynydd

ENJOY: Castell-y-blaidd, Moel Dod, Ysgwd-ffordd, Dyfaenor, Abbeycwmhir

Felindre is a pleasant but unremarkable place, the English border just a stone's throw beyond the river to the east of the village. Hopefully fortified by a good full Welsh/English border breakfast, you now head westwards; inevitably you start the day with a climb, albeit a most agreeable one, with beautiful views to the Teme valley opening out almost at once. There is then a descent to the farm buildings at Rhuvid, followed by another climb along a clearly defined path which goes forward to Hope's Castle Farm where you join a road and descend with it. The going is excellent, the sense of peace and timelessness is palpable and the lush green countryside and surrounding hills, while unspectacular, are very beautiful. As the road bends right, you turn hard left off it onto a clear track; don't be tempted to continue along the alluring track, but continue south-eastwards as directed by the waymark, through rougher terrain, passing a pond and an area of woodland and gaining height gradually to reach some 1500 ft above sea level.

Your route swings from south-east to south-west to pass a very prominent hill standing to your right, the site of the unfinished thirteenth-century Castell-y-blaidd, translated as 'castle of the wolf'. Despite its forbidding name, its surroundings are extraordinarily peaceful. Now proceeding more resolutely south-westwards, you go forward to arrive at a road, and follow this downhill to Llanbadarn Fynydd, the only settlement between Felindre and the next obvious staging post, Abbeycwmhir. It seems tempting and logical just to stick to the road all the way, but near the bottom a waymark sign directs you to leave the road and proceed rather less confidently along adjacent fields – to arrive at the road again. One would have to have an awfully tyrannic conscience to be disturbed one iota by having stuck to the road throughout rather than embark on some rough and fiddly field walking. Especially if it was raining and a member of the party had identified the New Inn pub as one of Llanbadarn Fynydd's more dominant features.

The Way turns left on to the A483 – one of the major trunk roads bisecting Wales from north to south – to pass southwards through Llanbadarn Fynydd (23.25), which, at the time of writing, boasted a pub but not much else. The route then bears sharp right, northwards, along a minor road to cross the river Ithon and pass the very pretty village church, then swings sharply westwards with the road and now proceeds uphill. This is a laborious climb, and it is a relief when you are waymarked left, firstly south-westwards then swinging south-eastwards, into the moorland on the west side of Moel Dod. Do watch very carefully for waymarks here, as initially the path is very poorly defined on the ground – in mist, you may need the help of a compass – but in due course, as you edge round Moel Dod, it becomes clearer. A really magical walk now follows, as you veer south-westwards again, before swinging south-east once more, along the conifer-clad hillside, with quite glorious views across the Ithon valley to your left including sight of Tinboeth, a late thirteenth-century castle which stood until 1322. This is long-distance footpath walking at its very best.

Sadly you must leave the hillside, turning sharply left, eastwards, to drop steeply to the buildings of Tynypant, but having crossed the road here and swung southwards, you quickly regain the lost height. There's a brief road walk here, but soon you join a path which continues southwards and provides some of the finest walking on Glyndwr's Way, with beautiful views in all directions. Although the Way doesn't visit it, it's almost mandatory to detour briefly to the right (westwards) to the triangulation point of Ysgwd-ffordd; if you are walking from Felindre to Abbeycwmhir in one day, this may be a splendid spot for a picnic. The walking remains exhilarating, and quite dramatic as you reach a junction and plunge southwestwards down a thickly wooded hillside. Enjoy the moment, as although there is plenty more splendid walking immediately ahead, you won't have anything quite as magnificent as this for many miles. You pass the buildings of Neuadd-fach, cross the Bachel Brook and turn left for another piece of road walking. If time was short and/or the weather was very bad, you could actually use this road, and the one to which it leads, to walk westwards all the way to Abbeycwmhir.

However, Glyndwr's Way prefers a more adventurous route, leaving the road at a fine house named Dyfaenor which dates back to the Civil War. Initially it follows a modest and rather unpromising path, but having negotiated an impressive wooded river crossing it goes forward to Brynmoel to pick up a track that proceeds easily through the woods to Abbeycwmhir (31.5). This, at roughly the most southerly point on Glyndwr's Way, is a magical, secluded place, surrounded by great hills and forests and seemingly forgotten by the march of so-called progress. The bad news for walkers is that amenities here will not necessarily be easy to come by, although at least one B & B in a neighbouring village offered a pick-up service for walkers at the time of writing. Its chief feature of historic interest is the ruins of a twelfth-century Cistercian abbey, which ironically was burnt by Owain Glyndwr in 1401 as it was under English patronage at the time, and was subsequently dissolved by Henry VIII. Parts of it survive elsewhere, the house at Dyfaenor being partially built from stone from the abbey, and some materials being incorporated into the rebuilt church at Llanidloes which you will visit a few miles further on. The village also had, at the time of writing, a pub with the strange name of the Happy Union, and a pretty church which, perhaps recognising the paucity of readily available refreshment facilities round the clock, offered at the time of my visit a kettle and supplies of coffee and tea. A wonderfully thoughtful gesture.

Abbeycwmhir to Llanidloes (16.25 miles) via Blaentrinant

ENJOY: Upper Esgair Hill, Cwm, Nant-y-Bradnant, Llanidloes

The first part of the walk from Abbeycwmhir to the next settlement of substance on the route, Llanidloes, is quite spectacular, the Way heading north-westwards uphill through the forest, but slight anticlimax sets in as the trees relent and you find yourself proceeding through unspectacular farmland. As you continue north-westwards, the going improves with a fine climb up Upper Esgair Hill, but sadly your hilltop promenade is short-lived, as you then swing north-eastwards to make a very steep, very muddy descent to the little village of Bwlch-y-sarnau. Now you swing north-westwards again, initially along a sunken track in open country, and then through an area of forest; emerging from the trees, you join a road which proceeds north-westwards past the buildings of Waun and then into another large area of woodland. Leaving the tarmac, the Way then turns right, north-eastwards, to follow a clear track along the extreme western edge of the forest to hit another road at Blaentrinant. The lofty hillside of Crugyn Llywd lies to your right, but the Way stays to the left of it, following a minor road briefly north-westwards then turning right at the buildings of Grach to head north-westwards along the hillside. A nondescript road walk now follows as the Way turns sharply westwards and then north-eastwards, skirting the western slopes of Pegwm Bach, while above you, you can see a wind farm has been created on the hilltops.

The best walking of the Abbeycwmhir-Llanidloes section now ensues, as you descend towards the buildings of Cwm, through quite magnificent scenery consisting of steep wooded hillsides plunging down to the valleys. There is now definitely the feeling of having left the gentler border country and moving into the heart of Wales. As you approach Cwm in the valley, look out for a crucial left turn which now takes you south-westwards, initially on the valley floor in the shade of trees, and then up a hill of almost inhuman severity. It's one of the steepest you'll meet on Glyndwr's Way and you will need to pause frequently for breath, but the views are tremendous. At the top, you swing right, north-eastwards, to follow initially a road then a path, continuing to enjoy fabulous views; again you must watch for a sharp south-west turn to follow an enjoyable hillside path with an area of woodland to your right.

Slight anticlimax follows: the Way continues largely south-westwards along the southern edge of a hill named Moelfre, and then north-westwards to hit a road at Prospect Farm, but although there's a fine descent to a wooded river crossing just under half a mile shy of the road, this is largely uninteresting fiddly walking through fields and farmland. Turning right, north-east, on to the road, you go steeply downhill and are shortly directed left, north-westwards, at Newchapel, enjoying an excellent view and passing the handsome Chapel Baptist Church building; you may perhaps wonder from where its congregation has been drawn, having regard to the comparatively remote surroundings. It was rebuilt in 1957 after a fire three years earlier, but a church has stood on this site since 1740. Now, continuing north-westwards, you shortly leave the road and descend into a lovely wooded valley, crossing the stream of Nant-y-Bradnant, which is an ideal spot for a picnic.

Climbing up quite steeply through the woods, following the path carefully, you shortly hit a road that takes you peacefully and easily into the town of Llanidloes (47.75), pronounced 'Chlan-id-loyce'. Here you will see your first on-route shops since you left Knighton, plus an excellent range of accommodation and eateries, and once you've queued with the locals in Somerfield, and found somewhere to stay, you can enjoy looking round what is a most picturesque town.

Llan-id-loyce

Its Market Hall, built around 1600, is the only remaining half-timbered market hall in Wales; its principal church boasts a fine decorated roof, fourteenth-century tower and a thirteenth-century arcade that was taken from Abbeycwmhir (see above); although the railway has long shut down, there is a fine nineteenth-century station building; and a town hall built in Classic Renaissance style dating back to 1908.

Llanidloes to Machynlleth (27.75 miles) via Afon Biga and Aberhosan

ENJOY: Van Pool, Bryntail, Clywedog, Dylife, Foel Fadian, Rhiw Goch, Machynlleth

The section from Llanidloes to Machynlleth is the most logistically challenging aspect of the walk, consisting of nearly 28 miles with virtually no amenities and very limited accommodation opportunities, so rucksacks will need to be filled and loins girded before the start of the journey. It is just about do-able within a day, if you are fit and well prepared, but it will be a long day and good weather and plenty of daylight are essential. The walk begins innocuously enough with a climb out of Llanidloes on a good path through woodland, taking you north-eastwards initially then swinging westwards round the edge of a golf course and downhill, seemingly losing all the height you gained since breakfast! A pastoral ramble now follows as you head westwards, with fine views north to a prominent summit called the Fan with a lake immediately in front of it, known as Llyn y Fan or Van Pool; adjacent to the lake there was a mine which opened in the 1850's and closed in 1921, once the most productive lead mine in Wales.

You turn right onto the Llanidloes-Machynlleth road – if the weather got really bad, this could provide an important safety net – and after a rather laborious uphill road walk, you turn left to head westwards along a driveway. This passes beside farm buildings then plunges downhill to the remarkable old mineworkings at Bryntail, which like the mine beside Van Pool was a rich source of lead during the latter part of the nineteenth century, and continues on beside the awesomely large Clywedog Dam which when completed in 1967 was the tallest in Britain. Another climb on tarmac leads to the Clywedog Reservoir, one of the principal providers of fresh water for Wales, housing some 11 billion gallons of water. For a couple of miles you endure some quite fiddly walking as you proceed along the western side of the reservoir using a mixture of roads, tracks and paths; at one point you find yourself picking your way along a thin muddy path as you negotiate a tree-clad inlet, and a while later you play hunt-the-waymark as your route clambers up a hillside that is thick with vegetation but confusing for walkers as there is little trace of any path on the ground at all. The reward, however, is a constantly changing view of this reservoir which seems to assume a greater majesty and beauty the further you proceed along it.

Eventually you strike out south-westwards, bidding farewell to the reservoir and crossing open country to pass through a surprisingly dark forest and then along a track through a younger forest plantation. Now swinging northwards, the route emerges into more open fields before dropping down gently to the thickly-forested picnic area by the crossing of the Afon Biga (56.75). With road access nearby, this may be a good place to break if you don't feel up to completing the walk to Machynlleth in a day, as you are still only a third of the way from Llanidloes to Machynlleth.

A straightforward forest walk ensues, initially along a path and then a road. You keep to the road which emerges from the trees, heading northwards, but in due course you leave the comfort of tarmac to follow a track that takes you above the valley floor; shortly you descend and find yourself walking through a charming valley, passing the farm at Llwyn-y-gog and going forward to Felin-newydd. Now, suddenly, everything changes. A steep climb lifts you out of the valley and onto a clear track which now heads resolutely north-westwards, climbing all the time and providing sensational views across a landscape which seemingly in seconds has been transformed from lush and homely to stark and spectacular. To your right the isolated pub at Dylife (pronounced Dillivai) comes into view, and a footpath provides the means of getting to it; in bad weather, this hostelry may prove to be something of a lifeline! The sense of remoteness is now quite palpable and the landscape is all the time getting more rugged, with a very steep valley to your left, and more lead mineworkings – again reaching their peak of production in the latter part of the nineteenth century – close by, but the way remains well defined.

There is a dramatic footbridge crossing, beyond which you strike out into a barren moorland landscape that may recall memories of the early part of the Pennine Way. You swing northwards and now need to watch signposts and the map carefully as the route alternates between a clear track and heather moorland where the path is quite unclear on the ground and you may need to rely on a compass if the mist comes down. Shortly, however, you come to a more obvious track on to which you turn right, with the beautiful Glaslyn lake to your left; ahead of you is the massive Foel Fadian, 1850 ft above sea level, and your track heads straight for it, but rather coyly forks left just short of the mountainside and proceeds north-westwards round the edge of it. A detour to the summit is possible but if it's now lunchtime and you have to be at Machynlleth that evening, is probably best left out. This is the highest point of Glyndwr's Way in every sense, and as you begin your descent the most wonderful view presents itself, providing just reward for the effort you've put in since Afon Biga. But do be careful: the rock here is hideously slippery, and it would be tragic for your walking adventure to end here because of the injudicious placing of a boot as you tried to see if you could make out Cardigan Bay through your state-of-the-art binoculars.

It's a riproaring north-westerly descent to a delightful green road which takes you past the incredibly isolated house at Cwm-hafod-march and the larger Esgair-fochnant to reach a road where you must climb steeply, skirting the amenity-less village of Aberhosan (66) which lies two thirds of the way from Llanidloes to Machynlleth. You are winning! Easy walking follows, with a descent through woods to a road that takes you to a river crossing at Felindulas, then a stiff road climb takes you south-westwards; it seems inconceivable after Foel Fadian that you should be climbing again, but having left the road at Cleriau-isaf you now proceed steadily uphill, on a good track. The reward is a fabulous view back across to Foel Fadian. You now begin to descend, still heading south-westwards through open green countryside and then through an area of forest, emerging and continuing on down to Talbontdrain with the possibility of accommodation. You proceed briefly along tarmac, then swing south-eastwards and brace yourself for yet another climb, and a very severe one at that, to the woodlands at Rhiw Goch, swinging westwards again. If you're doing the whole walk from Llanidloes to Machynlleth in one go, this really will seem a tough climb – the relief when you reach the top and join a clearer track is huge – but the views as you climb are quite fantastic. You enjoy much easier walking as you head north-westwards downhill through the forest. You are sharing your route with a mountain bike trail, so do listen intently for feverishly sounded bicycle bells, and keep the sunglasses primed for sudden blinding flashes of bright yellow and orange lycra.

Emerging from the forest, you really do feel on top of the world. The track levels out and with the signposting leaving you in no doubt as to the way ahead, you continue north-westwards, enjoying superb views to the spectacular valley on your left; to your right, the combination of steep bare hillsides and extensive forest plantations is also exhilarating, and it's hard to believe that soon you will be back in civilisation. Passing the slopes of Mynydd Bach, you begin to lose height and reach a T-junction of paths, at which you turn right and plunge downhill, heading north-eastwards. Very soon, however, a sharp left turn at the bottom of the hill takes you northwards, climbing again; the route is far from clear on the ground, but matters are clarified as you find yourself at the southern end of a thin forest plantation, the ground falling away dramatically to the right and more open country, including the isolated lake Llyn Glanmerin, ahead. You enter the forest and now proceed along the track which is quite rough and claustrophobic, and you will be glad of the reassuring waymarks.

Emerging from the woods, you now swing westwards and get your first view of the lovely Dyfi valley, which will become a good friend to you for the next 20 miles or so, and the welcome oasis of Machynlleth. With the town tempting you down, your traverse of the hillside, on what isn't always a very well-defined path, seems a lot longer than one thinks it should be, and there is slight anticlimax as you continue westwards, seemingly away from the town, past the buildings of Bryn-glas. At last, as if tired of playing games, your route swings right and heads north-eastwards, descending via the slippery so-called Roman Steps into Machynlleth (75.5). The Way eschews the main centre of the town, preferring a walk through a quieter area passing what at the time of writing was the Celtica visitor centre, a celebration of Celtic culture and history, and eventually reaching the main street (A489) and turning right.

Machynlleth would seem welcoming to the walker whatever it was like, but it is in fact a delightful town with many fine buildings, a plethora of good shops, museums including the splendid Tabernacl Museum of Modern Art, craft centres and restaurants, and the famous Centre for Alternative Technology, established in 1975 to research renewable sources of energy. It was at Machynlleth that Owain Glyndwr summoned a parliament in 1402 and made the town his capital, and it was this that helped the town onto the shortlist of prospective capitals of Wales in the 1950's. And although it does not enjoy that distinction in the twenty-first century, it boasts all the amenities a walker could wish for.

Machynlleth to Llanbyrnmair (15.5 miles) via Cemmaes Road

ENJOY: Bryn Wg, Abercegir, Cefn Coch, Commins Gwalia, Ffrid Pentrecelyn

The Way leaves Machynlleth deceptively easily, following the A489 briefly then turning right on to a minor road and proceeding south-eastwards along the road to the village of Forge; further road walking and a gentle traverse of farmland bring you back to the main road at Penegoes with its splendid restored seventeenth-century watermill right on the route. A little to the west off route, on the road to Machynlleth, is the village church, close to which the head of Egoes, a Celtic saint, is said to be buried. Soon leaving the main road to the right, you head eastwards and begin to climb, following a good path with views already opening out behind you. From here you swing dramatically left and after a short sharp climb enjoy an exhilarating walk round the edge of Bryn Wg, with dramatic views across the Dyfi valley. The going becomes rough as you follow the hillside, taking care not to descend the steep slope; there is one stile which is almost completely smothered with bracken, and you will need to keep your wits about you to spot it. Looking ahead, there is now a view to the village of Abercegir, set snugly at a junction of three valleys with wonderful hills rising up behind, but the descent to the village is long and slow, following a very narrow hillside path where it is essential to watch where you are putting your feet. At length you reach the valley bottom and can appreciate more fully this very pretty village (80.25) where time does seem to have stood still and you half expect to see BBC cameras filming a period Sunday teatime serial. Its name translates as 'mouth of the Cegir stream' and not an on-route invitation to sample the finer products of Messrs Benson and Hedges.

There is a long climb out of Abercegir, first north and then north-eastwards round Rhos-y-Silio, and the views just get better and better with the mountains of Snowdonia as well as the Dyfi valley on display. Care is needed as you pick your way past waymarks when the track peters out, but there follows easy and very rewarding walking on a green road towards the top of the Cefn Coch hillside; particularly enticing is the view of the Dyfi valley towards Dinas Mawddwy and the summit of Cadair Idris, the closest you will get to them on this route. Sadly the green road gives way to rather rougher terrain, and there follows some fiddly walking as far as the top of a lane, due south of which – a mile or so away – is Darowen, close to the point where Owain Glyndwr is believed to have died. Swinging from eastwards to north-westwards you head initially along the lane then strike out across pasture and plummet down to hopefully hit the valley at Cemmaes Road, also known as Glantwymyn (84.25). This is an important road junction – the railway also runs through the village – and there is a shop and a pub.

From Cemmaes Road the route heads initially north-eastwards along the A470 then strikes out south-eastwards, following a clear track and then climbing; the climb gets more intense as the marked route leaves the main track and joins a subsidiary one, but there are excellent views to the south-west. There is then a short descent to the farm buildings of Rhyd-yar-aderyn but the climbing resumes with a vengeance as you heave yourself up past the hills of Gwern-y-Bwlch and Commins Gwalia. From here there are first-rate views to Moel Eiddew ahead, but you may be relieved to know that the Way will skirt the south of this hillside.

There follows a brief respite with some gentle road walking, but save for another short section of road the going becomes rough and often boggy, with plenty more climbing, as you pass beneath Moel Eiddew. There is a real sense of remoteness here. Soon you enter the Gwern-y-bwlch Forest, which offers some nature trails – if your Glyndwr's Way walk isn't enough for you – and in due course you emerge from the trees to turn right on to the slopes of Ffrid Pentrecelyn. To begin with you seem to be picking your way rather gingerly through a hilltop no-man's land, initially clinging like a limpet to the fence to your right, then moving away left, aiming for a mast. Now suddenly a quite spectacular scenic panorama opens up in front of you, and, as on the approach to Cemmaes, you find yourself skipping down the grassy hillside with joyous abandon. To your left (north-east) at the meeting of two valleys is a mansion named Plas Rhiw Saeson which has traditionally attracted great poets including Richard Davies among whose works is the well-known *Sospan Fach* ('the little saucepan'). Slight anticlimax follows as you drop down to the valley bottom and proceed towards Llanbrynmair, but on arrival there (91) you'll find it provides the most comprehensive range of amenities since Machynlleth, including the welcome Wynnstay Arms and the fascinating Machinations museum which at the time of writing housed an excellent tearoom. Following the closure of the old railway crossing the route now bypasses the village, using a brand new road, but you would have to be very strong-minded and determined to pass it by; to access it, simply turn south when you reach the junction with the Llanbrynmair-Plas Rhiw Saeson road.

Llanbrynmair to Llanwddyn (16.75 miles) via Llangadfan

ENJOY: Pen Coed, Llanwddyn, Lake Vyrnwy

Leaving the pleasant surroundings of Llanbrynmair, the route then goes north a little way along the Plas Rhiw Saeson road before striking out south-eastwards for what is initially an innocuous valley-bottom ramble, but soon things get tougher with quite a steep ascent. The original approved route of Glyndwr's Way now zigzags uphill and continues northwards via Esgair Fraith and Bwlch Gwyn, providing absolutely unforgettable views to the west – you may think it was worth all the effort to get here just for this moment – then heads north-eastwards over Cerrig y Tan and enters an expanse of moorland interspersed with dense patches of forest. However, at the time of writing it is possible that the approved route could be changed and you may find yourself faced with a rather tamer promenade through lower lying farmland before hitting the forest. All being well, whether on the original route or amended one, you will arrive at the Talerddig-Llanerfyl road which snakes across the moors and takes you forward north-eastwards to Neinthirion where there is a chapel.

More road walking takes you north-east to the farmstead at Dolwen, where the reassuring tarmac is left behind and you strike out north-eastwards between Moel Frrid-ddolwen and Moel Ddolwen before tackling the slopes of Pen Coed. The views are still pleasant, and although the spectacular slopes of the Dyfi valley and Snowdonia are now out of vision, the hillside, populated by ponies, is most attractive. The descent that follows is messy and confusing, with, when I walked the route, a distinct paucity of waymarking at crucial moments. You swing north-westwards to descend to a stream, then swing north-eastwards through largely pathless and squelchy areas of rough pasture which all comes as a sad anticlimax after the splendid walking a few miles back. All being well, if you set off from Llanbrynmair first thing, you'll arrive at Llangadfan (101.25) around lunchtime and perhaps enjoy refreshment here. It has become well known for its pub with the most extraordinary name, the Cann Office, believed to derive from Cae'n y ffos, translated as 'fortified enclosure.' It may be possible to visit the enclosure itself, a twelfth-century earthwork in the hotel garden. But this assumes that you have not been, as I was, caught out by the rerouting between Bwlch Gwyn and Neinthirion, been sucked down to Talerddig and faced with a longer walk to your ultimate objective than you were at breakfast time.

Having crossed the A458 at Llangadfan, you are faced with largely unexciting road and field walking for the first mile or so, and the going gets wet and rough for a while with no views to speak of. Then, however, things improve greatly, as having climbed steeply to cross the road at Penyffordd and admired a much improved view from here, you join a hilltop forest track heading north-west; not only are the views excellent but the walking is easy and progress rapid. Almost too soon, it seems, you find yourself beginning a descent, soon leaving the forest track on to a much narrower path with thick woodland and the refreshing sound of running water to your right. You share your route briefly with that of the stream, but shortly the stream is forsaken for a lane along the eastern fringe of extensive woodland, and once again the walking becomes quick and straightforward as you continue north-eastwards to Ddol Cownwy. This little settlement, dominated by a large caravan park, is barely a mile from Lake Vyrnwy, the next significant staging post on your journey, but you still have work to do; beyond Ddol Cownwy you have a stiff climb up a steep wooded hillside, which seems a lot more arduous at the end of a long day's walk. After swinging north-westwards you find yourself descending, initially through woods and then along a field edge, turning north-east for the final plunge to Llanwddyn on the shores of Lake Vyrnwy (107.75). The view of the lake and the dam when you emerge from the wood is fantastic. Llanwddyn is a super place to stop and linger, with, at the time of writing, a most useful and friendly shop/cafe, a number of accommodation opportunities, a splendid craft centre, RSPB birdwatching centre, nature trails, sculpture trail, trout fishing, cycle hire and of course Lake Vyrnwy itself. The dam at the village end of the lake is a spectacular construction, the Lake Vyrnwy Experience may be able to offer an audiovisual virtual tour of the lake, and if you have the energy after the walk from Llanbrynmair there are ample lakeside paths. Or you can simply sit in a lakeside pub, watching the sun going down over the water and reflect that this must be one of the top ten candidates for Best Place In Wales To Eat A Plate Of Gammon And Chips.

Llanwddyn to Meifod (15.25 miles) via Pont Llogel and Dolanog

ENJOY: Ann Griffiths Walk, Allt Dolanog, Vyrnwy walk, Pontrobert

It will be an effort to pull yourself away from Llanwddyn, but the route continues by going eastwards along the north edge of woodland to the adjacent village of Abertridw, before swinging southwards along the B4393. It leaves the road shortly at a hairpin bend and now continues south-westwards along initially a good forest track interspersed with a short stretch of road, then climbs very steeply up to join another, clearer forest track, now heading a little west of south. The path emerges from the woods to provide beautiful views of the surrounding hills, although sadly Lake Vyrnwy is now lost to sight. A steep rather messy descent follows, swinging south-eastwards and skirting further woodland, with one particularly awkward clamber down the side of a very steep grassy slope, and from here you pick your way through rough grass, swinging now eastwards to arrive at Pont Llogel. There is a very prominent church here, and it's a good place to pause and draw breath before embarking on the long haul to Dolanog, the next (and amenity-less) village. Near to the church there was once a deer park owned by the Fychan family, and here is another link with Owain Glyndwr, for Sir Gruffudd Fychan was one of Glyndwr's allies during the uprising.

You make your way down the road to the bridge and begin a really charming walk beside the river Vyrnwy, of which you'll see much more during the next few miles. This part of the walk coincides with the Ann Griffiths Walk: Ann Griffiths was a Calvinistic Methodist hymn writer who lived in the area and sadly died in childbirth in 1805 aged just 29. It is lovely, easy and relaxing walking in contrast to the messy tramping west of Pont Llogel, but all too soon you are directed north-eastwards away from the river and up through fields to a road, continuing just east of north through an area of woodland to Pentre. There's a short section of road now, followed by a tramp eastwards along a path which could be very muddy, but the views really are magnificent. The surface does improve but just as you are beginning to get into your stride you are directed southwards, off the track and on to a less well-defined path that swings first south-east, then just west of south, to cross a road.

There then follows a splendid march round the eastern fringe of Allt Dolanog topped by an ancient hill fort, heading south-eastwards then swinging south-west. The path is initially poorly defined but by following the waymarks carefully you'll identify a track which becomes a delightful green road proceeding through the bracken. Offa's Dyke Path veterans may detect a similarity between this section of the walk and Hergest Ridge between Hay and Kington; the views are very fine indeed. A much narrower path takes you steeply down the hillside to hit a track that then brings you to the village of Dolanog ('the dale of the salmon') (116), where Ann Griffiths lived as a child. Sadly at the time of writing the only refreshment opportunity was the water coming out of the handbasin in the public toilets.

The next section, to Pontrobert, is one of the easiest on the whole route. The Way follows the road eastwards out of Dolanog then goes down to follow a riverside path; once again you're enjoying the river Vyrnwy at first hand, and this path is if anything even lovelier than the one at Pont Llogel, with a number of little climbs and descents and beautiful surrounding woodland. You are directed away from the river and up to an impressive house at Gwern-fawr, and here you join a lane which you follow all the way to the village of Pontrobert, just under 4 miles from Dolanog. Although you have lost the intimacy with the river, you can pick up some speed and not worry about direction changes or dodgy waymarking. It's always vaguely disconcerting to walk miles without seeing a waymark. It could of course be that the route is so obvious that no waymarking is needed. Or it could be that after six waymark-less miles you reach a locked gate with PRIVATE – NO ENTRY on it and are forced to choose between hours of backtracking or an attempted short cut requiring the negotiation of two rivers, a motorway, a sewage works and a military firing range.

Pontrobert

Pontrobert itself, named after the builder of the first bridge here in the seventeenth century, is a busier place than Dolanog, and offers the first pub since Llanwddyn. The map also shows no less than four places of worship in the village, including the John Hughes Memorial Chapel which was built in 1800. John Hughes, who became a full-time minister in 1814, transcribed the poems of Ann Griffiths which had been recited by Ann to his wife Ruth who had been a maid at Ann's home; the poems were published a year after Ann's death and each year in recent years 12 August has been celebrated here as an Ann Griffiths Day.

Beyond Pontrobert the going is initially easy, a good track taking you just south of east to Bryn-y-fedwen, but for those with half an eye on the time, the ensuing mile or so is frustrating and unrewarding.

Although the old Quaker Meeting House provides a moment or two of interest, there is a good deal of muddy farmland tramping, mainly in an easterly direction, a constant need to look out for the location of field exits with signposting not always brilliant, and lots of gates. Gates are the bane of the Glyndwr's Way walker, and seem to come in three varieties. There are those that open with one flick of the hand, and you are on your way before you know it. There are those with catches so stiff that you may well yield to temptation simply to climb over the thing and be on your way. And there are those overdue for replacement where the only thing securing them to the adjacent post is a piece of parcel string, and the moment you've prised the string off the post the whole structure crumples into a heap before your eyes.

It's a relief to hit a firmer surface at Coed-cowrhyd, and although you leave the lane again shortly afterwards to cut off a sharp corner, you're soon back on it again, leaving it to follow a field path and woodland path north-eastwards round the edge of Gallt-y-Ancr or Anchorite's Hill. Close to the hilltop is a pillow mound believed to be the burial place of the saint who founded the church in nearby Meifod, and a footpath is available for a detour to the summit. Glyndwr's Way steers round the edge, the field path becoming a better defined track which goes forward to meet a road that in turn takes you to the A495 in the centre of Meifod (123). This village boasts a neat collection of stone buildings, a few of which are whitewashed, and there is an ancient church which shelters a carved pre-Norman gravestone, while the church windows are notable for nineteenth-century glass which depicts coats of arms. It is a natural stopping place for those who've walked all the way from Lake Vyrnwy, while if you are simply stopping for a rest, it provides a good opportunity to obtain refreshment and gird up the loins for the final ten miles to Welshpool. Buses may also be available to Welshpool if you're intending to call it a day here.

Buses
Bus travel is an important amenity for walkers in more remote areas of the country where, courtesy of Dr Beeching, trains no longer run. However, buses can be disappointingly infrequent and irregular, and what looks like a promising service from a glance at the timetable can be anything but. You may be delighted to find a bus scheduled to leave at just the time you need – your delight is then tempered when you see that one or more of the six or seven symbols on the timetable relating to your journey, denoting anything from 'Schooldays only' or 'Terminates at Ponders Road on Fridays in July' to 'Does not run on the day after Bank Holiday Mondays or, if there is no Bank Holiday in the month, the second Tuesday in that month' means that actually your bus of choice doesn't exist after all, automatically doubling the length of your day's walk.

Meifod to Welshpool (10.75 miles) via Trefnant

ENJOY: Broniarth Hill, Y Golfa, Welshpool

You leave the A495 again shortly by turning left on to the Guilsfield road to arrive shortly at Broniarth Bridge and be reunited with your friend the Vyrnwy. This is a lovely spot and is popular with locals in summer. Now, after the rather nondescript and slow walking from Pontrobert, there's a big improvement; you can enjoy an easy roadside walk close to the Vyrnwy, then after a steep climb eastwards through the woodland on Broniarth Hill, you have a quite glorious hillside promenade, still heading eastwards, with the lovely lake Llyn Du to your right and a tremendous view of the Vyrnwy valley to your left. At Upper Pant-glas you join a road which you follow south-westwards, initially getting another even better view of the lake, but having rattled off an easy mile and a quarter, you then have a painfully slow and messy half-mile trudge south-eastwards past the buildings of Cefn-pentre. Things improve with a pleasant road walk through woodland past Bwlch Aeddan and a good march along a path eastwards through Kennel Wood, joining a lane that takes you up to the B4392; you follow this briefly south-westwards, then turn left on to a road that descends towards Trefnant Dingle, in due course leaving the tarmac and following field paths to reach the buildings of Trefnant, looking out carefully for the signposting which directs you westwards into Figyn Wood.

You proceed along what could be quite a squelchy path then turn left to climb very steeply southwards up the hillside through the trees along a path that is extremely poorly defined. Fortunately you are well rewarded for your labours, with really fantastic views from the top, and it is good also to see your final summit, Y Golfa, now clearly in view ahead. You make a steep descent, heading south-westwards through the Graig Wood Nature Reserve with a huge variety of trees, plants and wild flowers concentrated into a very small area, from ash to rowan, from hazel to crab apple. A bitty section follows, as you head towards Y Golfa through rather anonymous farmland and woodland, but at length you arrive at the edge of the golf course and proceed via marshland to join a very narrow, albeit well signposted, path that wends its way through the bracken. You will feel a little like an aeroplane taxi-ing before take-off, as your path goes westwards, seemingly away from the summit, before swinging round and climbing quite steeply up the bracken-clad hillside. As you head eastwards, the gradient eases and you now enjoy quite excellent views to the north, then as signposted you turn right and climb steeply uphill to reach the triangulation point on the summit of Y Golfa, 1120 ft high. The view from here, as might be expected, is magnificent – it really is the perfect climax to the Glyndwr's Way walk.

Now it is simply a case of using the signposting to help you off the summit, and proceeding rapidly downhill, just watching for a north-easterly swing near Pen-y-golfa where you pick up a more obvious track. The going is now extremely easy, the track becoming a tarmac road as you pass Llanerchydol Hall and go through an area of genteel parkland – quite a contrast to the terrain you were faced with a few miles back. You pass the Welshpool terminus of the Welshpool & Llanfair Steam Railway, which dates back to 1903, and shortly beyond the terminus you arrive in Welshpool itself, the end of your journey (133.75). It's a bustling and prosperous market town with a number of interesting buildings including St Mary's Church, the Montgomery Canal Centre which incorporates a museum and exhibition, and the magnificent restored medieval Powis Castle, a major visitor attraction. Glyndwr's Way officially ends at the commemoration stone in the gardens beside the well-signposted Montgomery Canal; it is an excellent spot to relax and think back on a walk of many contrasts with so much beautiful unspoilt scenery and a profusion of attractive towns and villages. Much better than going by road even though it has taken you a week longer.